A FIRST ENGLISH DICTIONARY for ESL Students

Raja T. Nasr
M.A., Ed.D., H.L.D., F.R.S.A.
Marymount University
Arlington, Virginia

UNIVERSITY
PRESS OF
AMERICA

Lanham • New York • London

University Press of America,® Inc.
4720 Boston Way
Lanham, Maryland 20706

3 Henrietta Street
London WC2E 8LU England

Printed in the United States of America
British Cataloging in Publication Information Available

Illustrations by Nancy Benson

Library of Congress Cataloging-in-Publication Data

Nasr, Raja Tewfik.
A first English dictionary : for ESL students / Raja T. Nasr.
p. cm.
1. English language—Dictionaries. 2. English language—
Textbooks for foreign speakers. I. Title.
PE1628.N3 1994 423—dc20 94–33030 CIP

ISBN 0–8191–9730–0 (cloth : alk. paper)
ISBN 0–8191–9731–9 (pbk. : alk. paper)

The paper used in this publication meets the minimum requirements of American National Standard for Information Sciences—Permanence of Paper for Printed Library Materials, ANSI Z39.48–1984.

TABLE OF CONTENTS

INTRODUCTION

A. ABOUT THIS DICTIONARY

A First English Dictionary: for ESL Students is a learner's dictionary for students whose native language is other than English. The features and characteristics of this dictionary are the following:

1. The total number of **entries** is just over 3,400, which is more than adequate for students in their first few years of English.

2. In the entry itself, if the word contains two or more syllables, the **primary stress** is indicated by underlining.

3. The **part of speech** is next shown in smaller type. If more than one part of speech occur, they appear in the following order: noun, verb, adjective, adverb, and then others. If the word is a *noun*, and the plural form does not take *s* or *es*, the full plural form is given. If the word is a *verb*, and the past and/or the past participle forms do not take *d* or *ed*, the full forms are given in this order: the present participle (with *-ing*), the simple past, and the past participle. If the word is an *adjective* or an *adverb*, and the comparative and superlative degrees do not take *er* and *est* (or *more* and *most*), the full forms are given.

4. The various **meanings** of the word in simple English are given in italics.

5. A **full sentence** is provided for each meaning to help the student learn how the word is actually **used**. In some cases, more than one sentence may be needed to clarify the meaning of the word.

6. Almost 600 **illustrations** are provided in the dictionary to help students with the meanings of the illustrated words.

7. The **information** at the end of the dictionary can be quite helpful as well.

This dictionary should prove to be a very useful and educational aid for ESL students.

B. HOW TO USE THIS DICTIONARY

The major learning devices in this dictionary are pointed out from the sample entries provided on this page.

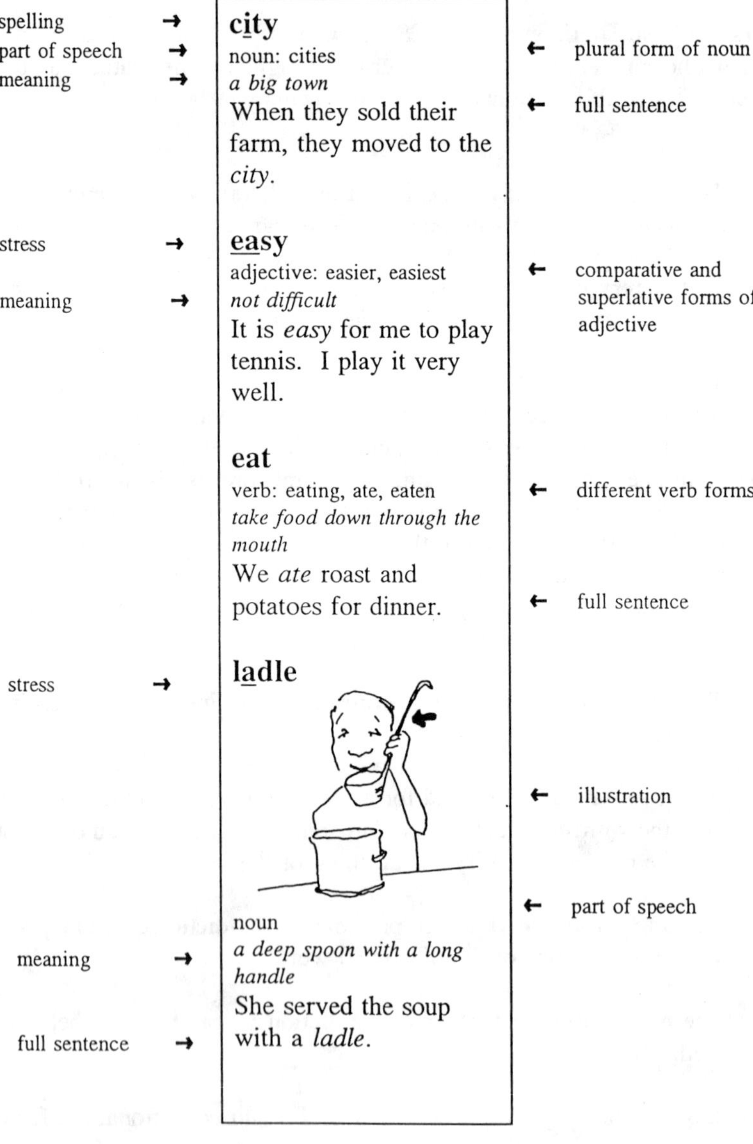

spelling →
part of speech →
meaning →
city
noun: cities
a big town
When they sold their farm, they moved to the city.
← plural form of noun
← full sentence
stress →
meaning →
easy
adjective: easier, easiest
not difficult
It is easy for me to play tennis. I play it very well.
← comparative and superlative forms of adjective
eat
verb: eating, ate, eaten
take food down through the mouth
We ate roast and potatoes for dinner.
← different verb forms
← full sentence
stress →
ladle
← illustration
← part of speech
noun
a deep spoon with a long handle
She served the soup with a ladle.
meaning →
full sentence →

Aa

a
indefinite article
Use *a* before words beginning with a consonant sound. Examples:
a book, *a* university. Use *an* before words beginning with a vowel
sound. Examples: *an* eye, *an* hour.
1. *one (of a kind)*
I have *a* pen in my bag.
2. *each (one)*
He works eight hours *a* day.

abandon
verb: abandoning, abandoned, abandoned
leave
He *abandoned* his family. He went to live in another city.

ability
noun: abilities
cleverness in knowing how to do things
They gave him more work to do, because they knew his *ability.*

able
adjective
1. *clever in doing things*
I know he is an *able* man. I have seen his work.
2. *can (do things)*
He studied his new English words well.
Now he is *able to* spell them.

aboard
adverb
on a boat, train, or plane
Thirty people were *aboard* the plane when it landed.

about
preposition
1. *just under or over*
She has *about* ten more minutes to speak.
2. *related to*
She talked *about* her country.

above
preposition
over
They have a nice clock *above* the table.

abroad
adverb
1. *in another country*
He is studying English *abroad.* He has been away for a year.
2. *to another country*
She is going *abroad* to look for a new job.

absence
noun
being away
We had an important lesson yesterday. She missed it because of her *absence.*

absent
adjective
away
She is *absent* from the office. She is at home.

accept
verb
agree to take or receive
They *accepted* our invitation to dinner.

accident
noun
an unexpected happening
Nobody was hurt in the car *accident.*
I met my old friend by *accident.*

accompany
verb: accompanying, accompanied, accompanied
be or go with
Will you *accompany* me to the train station, please?

accomplish
verb
complete successfully
He *accomplished* his duties on time.

according to
on the basis of
According to our rules, she did something wrong.

account
noun
1. *story*

Her *account* of what happened was very clear.
2. *a record of what one owes*
In the restaurant they put everything on my *account.*
3. *money in a bank*
She added $100 to her *account.*
4. *because of*
I don't need any help. Don't stay here on my *account.*
verb
show how something is spent
How do you *account* for your time yesterday afternoon?

accountant
noun
a person who keeps accounts
Their *accountant* prepares their tax forms.

accumulate
verb: accumulating, accumulated, accumulated
collect
They are very rich. They *accumulated* a lot of wealth.

accuse
verb: accusing, accused, accused
blame someone for doing something wrong
She *accused* her husband for not treating the children well.

accustom
verb
make someone used to something
We must *accustom* the new worker to our way of doing things.

ache
noun
pain
She has a slight *headache.*
verb: aching, ached, ached
hurt
The sad news *ached* her.

achieve
verb: achieving, achieved, achieved
1. *gain*
He *achieved* a fine reputation in his work.
2. *complete successfully*
She *achieved* her aim. She wanted a degree and she got it.

acquaint
verb
make known
We *acquainted* the new secretary with the office rules.

acquaintance
noun
a person just known
I don't know him well; he is only an *acquaintance* of mine.

acquire
verb: acquiring, acquired, acquired
get or gain
She *acquired* a knowledge of French when she lived in Paris.

acre
noun
land area of 4,840 square yards
Our school was built on six *acres* of land.

across
preposition
from one side to the other
They swam *across* the river.
adverb
to the other side
They could not drive to the island; so they swam *across.*

act
verb
1. *play a role*
She *acted* in the play; she was the maid.
2. *do something*
You know the rules. *Act* on them.

action
noun
1. *movement*
That child is full of *action.*
2. *something done*
They knew the rules. What *action* did they take?

active
adjective
able to move or do things
He is a very *active* person. He is always on the move.

activity
noun: activities
motion, being active
Things were not quiet here last night. There was a lot of *activity*.

actor
noun
a man who acts
Who is your favorite movie *actor*?

actress
a woman who acts
Who is your favorite T.V. *actress?*

actual
adjective
real
They did not spend $100. The *actual* amount was $96.00.

actually
adverb
really
She is neither shopping nor in her office; she is *actually* asleep at home.

add
verb
1. *put things together*
I *added* what I spent in three shops: $6, $11 and $16.
2. *say more*
He could not *add* to my story. I mentioned everything.

addition
noun
1. *adding numbers*
We learned *addition* in the arithmetic class.
2. *something added*
A fourth room was their new *addition* to the house.

address
noun
1. *where one lives*
His *address* is 415 Benjamin Street.
2. *a talk*
The principal gave a fine *address* to the parents.
verb
1. *write where one lives*
She *addressed* the envelopes correctly.
2. *give a talk to*
The principal *addressed* the parents.

adjective
noun
a word that describes (usually a noun)
Look at this short sentence. The word "short" is an *adjective*.

admire
verb: admiring, admired, admired
like and value
I *admire* honest people who work hard.

admit
verb: admitting, admitted, admitted
1. *say that something is true*
He *admitted* being wrong.
2. *let (someone) in*
The usher *admitted* the guests into the hall early.

adopt
verb
1. *take a person as a family member*
The couple *adopted* a boy and a girl when they couldn't have children of their own.
2. *take something and apply it.*
She *adopted* our principles and practiced them successfully.

adult
noun
a grown-up
Two *adults* were with the children on the bus.

advance
noun
money given ahead
She received an *advance*

of $100 before she left on her trip.
verb
move forward
The runner *advanced* to first place in the race.

advantage
noun
a strong point to help a person advance
Arriving early gave us an *advantage*: we could pick our seats.

adventure
noun
a new and exciting experience
Going through the forest was an *adventure* for us.

adverb
noun
a word that describes a verb, an adjective, or another adverb
Look at these sentences: He worked hard. He worked extremely hard. He was extremely intelligent. In these sentences, "hard" and "extremely" are *adverbs.*

advertise
verb
write or say something to help sell something
The shirt maker *advertised* his products on television.

advertisement
noun

something said or written to help sell something
I bought two shirts after listening to the *advertisement.*

advice
noun
ideas given to help someone do the right thing
I took his *advice* not to travel in bad weather.

advise
verb
give ideas to help someone do the right thing
He *advised* me not to travel in bad weather.

affect
verb
influence
The weather *affected* our decision not to travel.

affection
noun
feeling
She gave her talk with much *affection.*

afraid
adjective
fearful
She was *afraid* to walk through the forest. She is *afraid* of wild animals.

after
preposition
following
October comes *after* September, but before November.

afternoon
noun
the time between noon and sunset
We have tea at 4:00 o'clock in the *afternoon.*

afterwards
adverb
later
They studied their lessons first. *Afterwards* they watched a film.

again
adverb
once more
She liked the exercise so much that she did it *again.*

against
preposition
opposed to
They were *against* too much freedom for their children.

age
noun
length of life
I don't know his *age,* but he must be over thirty.

agent
noun
a person who does something for someone else
They bought their house with the help of a clever *agent.*

ago
adjective
in the past
She went to London two years *ago.*

agree
verb: agreeing, agreed, agreed
be of the same opinion
You think we shouldn't travel in bad weather. I *agree* with you.

agreement
noun
an accepted arrangement
We had an *agreement* not to start playing before three o'clock.

ahead
adjective
in front
He is very clever. He is *ahead* of his class.
adverb
in front
All of them are walking together, but the leader is walking *ahead.*

aid
noun
help
They could not do the work alone. They needed some *aid.* I came to their *aid.*
verb
help
I *aided* my friends when I saw they needed me.

aim
noun
goal, purpose
She had two *aims* in life: success and happiness.
verb
have a purpose
She always *aimed* to do her best.

air
noun
1. *the space around the earth*
Our kite flew high up in the *air.*
2. *the thing we breathe*
She wants to get some fresh *air* outside.

air-conditioning
noun
the method used to make a place cool
They have central *air-conditioning* at home.

airline
noun
a company that has airplanes
He always flies with his favorite *airline.*

airmail
noun
the way things are sent by air
I received a letter by *airmail.*

airplane

noun
the ship or vessel that flies
She flew on a small *airplane* with two engines.

airport

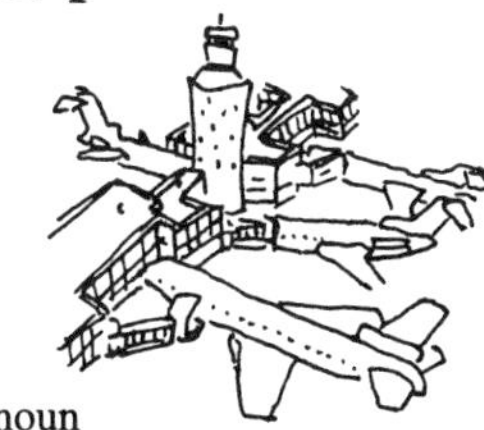

noun
The place where airplanes land
Our city has two big *airports.*
I can fly to London from either *airport.*

alarm
noun
a notice of danger
We left the building when we heard the fire *alarm.*
verb
give notice of danger or difficulty
The news about his failure *alarmed* us.

alien
noun
a foreigner
Fifteen *aliens* in our city want to become citizens.

alike
adjective
nearly the same
All three sisters look *alike.* It is hard to tell them apart.

alive
adjective
living
The cat was in a car accident. It was still *alive* when we saw it.

all
noun
the full amount or number
She ate *all* the food on her plate.
All the players were on the field.

allow
verb
let
The teacher *allowed* us to move around in class.

allowance
noun
money given to someone for use over a time
Parents usually give their children a weekly *allowance.*

all right
adjective
O.K., good
The food in that restaurant wasn't bad; it was *all right.*

almost
adverb
nearly
He is *almost* as tall as his brother. He is just half an inch shorter.

alone
adverb
by oneself
She sat *alone* in her room. She did not want anybody there.

along
preposition
in the same direction of
We walked *along* the river bank for an hour.
adverb
with
When she knew that I was going to the market, she wanted to come *along.*

aloud
adverb
in a loud voice
The teacher read the story *aloud* to the class.

alphabet

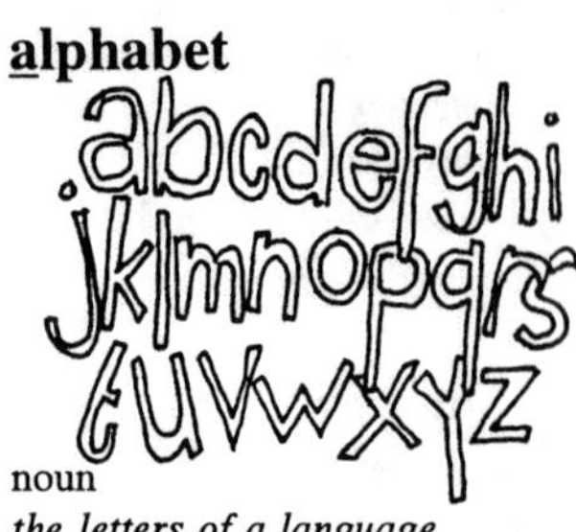

noun
the letters of a language
A, b, and c are three letters of the English *alphabet.*

already
adverb
1. *before*
She did not want to see the film with us; she had seen it *already.*
2. *by a certain time*
My friend was *already* in his seat when I arrived in class.

also
adverb
too
He likes cakes; he *also* likes ice-cream.

alter
verb
change

We *altered* our plans because of the weather.

although
conjunction
in spite of
Although it was raining, they still played outside.

altogether
adverb
on the whole, completely
His plan was *altogether* no good.

always
adverb
at all times
Her class starts at eight. She arrives at 8:15 every day. She is *always* late.

angry
adjective: angrier, angriest
not pleased
My brother was *angry* with me, because I was late.

appear
verb
1. *seem*
He *appears* to be happy today.
2. *come to be seen*
The sun *appeared* from behind the clouds.

appearance
noun
being seen
The sudden *appearance* of the sun made us go for a walk.

appetite
noun
a drive or desire (to eat)
She has a very good *appetite*. She is always ready for food.

apple

noun
a fruit
She made a nice pie with green *apples.*

apply
verb: applying, applied, applied
put into practice
They knew the rules very well, and they *applied* them well in their work.

appoint
verb
put (somebody) in some position
The Board *appointed* my friend manager of the company.

appointment
noun
1. *meeting time*
Our *appointment* with the chief was for 3:00 p.m.
2. *a position*
She got an *appointment* as a teacher.

approach
verb
come closer to
She *approached* her teacher to ask her a question.

approve
verb: approving, approved, approved
agree or accept
The captain *approved* our plan for the game.

apricot
noun
a fruit
My mother made us delicious *apricot* jam.

April
noun
the fourth month of the year
She was born on *April* 26, 1964.

are
verb
the form of the verb to be that goes with you, we, and they
We *are* students of English.

area
noun

a flat surface within certain lines
The farm had an *area* of six acres.

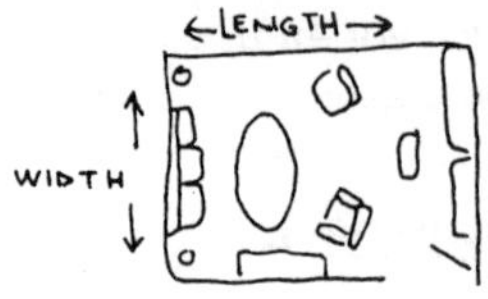

aren't
verb
are not
They *aren't* teachers; they're students.

argue
verb: arguing, argued, argued
speak or write in favor of or against an idea
They *argued* for a long time whether to go or not to go to London.

argument
noun
what is said or written in favor of or against an idea
I heard their *argument* to leave early, but I was not convinced.

arise
verb: arising, arose, arisen
happen or develop
An argument *arose* as they were discussing the subject.

arisen
See **arise.**

arithmetic
noun
the study of numbers in mathematics
We study addition in the *arithmetic* class.

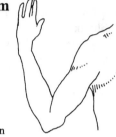

arm
noun
an upper limb of the human body
He wore a band on his right *arm.*

armchair

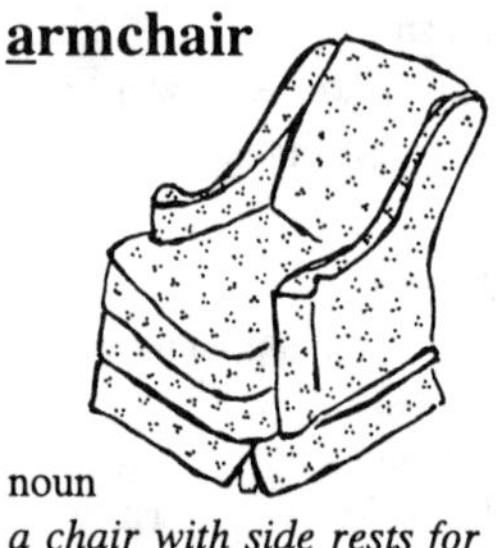

noun
a chair with side rests for the arms
He sat in an *armchair* all afternoon.

army
noun: armies
soldiers and land forces
My cousin was a captain in the *army.*

arose
See **arise.**

around
preposition
all the way on all sides
There were tall trees *around* the house.
adverb
here and there, about
I don't know where she is right now, but you'll find her playing *around.*

arrange
verb: arranging, arranged, arranged
plan
She *arranged* for us to see the president.

arrest
verb
stop and hold legally
The policeman *arrested* the thief and put him in prison.

arrival
noun
reaching or getting to a place
They left by taxi upon their *arrival* at the airport.

arrive
verb: arriving, arrived, arrived
reach or get to (a place)
Their plane *arrived* ten minutes late.

arrow
noun

1. *a sign to show direction*
Follow the *arrows* to reach the office.

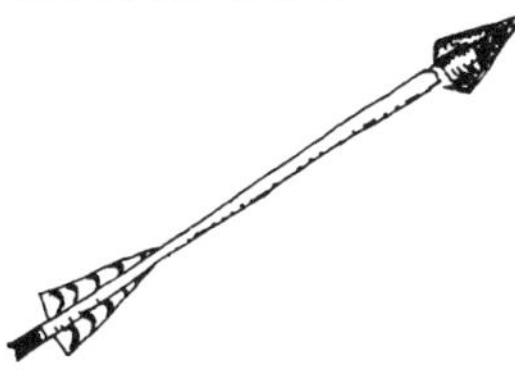

2. *a weapon used in old wars*
Some wars were fought with bows and *arrows.*

art
noun
things of beauty made
We saw nice paintings in the *art* museum.

artificial
adjective
not real
He acts in a very *artificial* way.

article
noun
1. *a part of speech*
A, *an*, and *the* are *articles.*
2. *thing*
I bought three *articles* from the shop: a book, a pen, and pencil.

artist
noun
a person who makes beautiful things
The *artist* painted a lovely picture.

as
adverb
like
Do *as* I do.
preposition
to the same extent
Our team is *as* strong *as* yours.

aside
adverb
on the side
They did not use the pen I gave them. They put it *aside.*

as if
conjunction
as though
He gives orders *as if* he is the boss.

ask
verb
state a question
"What is your name?" he *asked.*

asleep
adjective
sleeping
Lower your voices. The children are *asleep.*

as long as
conjunction
on condition that
He will give you the money now *as long as* he knows you will pay back the debt.

aspiration
noun
great wish
He has an *aspiration* to become a doctor.

ass

noun: asses
donkey
They have cows, horses, and *asses* on their farm.

assemble
verb: assembling, assembled, assembled
meet
The teachers *assembled* in the auditorium.

assembly
noun: assemblies
meeting
There was a student *assembly* at 9:00 a.m.

assignment
noun
a duty or piece of work given
The teacher gave the students a long reading *assignment*.

assist
verb
help
I couldn't do the work myself. I asked my friend to *assist* me.

assistance
noun
help
I finished my work early because of the *assistance* he gave me.

association
noun
people working or meeting together
My uncle and his friends have a successful business *association*.

assume
verb: assuming, assumed, assumed
accept as true
I *assume* you are coming to the meeting. I know you are interested in our work.

astronaut
noun
a person who goes in a space ship
Some *astronauts* have landed on the moon.

astronomy
noun
the study of the stars
A person who studies *astronomy* needs a telescope.

asylum
noun
shelter
The foreigner asked for *asylum* in this country.

at
preposition
1. *in (a place)*
They played *at* school yesterday.
2. *by or near*
She stood *at* the entrance before she walked in.
3. *(used to show exact time)*
They arrived *at* 3:00 o'clock.

ate
verb: past of eat
took food in
She *ate* her lunch at 11:00 o'clock.

athlete
noun
a person who does sports
Fast runners are good *athletes*.

atmosphere
noun
1. *the air around the earth*
The space ship flew through the *atmosphere*.
2. *spirit or climate*
There is a friendly *atmosphere* in our school.

attach
verb
connect or join
We *attached* the two metal pieces together.

attack
noun
a move against people or places
There was a military *attack* on the city.
verb
move against people or places
The army *attacked* the enemy camp before dawn.

attain
verb
reach or get
The company *attained* the profits they wanted.

attempt
noun
try
They made an *attempt* to reach the top of the mountain, but it was too hard for them.
verb
try

They *attempted* to climb the high mountain, but it was too difficult for them.

attend
verb
be present (somewhere)
We *attended* a very important meeting yesterday.

attention
noun
giving one's thoughts (to something)
The students paid *attention* to what the teacher was saying.

attitude
noun
a way in which a person feels (about someone or something)
You are likely to succeed more when you have the right *attitude* towards people.

attract
verb
draw (someone or something) towards
Her red dress *attracted* much attention.

attractive
adjective
being able to attract
What she was wearing made her look very *attractive.*

audience
noun
people attending a program
The popular movie attracted a huge *audience.*

August
noun
the eighth month of the year
My sister was born on *August* 23.

aunt
noun
the sister of a father or mother
My father has a sister; she is my *aunt.*

author
noun
the writer of a story, article, or book
The novel we read was written by a famous *author.* His name is Henry James.

automatic
adjective
being able to work by itself
We have an *automatic* washing machine at home.

autumn
noun
the season that comes after summer, the fall season
November is an *autumn* month.

avenue
noun
a road
We live on a wide and divided *avenue.*

average
noun
the mean of certain numbers
She received 75 and 85 on her tests. Her *average* was 80.
adjective
a normal level: not high and not low
He did *average* work in school.

avoid
verb
stay away (from someone or something)
Because she knew she had low grades in school, she *avoided* looking at her report card.

await
verb
expect, wait for
She *awaited* her husband's letter.

awake
adjective
not sleeping
He is still in bed, but he is *awake*; he can see you.

aware
adjective
knowing
She is *aware* that you are here; she will be with you soon.

away
adverb
1. *not here*
He cannot answer the phone now; he is *away.*
2. *towards another place*
I don't know where she is going, but she is walking *away* from her car.

awful
adjective
very bad
There was no water and no electricity in the house. It was *awful* there for two days.

awfully
adverb
1. *very badly*
He was in such a hurry that his work was *awfully* done.
2. *very*
He is *awfully* hungry; he will eat anything you give him.

awoke
See **awake**.

ax

noun
a sharp and heavy tool used to chop wood
We cut off a big branch with an *ax.*

axle

noun
the metal piece that connects two wheels
They needed a new *axle* for their car.

azalea

noun
a flower with a nice smell
They have many *azaleas* in their garden.

Bb

B.A.
the degree of Bachelor of Arts
She received her *B.A.* in English.

baby
noun: babies
a very young person or animal
She cannot walk; she is still a *baby.*

baby-sitter
noun
a person who looks after children
Her parents were going out for the evening; so she stayed with her *baby-sitter.*

back
noun

1. *the opposite of the front*
When they go to the movies, they like to sit in the *back.*

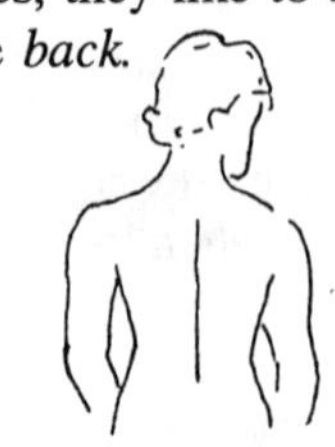

2. *The opposite of the front of the body*
He carried a heavy bag on his *back.*

adverb
the opposite of forward
She came up to the teacher to ask a question. Then she walked *back* to her seat.

backbone

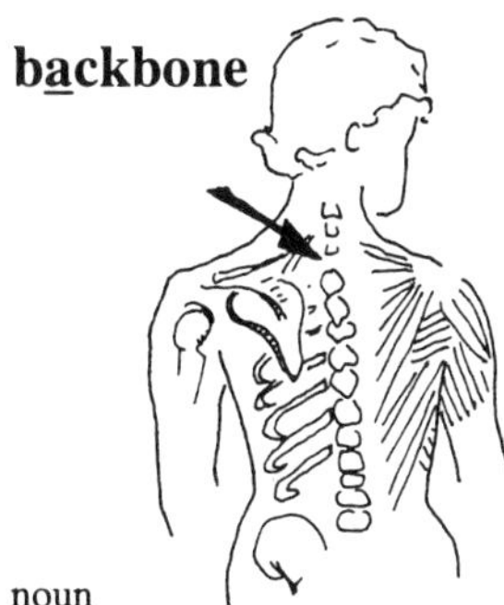

noun
the bone in the back that holds the body
The head is at the top of the *backbone.*

backward
adjective
not advanced
Some people who lived in jungles were rather *backward;* they had no schools or machines.

backwards
adverb
towards the back
Because he wanted to see me as he walked away, he walked *backwards.*

bad
adjective: worse, worst
the opposite of good
The weather is *bad* for a picnic today; it is cold and rainy.

badge

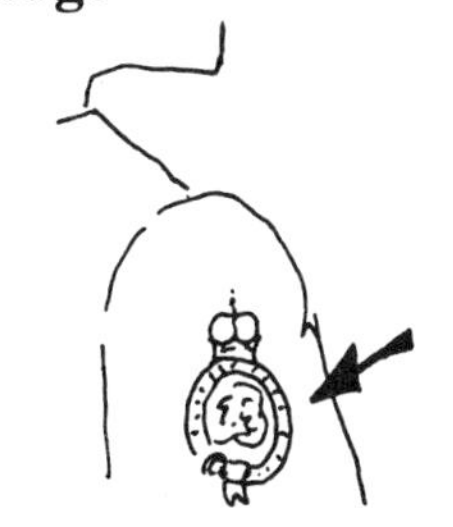

noun
a sign that one wears
I knew he was a scout from his *badge.*

bag

noun
a sack to put things in
The fruits I bought were put in two paper *bags.* My books are in my school *bag.*

baggage
noun
bags and suitcases for travel
Our *baggage* did not weigh much; each of us had one small suitcase.

bake
verb: baking, baked, baked
cook in an oven
My mother always *baked* delicious cakes.

baker
noun
a person who bakes
Our *baker* makes very good bread.

bakery
noun: bakeries
a place where one can buy baked goods
Our *bakery* always has fresh bread.

balance

noun
a tool used for weighing things
She used a *balance* to make sure she cooked only one pound of carrots.
verb
see that two things are equal in weight
She *balanced* her children's shares to be fair.

bald

adjective

without hair
Two of my uncles have hair and two are *bald.*

ball

noun
1. *a round play thing*
They used new *balls* when they played tennis.
2. *a big dancing party*
There were fifty couples at the *ball.*

balloon

noun

1. *a light play thing filled with air*
The children played with colored *balloons.*

2. *a vessel that goes up in the air filled with gas*
Two scientists went up in a *balloon.*

banana

noun
a fruit with yellow skin
Monkeys like to eat *bananas.*

band

noun
1. *a group playing music*
We listened to the *band* playing some nice music.
2. *a piece of cloth worn on the body*
Our football team wore a special *band* on their arms.

bandage

noun
a piece of cloth to wrap around a wound
The nurse put a *bandage* on his finger after he fell and cut it.

bank

noun
1. *a place where money is kept*
She cashed a check in her *bank.*
2. *either side of a river*
We walked along the river *bank* in the evening.

bar

noun
1. *a piece of wood*
They blocked the entrance with wooden *bars.*
2. *a long piece of something to eat*
He likes chocolate *bars;* his sister likes ice-cream *bars.*
3. *a place where people have drinks*
They had lemonade at the *bar.*

barbecue

noun
1. *an open place to cook meat or chicken*
We built a new stone *barbecue* in the garden.
2. food cooked on an open fire
We had a delicious *barbecue* for dinner.
verb: barbecuing, barbecued, barbecued
cook on an open fire
We *barbecued* our chicken.

barber

noun
a person who cuts hair
I had a nice haircut when I went to my *barber.*

bare
adjective
without cover
They walked with *bare* arms in the sun.

bargain
noun
a good deal
They bought their car for $2,000. It was quite a *bargain.*
verb
give and take on price
He wanted to sell the car for $1,000. We offered $500. We *bargained* and got it for $700.

bark
noun

1. *the cover of a tree trunk*
The squirrel ran up the *bark* of a tree.
2. *a dog's sound*
We heard the dogs' *barks* at night.
verb
make the sound of a dog
The dogs were hungry and they *barked* all night.

barn
noun
a depot on a farm where things are kept
The farmer kept the hay in a *barn.*

barrel

noun
a big round container made of wood or metal
They stored the oil in *barrels.*

base
noun
1. *the flat bottom of anything*
The vase stood firm because it had a wide *base.*
2. *one of the three corners in a baseball game*
He scored a home run by running from third *base* to home plate.
3. *a place turned into a center*
The navy had a *base* not too far away from the air force *base.*
verb
to rest an idea on
They *based* their business practice on their customers' needs.

baseball
noun
a ball game that uses a bat
Baseball is a popular game in the U.S.

basis
noun: bases
a starting point for an idea
She took the course on the *basis* that she needed new skills.

basket

noun
a container with a handle made of straw or wire
She put the eggs in a *basket* and sold them in the market.

basketball
noun
a ball game with a round metal goal that has a net under it
Tall people make good *basketball* players.

bat
noun

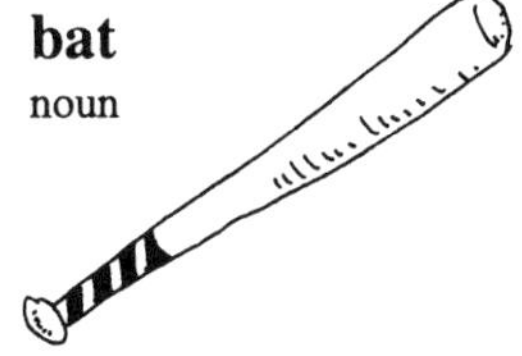

1. *the stick used in baseball or ping pong*
The baseball player hit the ball so hard that he broke his *bat.*

2. *a black bird that flies at night*
We saw many *bats* flying at night.
verb: batting, batted, batted
hit the ball in baseball or ping pong
She *batted* the ball very nicely when she played ping pong.

bath
noun
1. *a place where people wash themselves in the bathroom*
She put warm water in the *bath.*
2. *washing oneself*
I take a *bath* every morning.

bathe
verb: bathing, bathed, bathed
1. *wash a person or animal*
He *bathed* his dog in the garden.
2. *swim or dip*
We like to *bathe* in the sea.

bathroom
noun
the room where people wash and take baths
They have three bedrooms and two *bathrooms* in their house.

batter
noun
the baseball player who bats
The *batter* hit a home run.

battery
noun: batteries
a container that produces electricity
His car *battery* went dead because he left his lights on.

battle
noun
a fight
The army defeated the enemy in the *battle.*
verb
to fight
My brother and I *battled* over the ball.

bay

noun
a place where the sea goes into the land
The ships went into the *bay* because the sea was calmer there.

be
verb: am, is, are (present) was, were (past), being (present participle), been (past participle)
I *am* in school now. I have *been* here for a long time. I want to *be* a good speaker of English.

beach
noun
sea shore
We went to the *beach* to swim.

beam
noun
ray
We saw a *beam* of light coming from the house on the hill.

bean
noun
a white, red, green, or brown vegetable
I like baked *beans* with my hot dogs.

bear
noun
an animal
Bears like cold weather.

verb: bearing, bore, borne
stand something or someone
She can't *bear* to deal with dishonest people.

beard

noun
hair on the face
My grandfather had a long *beard.*

beast
noun
1. *an animal*
Lions are *beasts.*
2. *a wild person or animal*
She acted like a *beast* when she shouted at her children.

beat
noun
a strike
He felt his heart *beats.*
verb: beating, beat, beaten
1. *strike*
He *beat* himself on the chest.
2. *win over*
Our school *beat* your school in basketball.

beautiful
adjective
pretty, nice looking
The sunset looked *beautiful.*

beauty
noun
a beautiful thing or person
She won a prize for her *beauty.* There is a lot of *beauty* in nature.

became
See **become**.

because
conjunction
for, for the reason that
They did not go on a picnic, *because* it was raining.

become
verb: becoming, became, become
grow or develop to be
He is now a student. He wants to *become* a teacher.

bed
noun
1. *a piece of furniture to sleep in*
They sleep in twin *beds* in their bedroom.
2. *a place where flowers grow*
We planted some seeds in our flower *bed.*

bedroom
noun
a room used for sleeping
They have three *bedrooms* in their house.

bee
noun
an insect that makes honey

Bees are very busy insects. We can learn a lot from them.

beef
noun
cow meat
We had *beef* steak for dinner.

beehive
noun
the place where bees live
The farmer got the honey from the *beehive.*

been
See **be**.

before
preposition
ahead in time
The general fought in two wars *before* he died.
adverb
ahead in time
She doesn't want to see the film; she has seen it *before.*

beg
verb: begging, begged, begged
ask for help because of need
The poor child *begged* for some money.

began
See **begin**.

begin
verb: beginning, began, begun
start
He *began* his work in the morning and he finished it in the evening.

beginning
See **begin**.
noun
the start
He told the story of his life from the *beginning.*

beggar
noun
a person who begs
We noticed some *beggars* on the city streets.

begun
See **begin**.

behave
verb: behaving, behaved, behaved
act
She *behaves* well; she always does the right thing.

behind
adverb
further back
He is never with the other boys; he always runs *behind.*
preposition
opposite of in front of
The teacher cannot see the boy standing *behind* him.

being
See **be**.
noun
a living creature
Men and women are human *beings.*

belief
noun
something accepted as true
They have a strong *belief* in God.

believe
verb: believing, believed, believed
accept something as true
We *believed* his story; we know he is an honest man.

bell
noun
an instrument that rings
I opened the door when they rang the *bell.*

belong
verb
be for
This book *belongs* to me.

below
preposition
under
The desk is *below* the picture. The picture is above the desk.
adverb
in a lower place
We live on the top level. They live *below.*

belt

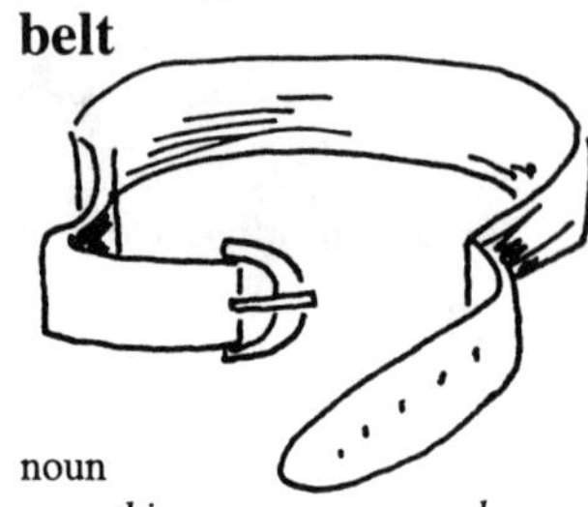

noun
something to wear around the waist
He bought a black *belt* for his gray trousers.

bench

noun
a seat made of wood or metal for more than one person
My friend and I had our lunch on a *bench* in the garden.

bend
verb: bending, bent, bent
turn or twist
The road *bends* around the school.

beneath
preposition
under
The book is *beneath* the box.

benefit
noun
advantage, good side
We finished our garden work before them, because we had the *benefit* of good weather.
verb
gain
We *benefited* from good weather.

bent
See **bend**.

beside
preposition
near, next to
My friend sits *beside* me in class.

besides
preposition
in addition to
Four people were in the room *besides* the teacher.

best
See **good**.
adjective
the highest good
Nobody received a higher grade in class than John. He got the *best* grade in class.

betray
verb
be insincere to
He *betrayed* his country by going over to the enemy.

better
See **good**.
adjective
the higher good
The blue car runs nicely. The red car doesn't. The blue car is *better* than the red one.

between
preposition
showing a position with one thing on one side and another on the other side
The boy is standing *between* the car and the tree.

beverage
noun
a soft drink or ade
They decided to have lemonade as the *beverage* with their meal.

beyond
preposition
further than
The city is *beyond* the river. You must cross the river to get to it.

bicycle
noun
a moving instrument with two wheels to ride on; a bike
She goes to school on her *bicycle.*

bid
noun
a price offer
Many people wanted to buy that old car, but we got it, because our *bid* was the highest.
verb: bidding, bade, bidden
wish
We *bade* them good-bye before they left.

big
adjective: bigger, biggest
huge, great
The box was too *big* to put in the car.

bike
noun
bicycle
She rode on her *bike* to school.

bill
noun
a statement about what one owes
I received the book I had ordered with a *bill* for $10.

billion
noun
a thousand million
1,000,000,000

The government spent a *billion* dollars on the new road.

bind
noun
fix
He is in a *bind*; he doesn't know what to do. His brother wants him to go with him, and his sister wants him to stay at home.
verb: binding, bound, bound
tie, put together
Can you *bind* the two parcels together? I want to carry only one parcel.

biology
noun
the study of living creatures
We learned about frogs in our *biology* class in school.

bird

noun
a creature that flies (or at least has wings)
The little *birds* flew out of their nest.

birth
noun
being born
They knew he was a clever child from the day of his *birth.*

birthday
noun
the day of the year that one was born
His *birthday* falls on November 27. They had a big *birthday* party for him last year.

bit
noun
small amount
I only ate a *bit,* because the food was too hot.
verb
See **bite**.

bite
noun
1. *something bitten or eaten*
He had a *bite* of food at midnight.
2. *biting*
The lion gave the hunter a *bite* on the arm.
verb: biting, bit, bitten
catch or cut something with the teeth
He *bit* his lip as he was eating.

bitter
adjective
not sweet
She didn't like the medicine she took, because it had a *bitter* taste.

black
noun
a dark color, the opposite of white
I don't like *black* as much as I like brighter colors like blue and green.
adjective
the opposite of white
She bought a *black,* white, and red dress.

blackboard
noun
the slate used in a classroom to write on with chalk
The teacher wrote the new words on the *blackboard.*

blade
noun
1. *the edge of a knife that cuts*
She couldn't cut the meat very easily. The knife *blade* was not sharp enough.
2. *a sharp and thin object used for shaving*
He needs new *blades* for his shaver.

blame
noun
responsibility for something that went wrong
If you don't study well and you fail, put the *blame* on yourself.
verb
say that someone or something was responsible for what went wrong

They *blamed* the new player for losing the football match, because he didn't play well.

blank
noun
empty space
The teacher asked us to fill the *blanks* in the sentences he gave us.

bla̲nket

noun
a warm cover for a bed
I use two wool *blankets* on my bed in winter.

blast
noun
explosion
The *blast* caused a hole in the roof.

blaze
noun
a quick burning fire
The firemen could not enter the burning house because of the *blaze.*

bless
verb
give grace and holiness
God *blesses* good people.

ble̲ssing
noun
grace and holiness
The believers asked for God's *blessing* on their new business.

blew
See **blow**.

blind
adjective
not seeing
Some dogs are trained to guide *blind* people.

bli̲ndness
noun
inability to see
The accident caused his *blindness* because his eyes were hurt.

block
noun
1. *building piece*
The wall was built with brick *blocks.*
2. *the area of buildings between two streets*
They live in the first *block* after the light.
verb
stop or prevent from passing
The police used their cars to *block* the road.

blood
noun
the red liquid in the body
Some *blood* came out when the boy fell and hurt his hand.

bloom
noun
a flower
The tree is in full *bloom.*
verb
come out with flowers
The cherry trees are *blooming.*

blo̲ssom
noun
a flower
Cherry *blossoms* appear in the spring; they are beautiful.
verb
flower or grow
Their friendship *blossomed* nicely.

blouse

noun
a woman's shirt
She bought a new white *blouse* to wear with her black skirt.

blow
noun
a hard hit
He fell on the ground when he received a *blow* on his head.
verb: blowing, blew, blown
produce a strong flow of air
The wind *blew* the leaves off the trees.

blue
noun
a color
I like *blue* and green more than black and red.
adjective
a color
This is a *blue* book.

board
noun
a flat piece
They used *boards* to block the entrance.

boast
verb
speak highly of oneself
He *boasted* about the high grades he received in school.

boat
noun
1. *a ship*
They went to New York by *boat.*
2. *a small vessel that uses oars, sails, or a motor*
I like to row a *boat.*

body
noun: bodies
1. *the physical part of a person or animal*
We must take care of our *bodies* by eating well and exercising.
2. *a mass*
In their travels they came across two *bodies* of water.

boil
verb
heat a liquid to 212°F (if it is water)
We *boiled* the eggs and used them in the salad.

bold
adjective
full of courage
He is not afraid of new experiences. He is very *bold.*

bolt
verb
fasten or lock
They *bolted* the doors at night.
They didn't want anyone to enter.

bomb
noun
a container full of explosives
The *bomb* exploded in the field.
verb
shoot or drop bombs
The enemy *bombed* the city at night.

bond
noun
a tie
Their partnership resulted in a strong *bond* between them.

bone
noun
the solid parts of the body that are made mostly of calcium
The football player fell and broke a *bone* in his arm.

book

noun
printed papers put together with covers and used for reading
I like to read history *books.*

bookcase

noun
a piece of furniture with shelves
I bought a new *bookcase* for my books.

bookstore
noun
a shop that sells books
I bought two new books from the *bookstore.*

boot

noun
a big shoe with a high top
She wears warm *boots* in winter.

border
noun
a line between two sides
We crossed the *border* between Virginia and North Carolina.
verb
be across a line from
Virginia and North Carolina *border* on each other.

bore
noun
uninteresting (thing or person)
They don't like their neighbor, because he is a *bore*. He talks about one thing all the time.
verb
See **bear** also.
1. *be uninteresting*
That old story *bores* me.
2. *make a hole*
She *bored* another hole in her belt.

bored
adjective
feeling a lack of interest.
They repeated the story many times. I felt *bored.*

boring
adjective
uninteresting
The story I read was *boring*. There was nothing new in it.

born
adjective
come to life in this world
The baby was *born* in a hospital.

borrow
verb
take and use for a time
I *borrowed* my friend's pen, because I had forgotten mine at home.

boss
noun
chief
He gives the orders in the office. He's the *boss.*
verb
act like a chief
The children don't like him, because he *bosses* his friends all the time.

both
pronoun
the two
We are missing John and Peter. *Both* are late.

bother
verb
annoy, trouble
He *bothered* his mother all afternoon. He was in her way all the time.

bottle

noun
a (usually) glass container with a narrow top
The baby drank milk out of a *bottle.*

bottom
noun
the lowest point
The ship sank to the *bottom* of the ocean.

bought
See **buy**.

bounce
noun
a spring or jump after hitting a surface
The boy caught the ball after the third *bounce.*
verb
spring or jump after hitting a surface
Basketball players know how to *bounce* balls well.

bound
adjective
sure
He is *bound* to leave soon because he has an important appointment.

bow
noun
a bending of the head or the body
They made a *bow* when the prince arrived.
verb
bend
They *bowed* their heads to the prince.

bowl

noun
a deep dish
She served the salad in a beautiful *bowl.*

box

noun
a cardboard, wood, or metal container
We offered them a nice *box* of chocolates.

boy
noun
a young male person
They have two *boys* and one girl in their family.

brackets [ ]
noun
square signs used around words or numbers
We use a lot of *brackets* in the mathematics class.

brain
noun
the gray matter in the head
The skull protects the *brain.*

brake
noun
the instrument that slows or stops a vehicle
He can stop his car in no time. He has good *brakes.*

branch
noun
1. *an arm of a tree*
The cat sat on a *branch* high up on the tree.
2. *a part or a section of a business or association.*
Our bank has many *branches* in the city.

brand
noun
a kind of a product
The only *brand* of chocolates she eats comes from Belgium.

brave
adjective
courageous, not afraid
The *brave* soldiers fought very well.

bread
noun
a baked food used to make sandwiches
She made a cheese sandwich with white *bread.*

break
verb: breaking, broke, broken
snap or separate by the use of some force
She *broke* the plate when she dropped it on the floor.

breakfast
noun
the morning meal
He likes eggs for *breakfast.*

breath
noun
the air we take in and give out when we breathe
The doctor asked her to take a deep *breath* and hold it.

breathe
verb: breathing, breathed, breathed
take air in and give it out through the nose or mouth
We *breathe* through our noses and mouths.

bride
noun
the lady getting married
The *bride* wore a white dress at the wedding.

bridegroom
noun
the gentleman getting married
The *bridegroom* wore a black suit at the wedding.

bridge
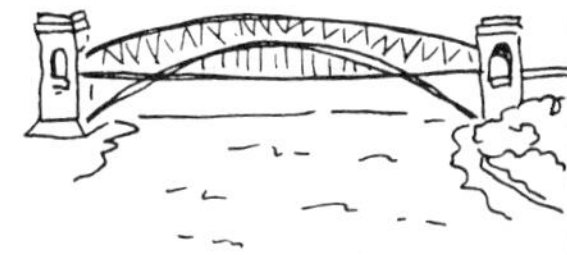

noun
a passage across a river or road
The government built a *bridge* to connect the city with the island.

brief
adjective
short
He gave a *brief* report about his trip. He did it in one minute.

briefcase
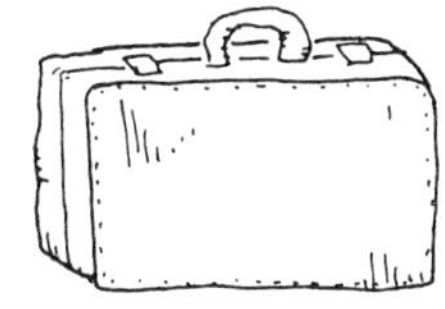

noun
a case for papers and books
My father takes his papers to the office in a *briefcase.*

bright
adjective
1. *with a lot of light*
The sun was very *bright* yesterday.
2. *clever*
Bright students receive high grades in school.

brilliant
adjective
very clever
The *brilliant* student received a prize from the school principal.

bristle
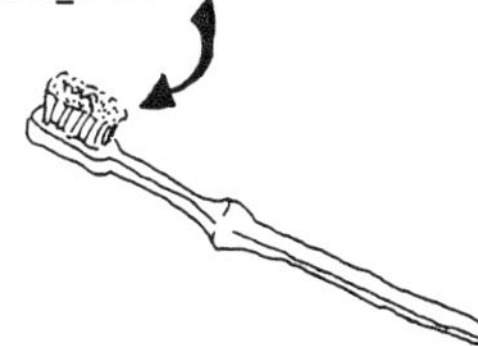

noun
a short thing like a hair on a brush
His new brush had strong *bristles.*

broad
adjective
wide
We drove along a *broad* avenue with four lanes.

broadcast
noun
a radio or television program
We learned about the weather from the news *broadcast.*
verb: broadcasting, broadcast, broadcast
air a program on radio or television
They *broadcast* the news after the game.

broke
See **break** also.
adjective
without money
He couldn't pay for the book. He was *broke.*

broken
See **break**.

brook
noun
a stream
They got some water from the *brook.*

brother
noun
masculine of sister
There are five children in the family: two *brothers* and three sisters.

brought
See **bring**.

brow
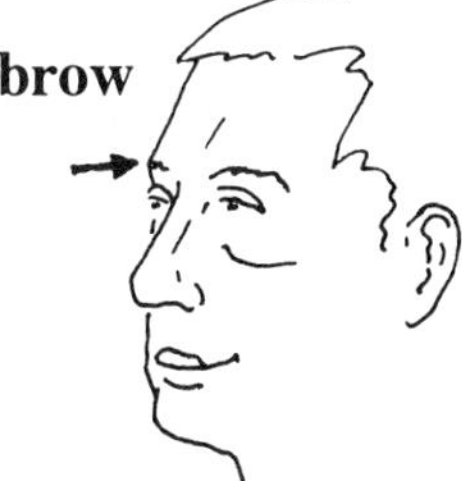

noun
the hair above the eyes
He moved his eye*brows* up and down.

brown
noun
a color
He likes *brown* for suits.
adjective
a color
This is a *brown* bag.

brush
noun
an instrument with bristles
She used a clothes *brush* to clean her coat.
verb
use this instrument
She *brushed* the dust off her coat.

bucket

noun
pail
She carried the water in a *bucket.*

bud
noun
a closed and young flower
We saw small rose *buds* in the garden.

bug
noun
an insect
We saw many *bugs* around the light.

build
verb: building, built, built
put together, construct
The children *built* a sand castle on the beach.

builder
noun
a person who builds
Our *builder* used stones on one side of our house.

building
noun
a house or bigger structure
There are ten apartments in our *building.*

built
See **build**.

bumper

noun
the piece of metal in the front and back of a car or truck
The driver hit the wall with his car *bumper.*

bunch
noun
a group of similar things together
I picked a *bunch* of grapes. I see a *bunch* of children playing together.

burden
noun
a load
There is a heavy *burden* on the donkey's back.

burn
verb: burning, burned or burnt, burned or burnt
1. *make black from heat or fire*
She *burned* the cake in the oven.
2. *catch and be on fire*
They *burned* the papers they didn't need.

burst
verb: bursting, burst, burst
break open
The boy's balloon *burst.*

bury
verb: burying, buried, buried
put underground
My grandfather was *buried* in the family cemetery.

bus
noun
a big vehicle that holds many people

They go to school on the school *bus.*
verb: bussing, bussed, bussed
move by bus
The students were *bussed* to school.

bush
noun
a plant that looks like a tree
They picked berries from a *bush.*

busier
See **busy**.

business
noun
1. *work, concern*
What he does with his money is his *business.*
2. *buying and selling*
They started a new *business* in town.

busy
adjective: busier, busiest
occupied
She is *busy* doing her homework.

but
conjunction
yet
He is short, *but* he is strong.
preposition
except
All *but* my friend are in class.

butcher
noun
a person who sells meat
We bought our steaks from the *butcher* near our house.

butter
noun
creamy fat used to cook with or to spread on bread
She makes delicious bread, *butter*, and cheese sandwiches.

butterfly

noun: butterflies
a colored insect
We saw beautiful *butterflies* in the field.

button

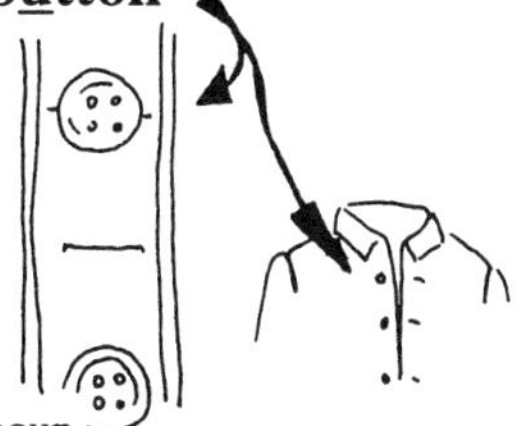

noun
a fastener used on clothes
She has three *buttons* on her jacket.
verb
to fasten with a button
She likes to *button* her jacket when she is standing or walking.

buttonhole

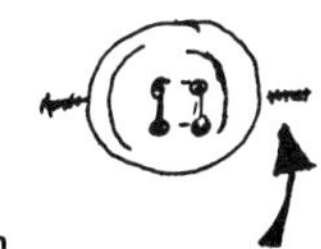

noun
the opening that a button goes through
This *buttonhole* is too small for the button.

buy
noun
a purchase
The car we got was a good *buy.*
verb: buying, bought, bought
to pay for something and get it
We *bought* some fruits and vegetables from the supermarket.

by
preposition
1. (*to show who did something)*
The book was written *by* my teacher.
2. *along*
They walked *by* the river.
3. *before*
They will be here *by* 5:00 o'clock.
4. *near*
He stood *by* the blackboard.

bye-bye
noun
good-bye
They said *bye-bye* before they left.

Cc

cab
noun
a taxi
When we landed at the airport, we took a *cab* to our hotel.

cabbage
noun
a red or green vegetable
She made a good *cabbage* salad.

cabin
noun
1. *a small house used as a resort*
They have a *cabin* near the beach. They live there in summer.
2. *a room on a ship*
Our *cabin* on the ship was near the dining room.

cable
noun
1. *a thick wire*
The electricity *cables* broke in the storm.
2. *telegram*
We received a *cable* telling us that they were arriving soon.
verb
send a telegram
They *cabled* us about their arrival.

cage
noun

a place surrounded by nets or wires where birds or animals are kept
She has two yellow birds in a *cage*.

cake

noun
a baked dessert
My mother baked a chocolate *cake*.

calculate
verb: calculating, calculated, calculated
figure out numerically
The student *calculated* his average by adding his three grades and dividing by three.

calendar
noun
a table showing the days, weeks, and months of a year
I checked my *calendar* to see what day of the week my birthday was on.

call
noun
1. *a shout*
I heard a *call* in the night.
2. *a telephone communication*
I received a *call* inviting me to the meeting.
verb
1. *shout or say aloud*
The teacher *called* the names of the students.
2. *make a telephone communication*
I *called* my friend at home last night.

calm
adjective
1. *steady, not rough*
The sea is *calm* today; we can swim easily.
2. *quiet*
The students were very *calm* in class; nobody moved or spoke.

came
See **come.**

camel

noun
an animal that lives in a desert
We rode *camels* in the desert.

camera

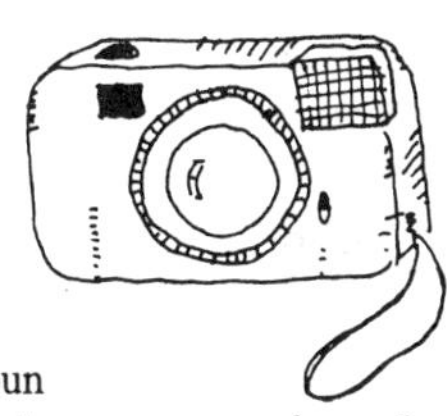

noun
an instrument used to take pictures
I put a new film in my *camera.*

camp
noun
an area with tents
The soldiers had five big tents in their *camp.*
verb
live in a tent
They *camped* on the top of the hill for a week.

can
noun
a tin container
We drank our juice out of a *can.*
auxiliary (helping) verb
1. *able to*
She *can* write very clearly.
2. *have permission*
The children *can* play on the grass here.

canal
noun
a water way made by man
The ship sailed through the *canal.*

candidate
noun
a person available or running for a position
Our *candidate* won the election.

candle

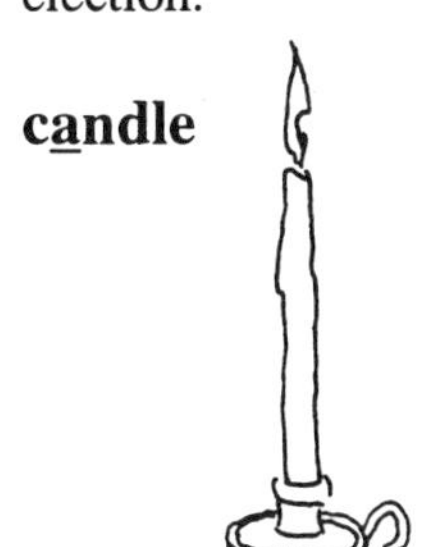

noun
a piece of wax with a wick to light up
She lit two red *candles* at dinner.

candy
noun
sweets
They offered us some chocolate *candy* in the cinema.

cannot
verb
negative of can
I am very busy; I *cannot* go to the movies.

canoe

noun
a small boat with a round opening for a person to sit in
They went down the river in *canoes.*

can't
verb
cannot
I'm busy; I *can't* go with you.

cap

noun
1. *a flat hat*
They wore *caps* to protect them from the sun.
2. *a top*
The juice bottle had a plastic *cap.*

capable
adjective
able, with ability
She will do the work well; she is very *capable.*

capacity
noun
ability to hold or contain
This hall has a *capacity* to seat sixty people.

cape
noun

1. *a piece of land stretching into the sea*
The ship sailed around the *cape.*

2. *a coat with no arms*
The lady wore a long *cape* over her dress.

capital
noun
1. *the main city of a country where the government is located*
Paris is the *capital* of France.
2. *big*
Use a *capital* letter when you write your name.

captain
noun
1. *a rank in the armed forces*
The *captain* led his soldiers into battle.
2. *The leading person or head of a team*
Our basketball *captain* wanted us to play together as a team.

capture
verb: capturing, captured, captured
1. *catch*
The cat *captured* the mouse.
2. *take and hold*
The army *captured* the city during the war.

car

noun
automobile
Our *car* has four doors.

card
noun
1. *a hard paper with a message*
She received fifteen birthday *cards* last year.
2. *a hard paper with numbers (1-10) or pictures (Jack, Queen, King) on one side*
The four of them played a *card* game together.

care
verb: caring, cared, cared
1. *show interest in and concern about*
That nurse works very hard; she *cares* for the patients.
2. *like*
Do you *care* to go with us?

career
noun
life work
He is interested in teaching as a *career.*

careful
adjective
showing care and attention
It is nice to ride with him; he is a very *careful* driver.

carefully
adverb
with care
He drives very *carefully.*

carpenter
noun
a person who makes things with wood
Our *carpenter* made us a big dining room table.

carpet

noun
rug
They have a *carpet* on their bedroom floor.

carriage
noun
a vehicle drawn by a horse or donkey that people ride in
Some *carriages* have two wheels and some have four.

carried
See **carry**.

carrot

noun
a vegetable
Rabbits like to eat *carrots.*

carry

verb: carrying, carried, carried
lift and hold in the hands or on the back
Students *carry* their school bags to school.

cart

noun
a vehicle with two wheels used to move articles
The farmer took the fruits to the market in a *cart.*

cartoon

noun
a funny picture
Children enjoy *cartoon* stories.

case

noun
a bag for papers, books, or clothes
She carried two *cases* with her on the plane.

cash

noun
money
He paid for his book in *cash.*

cassette

noun
1. *a tape*
She listened to some nice music on her *cassette.*
2. *a taped film*
We have a *cassette* of the war film.

cast

verb: casting, cast, cast
give
We *cast* our votes for our neighbor in the elections.

castle

noun
a big and fortified building
Princes lived in *castles* in the past.

cat

noun
an animal that catches mice
Our *cat* has two small kittens.

catch

verb: catching, caught, caught
receive and hold in the hand or hands
The basketball player *caught* the ball and passed it to a friend.

cattle

noun
the animals on a farm
The farmer sold his *cattle* and closed his farm.

caught

See **catch**.

cause

noun
reason
Laziness was the *cause* of their failure.
verb: causing, caused, caused
produce or lead to a result
The rain *caused* us not to leave.

cave

noun
an opening in the ground where people or animals can live or hide
In the past, people lived in *caves.*

cease
verb
stop
We can leave now; it has *ceased* raining.

ceiling
noun
the top inside surface of a room
The balloon rose to the *ceiling* of the living room.

cell
noun
1. *a prison room*
The police put the thief in a small *cell.*
2. *the smallest living thing*
Scientists study *cells* under microscopes.

cent
noun
penny
A dollar has 100 *cents.*

center
noun
1. *the middle point*
The boy stood in the *center* of the class and spoke.
2. *a place where things happen*
We swam in our activities *center.*
3. *a focus*
Money was the *center* of their attention.
verb
put in the middle
The lady *centered* the flowers on the table.

centigrade
noun
a temperature measure where water freezes at zero degrees and boils at 100 degrees
It is quite warm today. The temperature is 30°C (thirty degrees *centigrade*).

centimeter
noun
a measure which is one hundredth of a meter
He is one meter and 78 *centimeters* tall.

central
adjective
in the middle
The bank is in a *central* location in the city.

century
noun: centuries
a time of one hundred years
He lived 96 years. He lived for almost one *century.*

certain
adjective
1. *sure*
I am *certain* of one thing: it is not raining now.
2. *any, some*
There are *certain* people who are always late.

certainly
adverb
for sure, surely
I am *certainly* not going to help you with your homework. You must learn to do it yourself.

certificate
noun
an official paper stating that something has happened
The student brought a *certificate* from the doctor that he was in bed for two days.
When she finished her course of study, she received a *certificate* from the principal.

chain

noun
1. *a link of rings*
She wore a gold *chain* around her neck.
2. *a series of things*
There was a *chain* of accidents on the road.
verb
tie by using a chain
The prisoner was *chained* to the chair.

chair

noun
a seat for one person
We have six *chairs* around our dining room table.
verb
act as head
She *chaired* our meeting last week.

chalk
noun
the colored crayons used to write on a blackboard
The teacher used white and yellow *chalk* to write on the blackboard.

chamber
noun
room
The princess wanted to be alone in her private *chamber*.

champion
noun
1. *hero, the best*
Arthur Ashe was a tennis *champion*.
2. *supporter*
He is a *champion* of freedom.
verb
support
They *championed* more freedom for their children.

chance
noun
luck, unexpected happening
I was not expecting to see my cousin, but I met her by *chance* in the library.

change
noun
1. *a difference, a move to something else*
The old ways of doing things are not working; we need a *change*.
2 *a little money*
I had enough *change* for the parking meter; so I parked in the street.
verb: changing, changed, changed
do something different
They wanted to go to France. Then they *changed* their plans and went to England.

channel

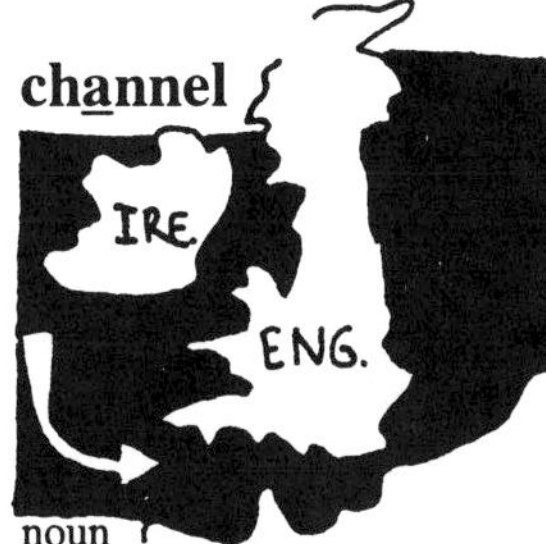

noun
1. *a seaway between two other bigger seas*
We crossed the *channel* by ship.
2. *a television station*
We watched the film on our local *channel*.
verb
send by way of
The students *channeled* their ideas to the principal through their teacher.

chapter
noun
a section of a book
Our history book has 25 *chapters*. Each *chapter* is about five pages long.

character
noun
1. *morality*
My father is a man of *character*.
2. *person in a play*
She was the leading *character* in the film.

characteristic
noun
a special quality
Touching her hair is one of her *characteristics*.

charge
verb: charging, charged, charged
1. *attack*
There was a lot of dust when the soldier *charged* on horseback.
2. *ask a price*

The restaurant *charged* us 15 dollars for our lunch.

charity
noun
giving to poor people
Their company gives a lot to *charity*. They do a lot of *charity* work.

charm
noun
delight
She shows her *charm* when she smiles and when she talks.
verb
delight (someone)
She *charmed* us with her smiles.

chart
noun
a map, graph, or picture
The *chart* showed that Boston is north of New York.

chase
noun
going after
The thief was caught after a long *chase*.
verb: chasing, chased, chased
go after
The police *chased* the thief through the city.

cheap
adjective
not expensive
Cheap things usually don't last very long.

cheat
verb
act in a dishonest way
The student who *cheated* on the test was punished.

cheater
noun
a person who cheats
The teacher caught a *cheater* and failed him.

check
noun
1. *a signed paper that can be cashed in a bank*
She cashed a *check* for 10 dollars.
2. *a stop*
The school put a *check* on new students.
3. *a mark*
I put a *check* on all the questions I knew.
verb
control
The guard *checked* everyone who entered. Only members were allowed in.

cheek

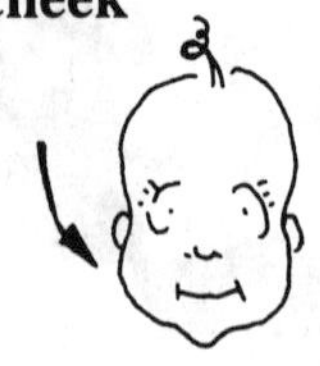

noun
the side of the face
She put some powder on her *cheeks*.

cheer
noun
a shout of joy
We heard the *cheers* when we scored a goal.
verb
shout with joy
The whole school *cheered* our team.

cheerful
adjective
happy
She is a very *cheerful* person; she is always smiling.

cheese
noun
a dairy product
Cheddar is a kind of *cheese*.
I like the taste of *cheese* sandwiches.

chemistry
noun
a science
We studied about oxygen and hydrogen in our *chemistry* class.

cherry
noun: cherries
a small fruit with a pit
We picked some *cherries* from the tree.

I like *cherry* pies.

chest
noun
1. *the top front part of the body*
Our hearts are in our *chests.*
2. *a box with a lock*
She put her jewels in a wooden *chest.*

chew
verb
break food with the teeth in the mouth
The old man could not *chew* his food well because he had a new set of false teeth.

chicken

noun
a bird that gives us eggs; a hen
We had a *chicken* barbecue for dinner.

chief
noun
head, boss
The men received their orders from their *chief.*
adjective
main
The *chief* problem they had was money.

chiefly
adverb
mainly
She sang *chiefly* to make us happy.

child
noun: children
1. *a young boy or girl*
We saw some *children* playing in the sandbox.
2. *a son or daughter*
They have five *children* in their family: two boys and three girls.

children
See **child.**

chill
noun
a cold feeling
The sick child has *chills* and a high temperature.
verb
make cold or put on ice
They *chilled* their drinks before dinner.

chimney

noun
the top part of a building that smoke goes through
In the winter you can see a lot of smoke coming from the *chimneys.*

chin
noun
the lowest part of the face
This boy hurt his *chin* when he fell.

chocolate
noun
a white or brown sweet made with cocoa
My mother baked a *chocolate* cake.

choice
noun
selection
The tallest person was my *choice* for team captain.

choose
verb: choosing, chose, chosen
select
She saw several pairs of shoes in the store. She *chose* a black pair with low heels.

chop
noun
a slice
I like the taste of lamb *chops.*
verb: chopping, chopped, chopped
slice, cut
They *chopped* their meat before they cooked it.

chorus
noun
a group of singers

The *chorus* sang a few nice songs.

chose
See **choose.**

chosen
See **choose.**

Christ
noun
the Messiah
Christ was born in Bethlehem.

Christian
noun
a person who follows Christ
Christians worship in a church.

Christmas
noun
the day Christ was born: December 25
People are very happy during the *Christmas* season.

church
noun
the place of worship for Christians
They attended a wedding in the *church* near their home.

cinema
noun
a place where films are shown
There is a *cinema* in our neighborhood.

circle
noun
1. *a round area*
There are three dots in this *circle*.
2. *a round line*
We drew a *circle* around the word.
verb: circling, circled, circled
go around
He is *circling* around the block on his bicycle.

circular
noun
a small publication which is sent around
We received a *circular* from the shop telling us about their new prices.
adjective
round
There is a *circular* road that takes you around the city.

circumstance
noun
condition
He was not feeling very well, and it was very cold outside. Under those *circumstances*, it was difficult for him to drive.

circus
noun
a funny show with funny people and dangerous acts
At the *circus* we saw a man doing tricks with three tigers.

citizen
noun
a member of a city or country
Our government treats the *citizens* very well.

city
noun: cities
a big town
When they sold their farm, they moved to the *city*.

civil
adjective
1. *kind and polite*
Her manner with people is very *civil.*
2. *relating to the citizens or people*
They are very good people; they follow both religious laws and *civil* laws.

civilian
noun
a person who is not in the armed forces
Civilians were not allowed to enter the military camp.

claim
noun
a demand
After the father died, the children had a *claim* over the business.
verb
demand

They *claimed* their father's business after he died.

clap
noun
the sound of hands hitting each other
I gave him a nice *clap* after he spoke.
verb: clapping, clapped, clapped
hit the hands together
The people *clapped* for the singer.

class
noun
1. *a number of students in a course*
Our *class* went on a trip to the zoo.
2. *a section of a plane, ship, or train*
They are rich people; they usually travel first *class.*

classmate
noun
a person in the same class
Two of my *classmates* and I studied together for the test.

classroom
noun
a room in which a class is held
Our *classroom* has one blackboard, 20 seats, and three windows.

clean
verb
make clean, remove dirt
She *cleaned* the house before her guests arrived.
adjective
opposite of dirty
He has washed his hands; now his hands are *clean.*

clear
verb
1. *move away (things)*
He *cleared* the books from the table before dinner.
2. *make free*
The police *cleared* the road before the president passed through.
adjective
1. *easy to understand*
His orders were very *clear*; all of us got the point.
2. *clean, spotless*
We drank the water from the river; it was very *clear.*

clearly
adverb
in a clear way
The teacher explained the lesson very *clearly.* We understood it.

clerk
noun
an employee who does written work
The company has a new *clerk* to keep a record of the goods.

clever
adjective
smart
He received an A on the test; he is a *clever* student.

client
noun
a person who buys things from a place
I always buy clothes from their shop. I am one of their regular *clients.*

cliff

noun
a steep place
The father and mother held their daughter's hand when they got to the top of the mountain. They did not want her to fall off the *cliff.*

climate
noun
the general weather of a place
The *climate* here is moderate; it doesn't get

too hot, and it doesn't get too cold.

climb
verb
go up walking
We *climbed* up the stairs; we like the exercise.

clinic
noun
a doctor's room or office
The patient saw the doctor in the *clinic* for an examination.

clock

noun
a time-telling instrument that sits on a table, hangs on a wall, or stands on the floor
The *clock* struck ten.
verb
time
The runner was *clocked* at 10.2 seconds.

close
verb: closing, closed, closed
shut
If you are cold, *close* the window.
adjective
near
This child is afraid to be alone. She is always *close* to her mother.

closet

noun
a built-in cupboard
We hang all our clothes in our bedroom *closet*.

cloth
noun
soft material made of silk, cotton, wool, or plastic
She bought a piece of silk *cloth* to make a new dress.

clothe
verb
cover with clothes
The mother *clothed* the baby after the bath.

clothes
noun
the things people wear
She always wears good *clothes*; she has beautiful skirts and dresses.

cloud
noun
the white, gray or black body of vapor hanging above the earth

Our plane flew high above the *clouds*.

cloudy
adjective: cloudier, cloudiest
full of clouds
It's not a good day to swim and sun bathe; it is very *cloudy*.

club
noun
1. *a stick*
Baseball batters used *clubs* to hit the ball. The guard carried a *club*; he did not carry a gun.
2. *a place where people meet for fun*
We had dinner in our country *club*.
3. *one of the four kinds of playing cards*
She had five cards in her hand: three hearts and two *clubs*.

coach
noun
1. *a bus*
My class went on a trip by *coach*.
2. *a person who trains others*
The football *coach* was happy that his players were winning.

coal
noun
the black stones used for burning
We burn *coal* in our barbecue.

coarse
adjective
rough
We drove slowly on the *coarse* road; the road was not smooth.

coast
noun
shore
The drive down the *coast* was beautiful; we had the sea on one side and the mountains on the other.

coat

noun
1. *a long warm jacket worn over other clothes*
She bought a new wool *coat* for the winter.
2. *a cover*
She put two *coats* of icing on the cake: one red and one blue.

cock
noun
male chicken, opposite of hen

We hear the *cocks* early in the morning on the farm.

code
noun
the use of numbers or letters to store or send signals or messages
Nobody could understand their letters, because they used a secret *code* in them.

coffee
noun
a dark drink made of roasted coffee beans
I like tea in the morning, but she drinks two cups of *coffee.*

coffin
noun
a wood or metal box in which a dead person is put
They opened the *coffin* to see their father before he was buried.

coin

noun
a metal piece of money
Nickels and dimes are American *coins.*
verb
make
The inventor *coined* a new word to give a name to his invention.

cold
noun
1. *a physical feeling of not being well in the head or nose or some other part of the body*
She can't go to school today; she has a *cold,* and she is in bed.
2. *a state of low temperature*
He wore a coat and went out in the *cold.*
adjective
low in temperature
We wear coats on *cold* days.

collapse
verb: collapsing, collapsed, collapsed
break and fall
The old hut *collapsed* in the storm.

collar

noun
the neck part of a shirt or blouse

He wore a shirt, but he left the *collar* button open.

collect
verb
gather
They *collected* some clothes to give to their poor neighbor.

collection
noun
1. *gathering, collecting*
I collect stamps. I have a big stamp *collection.*
2. *money received*
After she sang in the circus, she passed a basket around for a *collection.*

collector
noun
a person who collects (things)
I save the stamps I receive; I am a stamp *collector.*

college
noun
1. *an institution of higher learning*
Our *college* offers B.A. degrees.
2. *study after high school*
She plans to start her *college* education when she graduates from high school.

collide
verb: colliding, collided, collided
hit or strike (each other)
The two cars *collided* in the storm, but nobody was hurt.

collision
noun
the state of colliding
There was a car accident, but nobody was hurt in the *collision.*

colonel
noun
a rank in the armed forces
The army *colonel* led his men into battle.

color
noun
a quality that can be seen like red, blue, and yellow
The *color* of this car is red.
verb
to put or give a quality like red, blue, and yellow
She *colored* the tree green.

colorful
adjective
1. *full of color*
She wore a *colorful* dress to the party. It had more than five colors.
2. *varied, interesting*
He is a very *colorful* speaker. He gives many interesting examples.

column
noun
1. *a vertical section on a page*
There are three *columns* of words on this page.
2. *a tall and solid structure*
There are two stone *columns* at the entrance to this building.

comb

noun
a tool for fixing the hair
Her hair looked very bad; she forgot her *comb* at home.
verb
fix the hair
She *combs* her hair every time she goes anywhere.

combination
noun
mixture
She used a *combination* of vegetables for her salad.

combine
verb: combining, combined, combined
mix, join

Because our teacher was absent, they *combined* our class with another class.

come
verb: coming, came, come
1. *arrive*
The plane *came* in at 4:00 p.m.
2. *approach*
Come to the blackboard and write your name.

come back
verb
return
When are you *coming back* from your trip? We would like to see you.

comfort
noun
ease
They live in *comfort.* They have enough money to spend.

comfortable
adjective
providing ease
I have a *comfortable* bed; I can sleep in it all night very easily.

comic
adjective
funny
Children like *comic* books with pictures.

coming
See **come**.

comma
noun
a punctuation mark
If you want to know what a *comma* is, look at the *comma* between *is* and *look* in this sentence.

command
noun
order
The captain gave a *command* to all his men to return immediately.
verb
order
The captain *commanded* his men to return.

comment
noun
remark
The teacher had a few *comments* about my paper; he wanted me to correct it.
verb
remark
We *commented* on his talk; we said it was good and clear.

commerce
noun
trade
There is a lot of *commerce* between our two countries; we buy many things from each other.

commercial
noun
advertisement
I learned about the new beds from a television *commercial.*
adjective
having to do with business
He has a good *commercial* mind; he knows when to buy and when to sell.

commission
noun
1. *money paid to an agent*
He helped us buy the house, and he received his *commission.*
2. *duty, work*
The army had the *commission* of occupying the city.

commit
verb: committing, committed, committed
1. *do (something bad)*
The student *committed* three mistakes in his language class.
2. *dedicate (something) for a cause*
She *committed* her free time to helping old people.

committee
noun
a group of people (meeting)
The principal of our school asked three teachers to form a

committee to meet with the parents.

common
adjective
1. *usual, ordinary*
It is very *common* for them to go to the library. I see them there often.
2. *used or shared by all*
These are *common* grounds. Everyone can come here to sit or walk.

communicate
verb: communicating, communicated, communicated
give and take
They *communicate* by telephone every day.

communication
noun
1. *message*
I received their *communication* yesterday; they asked me to see them.
2. *giving and taking*
We had a short *communication* on the telephone; we discussed the weather.

companion
noun
a person who is with another
I don't like to travel alone; I prefer to have a *companion*.

company
noun: companies
1. *a business firm*
He works for a *company* that makes cars.
2. *companion*
She is good *company*; you are never bored with her.
3. *a group of people*
We have *company* for dinner tonight.

compare
verb: comparing, compared, compared
show or tell if something is the same or different
He *compared* the two cars for price and size.

compel
verb: compelling, compelled, compelled
force
The captain *compelled* his men to walk further.

complain
verb
say that one does not like something
They *complained* about the service in the hotel; nobody answered when they rang the bell..

complete
adjective
full, whole
We can play the game; my set is *complete*.

verb: completing, completed, completed
to make (something) full or whole
The teacher asked us to *complete* the sentences by adding the correct verbs.

compose
verb: composing, composed, composed
create, write, make
Mozart *composed* music.

composed of
verb and preposition
made up of, consisting of
The book is *composed of* three sections.

composition
noun
1. *creation*
Mozart's music *compositions* are famous.
2. *essay*
Our English teacher asked us to write a *composition* describing the school party.

compute
verb: computing, computed, computed
calculate
We *computed* the amount we had to pay by adding all our bills.

computer
noun

an instrument that receives and gives information fast
Our company does all its reports and business calculations on a *computer*.

conceal
verb
hide
He wore a coat to *conceal* his dirty shirt.

concern
noun
interest, business
His private life is of no *concern* to us.
verb
interest, worry
His low marks in school *concern* me; I want to help him.

concerning
preposition
with reference to, about
I had nothing to say *concerning* their problem; I knew nothing about it.

conclude
verb: concluding, concluded, concluded
1. *come to the end*
He *concluded* his talk by saying, "Thank you."
2. *come to a final decision*
From the way he talked about art, we *concluded* that he was an artist.

conclusion
noun
1. *end*
The program started at 6:00 p.m. and came to a *conclusion* at 8:00 p.m.
2. *final decision*
Three of us saw the film and came to the same *conclusion*: we did not like it.

condemn
verb
say that someone or something is bad
We *condemned* the father for shouting at his children.

condition
noun
1. *situation, circumstance*
It is cold and rainy; under such *conditions*, it is difficult to walk a long distance.
2. *basis*
He did not want to come with us at first. Then he said he would come on *condition* that we drive.

conduct
noun
manner
The child's *conduct* was good. He did not make any noise.

conduct
verb
lead
Our teacher *conducted* the tour to the museum.

conference
noun
a meeting
The teachers in our city had a *conference* to discuss teaching methods.

confess
verb
say that one has done something
The thief *confessed* to the police that he had stolen the car. He said, "I did it."

confession
noun
a statement that one has done something
The police heard the thief's *confession* about stealing the car.

confidence
noun
trust
We have *confidence* in our captain; he knows the game and he leads us well.

confident
adjective
feeling or having trust
I am *confident* that I will pass the test; I have studied very well.

confine
verb: confining, confined, confined
limit
The prisoner was *confined* to his room.

confirm
verb
say that something is so
I wondered if my friend had left. I telephoned his sister and she *confirmed* that; she told me that he had left.

conflict
noun
1. *a struggle, a war*
Three soldiers were wounded in the *conflict* between the two armies.
2. *a tie*
There is a *conflict* in our class schedule. Both history and science are scheduled at 8:00 a.m.

confuse
verb: confusing, confused, confused
make things unclear
We were talking about cars, but he *confused* us by talking about engines.

confusion
noun
a condition making things unclear
There was *confusion* in the hall when one teacher asked us to stay and another teacher asked us to leave.

congress
noun
1. *The American legislative body*
In the U.S., *Congress* makes the laws.
2. *meeting*
The doctors had a *congress* to discuss different diseases.

connect
verb
put together
My key chain broke, and I fixed it; I *connected* the two broken rings.

connection
noun
tie, relation
There is a *connection* between words and meanings.

conquer
verb
1. *defeat*
The enemies were very weak; we *conquered* them easily in the war.
2. *occupy and take*
The army *conquered* the city after a long struggle. Now the army rules over the city.

conscience
noun
the inner voice in people that tells them if they are doing the right or the wrong things
She wanted so much to take the money she was offered, but her *conscience* did not allow her to do that; she thought it was unfair.

conscious
adjective
knowing
I was saying something about my friend. I did not know that he was listening. I was not *conscious* of his presence.

consent
verb
agree
She asked her parents if she could go to her friends. Her parents *consented*; they allowed her to do so.

consequence
noun
result
If you spend too much money today, you will feel the *consequences* tomorrow.

consequently
adverb
as a result
He spent all his money last week.

Consequently, he had no money for a book today.

consider
verb
1. *give thought to*
They asked me a question, but I wanted to *consider* the matter before giving them an answer.
2. *look at*
I *consider* my brother as my best friend; we like each other, and we help each other.

considerable
adjective
quite a bit
We can play a game with you; we have a *considerable* amount of free time today.

considerably
adverb
quite a bit
Ask my brother to play with you. He has *considerably* more free time than I have.

consist
verb
be composed (of)
The salad *consisted* of lettuce, tomatoes, and carrots.

consonant
noun
a letter or a sound that is not a vowel
A, b, and c are letters. B and c are *consonants*.

constant
adjective
unchanging
We have *constant* warm weather in summer.

constantly
adverb
all the time
This child never rests; he is *constantly* moving.

construct
verb
build
The school *constructed* a new gym. The old one was torn down.

construction
noun
building
The company is planning the *construction* of a new office building.

consume
verb: consuming, consumed, consumed
use
The children *consumed* all the ice-cream we had at home.

consumer
noun
1. *user*
They are milk *consumers;* they drink a lot of it.
2. *buyer*
Shops usually consider the wishes of *consumers.*

contact
noun
connection
They had not seen each other for a long time. Then they made *contact* with each other through a friend.

contact
verb
get in touch with
I *contacted* my friend and asked her a question on the telephone.

contain
verb
has in it
This camera *contains* a new film.

content
noun
what a thing is made of or what it has in it
I emptied the *contents* of my bag; I had three books and a pencil inside it.

content
adjective
satisfied

I received a B on my test. I should have done better, but I am *content* with my grade.

contest
noun
race
Two persons want first prize in the race. We don't know who will win the *contest.*

continent
noun
a large part of the earth's land
North America and South America are two of the world's *continents.*

continue
verb: continuing, continued, continued
go on
They started their work at 6:00 p.m. and they *continued* with it till 11:00 p.m.

contract
noun
agreement
We signed a *contract* for one year when we rented the house.

contrary
noun
the opposite
He is not lazy; on the *contrary,* he works very hard.

contrast
noun
difference
These two cars are very similar; but can you see any *contrast* between them?

contrast
verb
show the difference
When we *contrasted* the cars, we found that one was a bit wider than the other.

contribute
verb: contributing, contributed, contributed
offer
She *contributed* some money to help the poor family.

contribution
noun
an offer
She made a money *contribution* to help the poor family.

control
noun
command
All the students behaved well; the teacher had good *control* over the class.
verb: controlling, controlled, controlled
have command
The teacher *controlled* the class well; he made sure the students did their work well.

convenient
adjective
suitable
It was not *convenient* for me to meet with them; I was very busy then.

conversation
noun
talk between people
We had a very interesting *conversation* with our guests; we talked about our school teams.

convince
verb: convincing, convinced, convinced
make someone think as you
He didn't want to study hard, but I *convinced* him that it was important for him to do so.

cook

noun
a person who prepares food
I know a restaurant that has very good food. They have a clever *cook.*

verb
prepare food
My mother *cooked* a delicious chicken dish.

cool
adjective
1. *not warm, but not too cold*
Our water was *cool* because we had it in the refrigerator.
2. *not tense and excited*
With all the heated argument, my brother kept *cool;* he was calm and he talked softly.

copy
noun: copies
an exact image
I sent my cousin a letter, but I kept a *copy* of it myself.
verb: copying, copied, copied
1. *imitate*
Monkeys like to *copy* people. They do what people do.
2. *write the same thing again*
The students *copied* what the teacher wrote on the blackboard.

cord
noun
a string
The lights went out because the electric *cord* broke.

corn
noun
1. *a kind of grain*
I like the taste of *corn*bread.

2. *a yellow vegetable*
We eat boiled *corn* with our meat and potatoes.

corner

noun
1. *the place where two walls meet*
This chair is in the *corner.*
2. *the place where two streets meet*
My friend met me at the *corner* of the road near our house.

correct
verb
make right
The teacher *corrected* our compositions. He showed us our mistakes.
adjective
right, opposite of wrong
I had no mistakes in my answers; they were *correct* answers.

correspond
verb
send and receive communications
My friend and I *correspond* with each other by mail.

correspondent
noun
a person who sends news and messages to a newspaper or magazine
The daily newspaper in our city received regular news from two *correspondents* who were with the army in the battle.

cost
noun
price
The *cost* of the book was too high for me; I didn't have enough money to pay for it.
verb: costing, cost, cost
That book *cost* too much; my friend paid a high price for it.

cottage

noun
a small house usually used for a vacation
My friends live in their *cottage* by the sea in summer.

cotton
noun
a kind of material made from the plant
I like *cotton* shirts; I don't like silk or wool shirts.

cough
noun
the sudden blowing of air through the mouth because of an illness or a problem in the throat or lungs
The doctor gave him a good medicine for his *cough.*
verb
make such blowing
He couldn't sleep well because he *coughed* all night.

could
auxiliary verb
can
Could you lend me your pen for a moment, please?
See **can.**
He *could* swim across the pool in ten seconds.

couldn't
auxiliary verb
could not
I *couldn't* walk as fast as he could.

count
verb
1. *call the numbers in order*
Her child can *count* to ten.
2. *rely*
You can *count* on me to be there; I will attend the meeting.

country
noun: countries
1. *a nation*
Our *country* has a nice flag.
2. *a rural area where there is no city or town*
They have a small cottage in the *country*; they go there a few times a year. We often talk walks in the *country*.

county
noun: counties
a section of a state in the U.S.
We elected a new sheriff in our *county.*

couple
noun
1. *two*
I bought a *couple* of apples yesterday.
2. *two people (usually a man and woman)*
Mr. and Mrs. Brown are a young *couple.*

courage
noun
daring, lack of fear
The soldier showed a lot of *courage* by rushing into battle.

courageous
adjective
daring, brave
The captain was very *courageous*; he faced the enemy without fear.

course
noun
1. *a school or college subject*
We learned about the Romans in our history *course.*
2. *the way a thing runs or goes*
You can reach the castle if you follow the *course* of the river.
3. *a part (a dish) of a meal*
Our dessert, a chocolate cake, was the last *course* of our dinner.
4. *certainly **(of course)***
When I asked her if she could play the piano, she said, "Of *course*, I can."

court
noun
1. *a place where legal matters are decided*
The judge listened to the lawyers in *court.*

2. *a field for a ball game*
We saw the players on the basketball *court.*

cousin

noun
the son or daughter of an uncle or aunt
I have six *cousins:* two boys and four girls.

cover

noun
a lid or a wrap
A blanket is a good *cover* for a bed.
verb
put a lid or a wrap
She *covered* the food to keep it warm.

cow

noun
an animal that gives us milk
The farmer fed his *cows* very well. He wanted them to give a lot of milk.

crack

noun
a slit, a split
She threw the glass away because there was a *crack* in it.
verb
slit or split
She *cracked* the glass when she was washing it.

crash

noun
1. *a bang*
We heard the *crash* when the car hit a tree.
2. *an accident*
Nobody was hurt in the car *crash.*
verb
hit suddenly
The car *crashed* on the side of a truck.

crawl

verb
1. *move on hands and feet*
The child *crawled* on the rug to get from one place to another.
2. *swim in a special way*
They *crawled* across the pool.

crazy

adjective: crazier, craziest
not sane, not logical
It was very dangerous to drive in such bad weather. He was *crazy* to do it.

cream

noun
a dairy product that has a lot of fat in it, the top part of milk
She likes *cream* in her coffee, and he likes *cream* on his dessert.

create

verb: creating, created, created
make something (from nothing)
The painter *created* a beautiful picture.

creature

noun
a living animal, bird, or insect
Our world is full of lovely *creatures* that live and move in different ways.

credit

noun
a plus in an account
He has a *credit* balance in his bank.
verb
add or put a plus to an account
I took a check to my bank, and they *credited* my account.

creep

verb: creeping, crept, crept
move on the stomach
The baby tried to *creep* on the rug.

crept

See **creep.**

crew

noun
the sailors on a ship or the officers on a plane

The plane we came on had 210 passengers and a *crew* of 12.

cried
See **cry.**

crime
noun
a very serious illegal act
Those who commit *crimes* are put in prison.

criminal
noun
a person who commits a crime
Criminals are put in prison.

crop
noun
a farm product
The bean *crop* this year was very good. We had a lot of beans.

cross
noun
1. *a bar with another shorter bar crossing it nearer to the top*
Some Christians wear *crosses.*
2. *a sign like an X*
The teacher put a check on our correct answers and a *cross* on the wrong answers.
verb
go from one side to the other
We *cross* the river by boat to reach the island.

crossing
noun
a place where someone can cross
There was a red light at the railroad *crossing*.

crowd
noun
a big number of people
We could not drive very fast because there were *crowds* of people in the street.
verb
fill a place with people
The students *crowded* the room when they came in.

crown

noun
the thing that kings and queens wear on their heads
The queen wore a *crown* at the meeting.

cruel
adjective
very rough and unkind to people or animals
I don't like people who are *cruel* to animals.
I like people to treat animals kindly.

cry
noun
a shout
The police heard a *cry*, and they found a boy needing help.
verb: crying, cried, cried
have or shed tears
The story they heard was so sad that many of them *cried* aloud.

cultivate
verb: cultivating, cultivated, cultivated
work on the land to make it ready to grow crops
The farmer knew how to *cultivate* his field to get the best crops.

cup

noun
a vessel used for tea, coffee, or soup
She had two *cups* of coffee with her breakfast.

cupboard

noun
a wood or metal cabinet to put things in
She keeps her canned food in her kitchen *cupboard.*

cure
noun
a remedy
The doctor had a *cure* for the sick girl; he gave her medicine that made her well.
verb: curing, cured, cured
remedy
The doctor *cured* the girl with the medicine he gave her.

curiosity
noun
the love of knowing and learning new things
His *curiosity* makes him ask so many questions.

curious
adjective
wanting to know things
He is very *curious* about animals; he wants to know all about them.

current
noun
a flow
When we opened the door and the window, we felt an air *current.*
adjective
present
The *current* price for our daily newspaper is 25 cents.

curtain

noun
the cloth that covers a window
They bought new *curtains* for their bedroom windows.

curve
noun
a turn
The driver was very careful when he drove around the *curve.*

custom
noun
habit
We have the *custom* of shaking hands with people when we meet them.

customer
noun
a person who buys things from a store
The shops in our city want to know what the *customers* like.

customs
noun
the official place where officers search suitcases at airports, seaports, and/or borders
The *customs* officer asked us if we had any fruits in our suitcases.

cut
noun
1. *a wound*
She had a *cut* on her hand when she fell.
2. *a drop*
The secretary had a *cut* in her pay when she was away.
verb: cutting, cut, cut
1. *wound*
She *cut* her hand when she fell.
2. *drop*
They *cut* her pay when she was away for a week.

cute
adjective
very pleasant, pretty
She looks very *cute* when she combs her hair back and wears a red dress.

cut out
verb
stop
The mother was tired of her son's jumping in the room. She said, "*Cut* that *out*, please." He did; he stopped jumping.

Dd

dabble
verb
deal with something for a short time
He *dabbled* with chemistry for a while; then he moved to astronomy.

dad
noun
father
My *dad* loved my sister and me.
So did my mom.

daddy
noun: daddies
father
He is a good *daddy* to his children.

daily
noun: dailies
a newspaper that comes out every day.
Our town has two *dailies.* I read one of them.
adjective
every day
His *daily* office hours are 8:00 to 12:00 and 2:00 to 4:00.
adverb
every day
Planes land at our airport *daily.*

dam
noun

a wall or border to stop water from flowing
The government built a *dam* across the river.

damage
noun
harm
The accident caused some *damage* to the car: one light broke.
verb: damaging, damaged, damaged
cause harm
The accident *damaged* a small part of the car. Only one light broke.

dance
noun
moving to music
People of different countries have different kinds of *dances.*
verb: dancing, danced, danced
move to music
First they listened to the music, then they *danced* together.

dancer
noun
a person who dances
The *dancers* wore colored dresses for their dance.

danger
noun
a situation that may bring harm
There may be *danger* in swimming alone; if you need help, you won't be able to get it.

dangerous
adjective
able to bring harm
It is *dangerous* to drive fast; accidents can happen.

dark
noun
absence of light
We cannot read in the *dark.*
adjective
1. *not light, deep in color*
This car has a *dark* blue color.
2. *not lighted*
We cannot read in a *dark* room. We need light to read.

date
noun
1. *a brown, red, or black fruit that comes from a palm tree*
My mother puts *dates* in some cakes. *Date* palms are quite tall.
2. *a given time*
The *date* of the party was June 25, 1994.

daughter
noun
a female child of a father or mother
Mr. and Mrs. Brown have five children: two sons and three *daughters.*

dawn
noun
the beginning (break) of daytime
In good weather, we get up at *dawn* and see the sunrise.

day
noun
1. *opposite of night*
He works very hard during the *day.* He rests and sleeps at night.
2. *twenty-four hours*
They were away for five *days* last week.

dead
adjective
not living
Our friends kept their bird outside all night. It was very cold. Now the bird is *dead.*

deaf
adjective
not able to hear
Deaf people use a special kind of sign language.

deal
noun
agreement, arrangement
My brother and I have a *deal:* he carries our bags one day and I carry them another.

deal with
verb
handle
I can *deal* with my own problems myself.

dear
noun
loved one
"You are my *dear,*" the mother said to her daughter.
adjective
1. *loved*
They are *dear* friends. I like them very much.
2. *expensive, costing a lot*
That coat is so *dear* that I cannot buy it myself.

death
noun
end of life
The war caused the *death* of many people.

debt
noun
what one owes
He borrowed so much money that his *debts* are growing. He is deep in *debt.*

deceive
verb: deceiving, deceived, deceived
cheat (someone)
He *deceived* me; he made me buy something I didn't need. He just wanted to sell it.

December
noun
the twelfth month of the year
December comes after November and before January.

decent
adjective
nice, good, and proper
We met a very *decent* gentleman; he was kind and he behaved very nicely.

decide
verb: deciding, decided, decided
make up one's mind
After I examined all three radios, I *decided* to buy the smallest one, because I wanted a radio to fit in my pocket.

decision
noun
making up one's mind
I can study or I can play with my friends. I think my *decision* will be to study. I will do well on my test, and

then I can play.

deck
noun

1. *a floor or level on a ship or plane*
Our seats were on the upper *deck* of the plane.

2. *a full set of playing cards (52 cards)*
We needed two *decks* for our card game.

declare
verb: declaring, declared, declared
announce to the public
The school principal *declared* all the rules to the students.

decline
verb: declining, declined, declined
1. *go down*
The prices of shirts *declined* when the stores discovered they had so many of them.
2. *refuse*
They invited us to dinner, but we *declined* because we were going to be out of town.

deduct
verb
reduce, take away from
When I told him that I could not pay ten dollars for the pen, he *deducted* two dollars from the price. I paid eight dollars for it.

deep
adjective
far down
They boy didn't go to the *deep* side of the pool; he didn't know how to swim.

deer
noun: deer
a big gazelle
The *deer* run very fast.

defeat
verb
beat
The stronger army *defeated* the weaker army.

defect
noun
a fault, something wrong
They could not sell the shirt because it had a *defect:* one sleeve was shorter than the other.

defect
verb
leave, desert
One soldier *defected* from the army, and he was punished.

defend
verb
protect
The wall they built helped to *defend* the city.

defense
noun
protection
They built a wall for the *defense* of the city.

definite
adjective
exact, precise
She had a *definite* answer to our question; she knew what to say.

degree
noun
1. *a level of temperature*
The temperature today is 80 *degrees* Fahrenheit; it is warm.
2. *a university or college diploma*
She has an M.A. *degree* in History.

delay
noun
keeping till a later time
We arrived late because of a *delay* on the way; the traffic was heavy.

verb
keep till a later time
The traffic *delayed* us; we arrived late.

delete
verb: deleting, deleted, deleted
take out
There were ten names on the list. Then one name was *deleted.* Now we have nine names on the list.

delicate
adjective
1. *soft and nice*
She wore a *delicate* lace dress.
2. *sensitive*
She is a *delicate* person; a wrong word or a wrong move can hurt her.

delicious
adjective
having a nice taste
My mother baked a *delicious* cake; I loved it.

delight
noun
joy, something liked very much
The chocolate cake we had was a *delight*; it was soft and delicious.
verb
make someone enjoy something very much
They *delighted* us with their music and dances.

delightful
adjective
very nice, very enjoyable
We had a *delightful* evening listening to music and nice stories.

deliver
verb
1. *speak or read*
The school principal *delivered* a good speech to the students.
2. *take something to someone*
The mailman *delivered* three letters to our address.
3. *give birth*
His wife *delivered* a baby boy in the hospital.

demand
verb
1. *need*
Baking *demands* an oven.
2. *make a request*
The teacher *demanded* silence in the library.

democracy
noun: democracies
a system of government where the people make decisions
The United States is a *democracy*.

Democrat
noun
a member of the Democratic Party in the U.S.
President Clinton is a *Democrat*.

democratic
adjective
having the nature of democracy
The teacher was very *democratic* with the students; he allowed them to make certain decisions.

denied
See **deny.**

dental
adjective
having to do with teeth
She has a *dental* problem; one of her teeth is broken.

dentist
noun
a doctor who treats teeth
When she broke her tooth, she went to see her *dentist*.

deny
verb: denying, denied, denied
say that something isn't so
They thought that she had eaten the last apple. She *denied* it. She said that her brother was the one who ate the apple.

depart
verb
leave
They arrived early, but they *departed* before the end of the game.

department
noun
a division of an organization
The English *department* in our school has eight teachers.

department store
noun
a store with divisions for shoes, clothes, toys, etc.
He bought a new suit from a famous *department store* in the city.

depend on
verb
trust, lean on
I *depend on* his ideas. He is very wise.

deposit
noun
1. *a first part payment*
I didn't have enough money to pay for the suit; so I paid a small *deposit* on it.
2. *something put somewhere*
She made a *deposit* of $100 in the bank.
verb
put down
She *deposited* the plates on the table and left. We put them in their right places.
He *deposited* some money in the bank.

depth
noun
the measure of how deep a thing is
The *depth* of the pool was five feet. It is five feet deep.

descend
verb
go down
They climbed up the mountain last week, and they *descended* today.

descendant
noun
a person who is a child of a child of a child (of somebody)
She thinks she is a *descendant* of Napoleon.

describe
verb: describing, described, described
give the features or characteristics of something
She *described* the thief so well that the police were able to find him.

description
noun
the features or characteristics of something
Her *description* of the thief was so good that the police were able to catch him.

desert

noun
a dry land with sand
The best way to travel in a *desert* is on a camel.

desert
verb
leave, abandon
The soldier was punished because he *deserted* the army in a time of war.

deserve
verb: deserving, deserved, deserved
be worthy of (something)
He *deserved* the prize because he was the best player.

design
noun
plan
The engineer had a good *design* for the new building. We saw his *design*.
verb
plan
The engineer *designed* the new building.

desire
noun
wish, want

His *desire* is to become a doctor.
verb: desiring, desired, desired
want, wish
He *desired* a seat in the front row.

desk

noun
a table to study or work at
The secretary had a typewriter on her *desk*.

desperate
adjective
without hope
He became *desperate* when he lost his money. We tried to comfort him.

dessert
noun
the sweet course of a meal
We had ice-cream for *dessert*.

destroy
verb
ruin, spoil
The building was *destroyed* in the fire.

destruction
noun
ruining, spoiling
The war caused the *destruction* of the city.

detail
noun
an individual fact
The teacher asked us to give him the *details* of our school trip.

detailed
adjective
with all the small facts
We gave the teacher a *detailed* picture of our school trip.

determination
noun
a strong will and decision
He does his work with *determination*; he knows what he wants, and he works hard.

determine
verb: determining, determined, determined
make a strong decision
She *determined* to continue her studies; she wanted to become a nurse.

determined
adjective
decided
She is *determined* to become a nurse; nothing will stop her.

develop
verb
1. *grow and change*
The little chick *developed* into a big hen.
2. *turn into photos*
We *developed* our film and saw pictures of our trip.

development
noun
1. *growth and change*
The parents observed the fast *development* of their children.
2. *turning into photos*
We took our film to the photographer for *development*.

device
noun
an instrument
A thermometer is a *device* to measure one's temperature.

devil
noun
a bad person or being
The little boy behaved like a *devil*; he broke all the dishes.

devote
verb: devoting, devoted, devoted
set (something) aside for a purpose
She *devoted* all her time to helping old people.

devoted
adjective
loyal, sincere

She is *devoted* to helping old people.

devotion
noun
loyalty, sincerity
Old people love her for her *devotion* to them.

dew
noun
water drops that are found on plants, cars, and other places on a cold night
It was so cold at night that our car was wet because of the *dew.*

diagnose
verb: diagnosing, diagnosed, diagnosed
examine and find out, analyze
The teacher *diagnosed* the student's English problem as a matter of spelling.

diagnosis
noun
analysis, finding out
The teacher's *diagnosis* of the problem as a matter of spelling was right.

diagonal
adjective
going from the first to the third or from the second to the fourth corner of a shape with four sides
We drew a *diagonal* line to divide the square into two triangles.

diagram

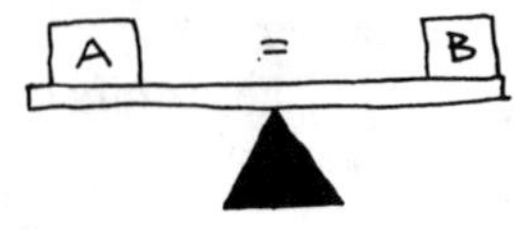

noun
a drawing that represents something
The teacher drew a *diagram* to show us how a balance works.

dial

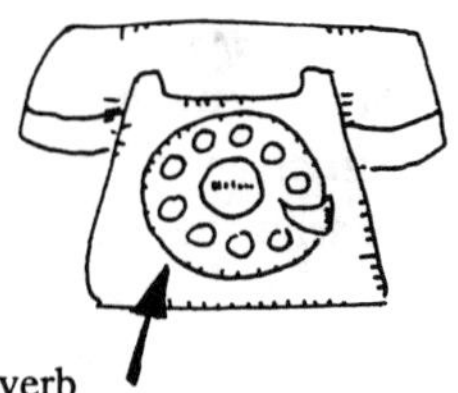

verb
turn the disk on a telephone to make a call
I couldn't speak with my friend on the telephone, because I *dialed* the wrong number.

dialog
noun
an oral (or written) exchange of ideas
The two groups came to a common understanding after a long *dialog* between them.

diamond
noun
a precious stone
The rich lady wore a beautiful *diamond* ring.

diary
noun: diaries
a book or notebook with dates for daily notes
He writes down all his appointments in his *diary*.

dictionary
noun: dictionaries
a book like this one with words and their meanings
When I don't know a word, I look it up in my English *dictionary.*

did
See **do.**

didn't
auxiliary verb
negative of did, did not
She *didn't* eat her food; she wasn't hungry.

die
verb: dying, died, died
stop living
The plants *died* without water.

diet
noun
a plan of what foods to eat
The doctor put the patient on a special liquid *diet.* She went on a *diet* to lose weight.

differ
verb
be not the same
My friend and I *differed* in our ideas about the film.

difference
noun
the thing which is not the same
They looked alike, but the *difference* between them was their height: one of them was tall; the other was short.

different
adjective
not the same
The two sisters are very *different*: one is fast and one is slow.

difficult
adjective
not easy
The teacher asked us four questions. I answered three correctly, but one question was *difficult* for me.

difficulty
noun
a matter of not being easy
I faced some *difficulty* with one question only. The other questions were easy for me.

dig
verb: digging, dug, dug
make a hole in the earth
Some animals *dig* in the earth and hide things.

digest
verb
change food in the stomach so that it can become a part of the body
We can't *digest* a stone if we swallow one.

dig for
verb: digging for, dug for, dug for
go into the earth to look for something
They are trying to *dig for* oil.

dig into
verb: digging into, dug into, dug into
study very well
The school principal is *digging into* the problem we had with one student.

digit
noun
a number: 1, 2, 3, 4, 5, 6, 7, 8, 9, 0
The second digit in the number 457 is 5.

digital

adjective
showing numbers
I have a *digital* alarm clock.

dignity
noun
grandness of character
That prince moves with *dignity*; one can see that he is very noble.

dig out
verb: digging out, dug out, dug out
get out of the earth
A man hid some money in the garden. A week later he *dug* it *out*.

dim
verb: dimming, dimmed, dimmed
make darker (with less light)
They *dimmed* the lights in the hall when the play started.
adjective: dimmer, dimmest
not bright
You can't read well if the lights are *dim*.

dime
noun
a coin of ten cents
She has a quarter, a *dime*, and a nickel in her pocket; she has 40 cents.

dine
verb: dining, dined, dined
eat a main meal

They *dined* in a restaurant last night.

dining room
noun
the room in the house in which one eats
They have a living room, a *dining* room, and two bedrooms in their house.

dinner
noun
the main meal of the day
During the week, we have our *dinner* in the evening; on Sunday, we have it at noon.

dip
noun
going into the water for a short time
We took a *dip* in the sea first; then we sat on the beach all day.
verb: dipping, dipped, dipped
go into the water
The little boy dropped his toy in the pool; his father *dipped* his hand in the water and got it for him.

direct
verb
lead, show the way
The teacher *directed* us to the library.
adjective
straight
She gave me a *direct* answer to my question.

direction
noun
1. *leadership*
We played well under the *direction* of our captain.
2. *way*
He showed us which *direction* we should go to get to the train station.

directions
noun
points or ways to follow
She gave us *directions* on how to make a cake.

directly
adverb
straight
They came to us *directly* after the play; they did not stop anywhere else.

director
noun
leader, chief
The company has a good *director;* he treats everybody very well.

dirty
verb: dirtying, dirtied, dirtied
make unclean
She *dirtied* her hands playing in the mud.
adjective: dirtier, dirtiest
not clean
Wash your hands if they are *dirty*.

disagree
verb
have a different idea
They wanted to eat first and then play. I *disagreed*; I wanted to play and then eat.

disagreement
noun
a difference in ideas
Our *disagreement* didn't last long; I changed my mind and followed them.

disappear
verb
move away and not be seen
The sun was very hot for a time; then it *disappeared* behind the clouds.

disappearance
noun
moving out of sight
The *disappearance* of the child worried the parents until he was found.

disappointed
adjective
not happy for not getting what was expected
We had a strong team; we thought we were going to win the game, but we were *disappointed* when we

lost.

disappointment
noun
unhappiness for not getting what was expected
We had a strong team, and we couldn't hide our *disappointment* when we lost the game.

disaster
noun
a bad and serious happening
The floods they had in their area were a *disaster*.

discharge
verb: discharging, discharged, discharged
send out
His old car *discharged* black smoke. He was *discharged* from his job; he wasn't doing well.

discourage
verb: discouraging, discouraged, discouraged
try to stop something by showing its bad effects
I *discouraged* them from driving at night, because the road was not good.

discover
verb
find something new
The tourists *discovered* a new way over the mountain. Nobody had seen it before.

discovery
noun: discoveries
something new found
The *discovery* of America took place in 1492.

discuss
verb
talk about
There were five questions at the end of the chapter. We *discussed* them with our teacher before the test.

discussion
noun
talk between people
We had an interesting *discussion* about the film. Everybody gave a different idea.

disease
noun
illness
The doctor gave the patient a new medicine to cure his *disease*.

dish

noun
plate
My mother served the fish on a *dish*.

dishonest
adjective
not honest
The boy was *dishonest* in what he said; he told some lies.

dishonesty
noun
lying, not telling the truth
The boy's *dishonesty* was clear; he did not tell the truth.

dislike
verb: disliking, disliked, disliked
not like, hate
She *dislikes* cold weather; she prefers warm weather.

dismal
adjective
sad
After his accident, he told us a *dismal* story; some of us had tears in our eyes.

dismiss
verb
let (something or someone) go
The school *dismissed* the student who cheated on the test.

disobedient
adjective
not obedient, not following

rules or instructions
The teacher told us not to leave the classroom before 10:00. One student was *disobedient;* he left at 9:40.

disobey
verb
do something against rules or instructions
The child *disobeyed* his parents. He went out of the house when they wanted him to stay in.

disperse
verb: dispersing, dispersed, dispersed
scatter
The police *dispersed* the crowd of people in the street.

display
noun
a showing of things to the public
The students had a *display* of their art work in school. The parents came to see the *display*.
verb
show publicly
The students *displayed* their art work.

disprove
verb: disproving, disproved, disproved
show that an idea is wrong
I *disproved* his theory when I presented the facts. He then knew that he was wrong.

dispute
noun
disagreement
My neighbors and I had a *dispute*; we did not agree on how to keep our street clean.

dissolve
verb: dissolving, dissolved, dissolved
turn into liquid
The sugar *dissolved* in the tea.

distance

noun
a measure of space
The *distance* between school and my home is three miles.

distant
adjective
far
The stars we see at night are very *distant* from the earth.

distinct
adjective
1. *different, having a different quality*
Our cars are very *distinct* from each other: mine is large; his is small.
2. *clear*
Her words were very *distinct* when she spoke. We understood everything she said.

distinction
noun
1. *difference*
Know the *distinction* between the two cars before you decide on one of them to buy.
2. *excellence*
He received his degree with *distinction.*

distinctive
adjective
standing out as different
She wore a very *distinctive* ring; we had never seen anything like it.

distinguish
verb
see or show a difference
She can *distinguish* the two brothers by the color of their eyes.

distract
verb
take someone's attention off something
The loud music

distracted them from their work.

distraction
noun
taking one's attention off something
We tried to finish our homework, but the music was a big *distraction*. We stopped working for a time.

distress
noun
great pain
The fighting in the city caused the people much *distress;* they felt afraid and hurt.

distribute
verb: distributing, distributed, distributed
1. *spread around*
The newspaper is *distributed* all over the country.
2. *divide and share*
The manager *distributed* the profits among the partners.

district
noun
an area of a country
There was a lot of snow in the country, but our *district* was dry.

disturb
verb
interrupt a situation
I wanted to study, but my little brother kept *disturbing* me with his questions.

dive
noun
a jump into the water with the head first
The swimmer stood on a rock and took a *dive* into the sea.
verb: diving, dived or dove, dived
Make sure the water is deep enough if you want to *dive* in.

divide
verb: dividing, divided, divided
1. *cut, break, or separate*
She *divided* the apple between us.
2. *do an arithmetic calculation*
When you *divide* 60 by 10, you get 6.

divine
adjective
holy
Most religions have *divine* teachings.

division
noun
1. *department or section*
Their school has two *divisions*: elementary and secondary.
2. *an arithmetic calculation*
In the arithmetic class, we learned how to do *division*: 60 / 10 = 6.

do
verb: doing, does, did, done
perform, work
I *did* my homework and gave it to my teacher.
auxiliary verb: (does) did
I *do* not go to school every day.
Did you read the notice?

doctor

noun
1. *physician, a medical person*
If you get sick, see your *doctor*.
2. *a person who holds that degree*
She is a Ph.D. (*doctor* of philosophy).

does
See **do**.
He *does* his work well.
He *does* not waste his time.

doesn't
See **do.**
negative of does, does not
He *doesn't* know my name.

dog

noun
an animal that people keep as a pet
They have two *dogs* and a cat at home.
Their *dogs* like bones.

doing

See **do**.

doll

noun
a toy in the shape of a person
Their daughter dresses her *dolls* and feeds them every day.

dollar

noun
a piece of money worth 100 cents
I have five *dollars* and sixty cents in my pocket.

domestic

adjective
1. *related to the home*
They have a *domestic* problem: the family income is very low.
2. *related to one's country*
Roads and schools are *domestic* responsibilities.

dominant

adjective
main and controlling
Most of the people on the bus came from France. The French people were the *dominant* group on the bus.

done

See **do.**
adjective
1. *finished*
My work is *done.* Now I can play.
2. *cooked enough*
She served the dinner when she thought the meat was *done.*

donkey

noun
ass
This boy is riding a *donkey.*

don't

auxiliary verb
do not
Don't do foolish things.

door

noun
a barrier that opens and leads out of or into a cupboard, a room, or a house
Our living room has one *door* and two windows.

doorway

noun
the place where a door is that leads into and out of a room or house
Our guests stood in the *doorway* until we asked them to come in.

dot

noun
a spot
She has a blue *dot* on her dress from her pen.

verb: dotting, dotted, dotted
put spots
We *dotted* the map to show the places we would like to visit.

double

noun
twice the amount
We offered him five dollars for his pen. He wanted *double* the amount: 10 dollars.
verb: doubling, doubled, doubled
make an amount twice what it is
I offered him five dollars for his pen, but he asked me to *double* it to 10.

doubt

noun
a question in one's mind about a fact or an idea
Some people think that our neighbor is an honest man. Others have some *doubt* about that; they think he may not be very honest.
verb
raise a question about a fact or idea
Some people are sure he is honest. Others *doubt* his honesty.

down

adverb
opposite of up
First they went up the mountain; then they came *down.*
preposition
opposite of up
The children ran *down* the hill to the sea.

downstairs

adverb
on a lower level of a building
We live on the top floor. Our neighbors live *downstairs.*

dozen

noun
twelve
I bought a *dozen* apples: six red and six green.

Dr.

noun
doctor
My dentist's name is *Dr.* Brown.

drag

verb: dragging, dragged, dragged
pull along the ground or floor
She could not carry the heavy bag; so she *dragged* it to her car.

drain

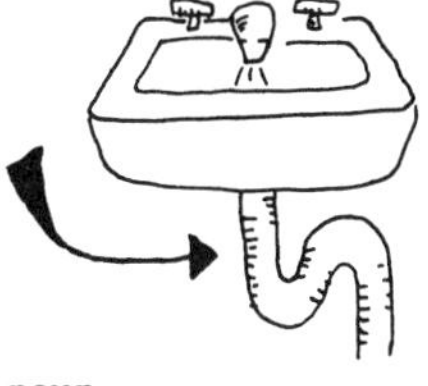

noun
a pipe that takes water out
The *drain* in the bathroom was blocked; the water was not going through.
verb
take water out through a pipe
The rain flooded our basement. We had to *drain* the water out.

drank

See **drink**.

drape

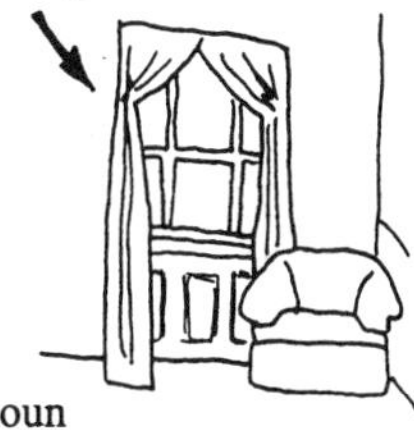

noun
curtain
The lady put new *drapes* on her bedroom window.

draw

verb: drawing, drew, drawn
1. *make figures on paper*
The little girl *drew* a cat and a dog in pencil.
2. *pull*
She *drew* the drapes to make the room darker.
3. *take out*
He needed some money; so he *drew* some of his money from the bank.

drawer

noun
a container in a table or cupboard that can be drawn in or out
He has all his socks in one *drawer.*

drawing

noun
a figure made on paper
She showed me her own *drawing* of a cat.
See **draw** also.

drawn
See **draw.**

dread
verb
be afraid of
She doesn't like darkness. She *dreads* the nights.

dreadful
adjective
fearful, very bad
He had a *dreadful* story to tell us about the dangers he met.

dream
noun
visions a person sees while asleep
I had a *dream* last night. I saw myself flying in the air.
verb: dreaming, dreamed or dreamt, dreamed or dreamt
see visions while asleep
I *dreamed* that I was flying in the air last night. When I woke up, I knew it was only a dream.

dreamt
See **dream.**

dress

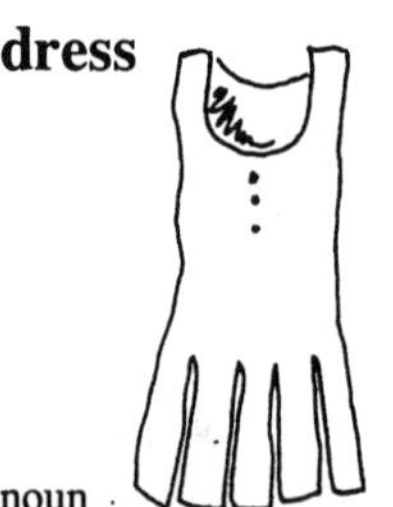

noun
a woman's wear
She bought a nice red *dress* for the party.
verb
put clothes on
The mother *dressed* her baby in a pretty yellow suit.

drew
See **draw.**

dried
See **dry**.

drier
noun
a machine that dries clothes
After she washed the sheets, she put them in the *drier* to dry.

drink
noun
a liquid that one drinks
She was very thirsty; she asked for a *drink* of water.
verb: drinking, drank, drunk
take a liquid down through the mouth
She was very thirsty; she *drank* two glasses of water.

drive
noun
a trip by car or bus
They took us for a long *drive* up the mountain in their car.
verb: driving, drove, driven
1. *steer and guide a car or bus*
They *drove* us up the mountain in their car.
2. *push or knock or force (something)*
He *drove* a nail into the wall to hang a picture.

driven
See **drive.**

driver
noun

a person who drives
I felt very safe in his car. He is a very good *driver.*

drop
noun
1. *a small liquid ball*
You can see the *drops* of rain when they fall.
2. *a fall*
The boy fell from the wall. It was a *drop* of about three feet.
verb: dropping, dropped, dropped
let go (to fall)
The player *dropped* the ball from his hands and lost it.

drove
See **drive.**

drown
verb
die in the water
Two children *drowned* in the pool. They didn't know how to swim, and there was nobody else there.

drum

noun
a musical instrument that is hit with sticks
I like the sound of *drums* when I listen to music.

dry
verb: drying, dried, dried
make (something) stop from being wet
The lady *dried* the clothes after she washed them.
adjective
not wet
The shirts were wet. We put them in the sun. Now they are *dry.*

duck

noun
a bird that likes to swim
We saw some *ducks* swimming in the river, and we fed them.

duckling

noun
a young duck
We saw big duck*s* and little *ducklings* swimming in the river.

due
noun
a person's right to something
We must thank him for his help. This is his *due* for what he did.
adjective
needing to be paid or given
His debt is *due* today. The book I borrowed from the library is *due* next Monday.

dues
noun
payment for something
He is a member of a club. He pays his *dues* twice a year.

dug
See **dig.**

dull
adjective
1. *not bright*
I didn't like the color of the car. It was a *dull* blue.
2. *not sharp*
It was difficult to cut the meat, because the knife was *dull.*

dumb
adjective
not able to speak
She was *dumb* from the shock of hearing the sad news.

during
preposition

in the time of
In the morning, it was sunny, but the roads were wet. It had rained *during* the night.

dust
noun
small particles that collect on surfaces
They did not clean the house for a week. There was a lot of *dust* on the floor and the tables.
verb
remove the dust
They *dusted* the books when they took them off the shelf.

duty
noun: duties
obligation, something that one has to do
It is our *duty* to keep the streets clean. Everybody must do his share.

dwell
verb
live
They *dwelled* here for two years; then they moved to another city.

dwelling
noun
a place to live in
This small room was their *dwelling* for a month.

dying
See **die**.

dynamic
adjective
active
He is a *dynamic* person; he is always doing something.

Ee

each
pronoun
every one
My friends and I are in the play. *Each* of us has a role to play.

eager
adjective
highly interested
She is *eager* to become a nurse. She has always wanted to be one.

eagle

noun
a strong bird that flies high and eats meat
The *eagle* caught a rabbit and ate it.

eaglet
noun
a baby eagle
The *eaglets* flew out of their nest.

ear

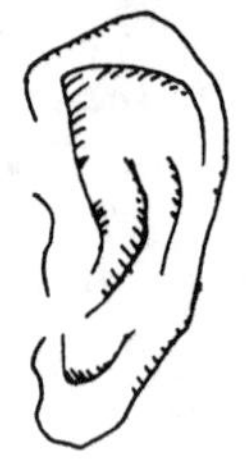

noun
part of the body that we hear with
We see with our eyes and hear with our *ears.*

early
adjective: earlier, earliest
before time
The meeting started at 10:30. They arrived at 10:15. They were *early.*

earn
verb
receive for work done
The children *earned* ten dollars each for helping their parents.

earnings
noun
the total amounts received for work
His *earnings* were more than what he spent. He could save a bit.

earring

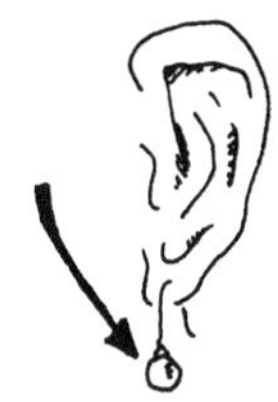

noun
an ornament worn on the ear
She wears different *earrings* with different dresses.

earth
noun
1. *soil*
The plant needed a little more *earth* in the pot.
2. *the world*
Our life on this *earth* is interesting.

ease
noun
comfort
He was weak, and he couldn't walk. Now he is well, and he can walk with *ease*.

easier
See **easy.**
adjective
more easy, opposite of more difficult
It is *easier* to do subtraction than to do division.

easily
adverb
with ease
She knows English very well. She can speak it and write it *easily.*

east

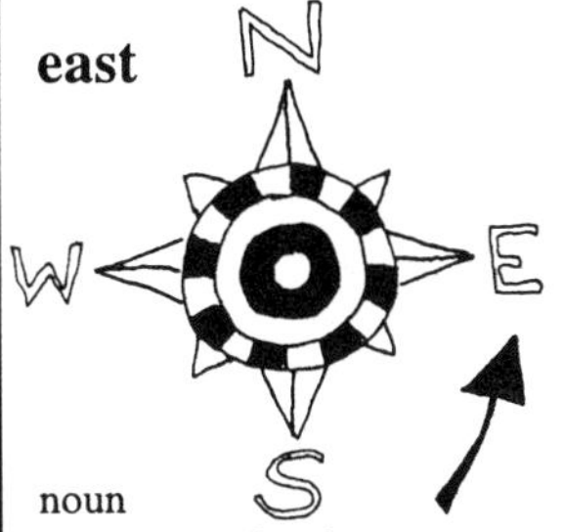

noun
the right side of a map
New York is in the *east* and California is in the west of the U.S.
adverb
towards the right side of a map
My friends in California wanted to go *east* for a vacation.

eastern
adjective
related to the east
New York is an *eastern* state in the U.S.

easy
adjective: easier, easiest
not difficult
It is *easy* for me to play tennis. I play it very well.

eat

verb: eating, ate, eaten
take food down through the mouth
We *ate* roast and potatoes for dinner.

echo
noun
a sound coming back repeating the first sound
We heard our own *echo* in the valley.
verb: echoing, echoed, echoed
repeat
The child *echoed* the singer's voice.

economic
adjective
related to business, money, and trade
The *economic* situation is good now: more people are working, and we are selling more products abroad.

economical
adjective
spending less and saving more
He is a very *economical* person; he knows when and how much to spend.

economics
noun
the study or science of economic matters
My cousin is studying *economics* in the university.

edge
noun
the end part, the border
The poor man stood on the *edge* of the road.

edit
verb
make corrections and changes to a written piece
The author wanted someone to *edit* his book before it was printed.

editor
noun
a person who edits
I know the newspaper *editor.* He makes sure everything printed is correct.

education
noun
1. *teaching*
She is studying *education* in college. She wants to become a teacher.
2. *learning*
His children are getting a good *education.* Their school is excellent.

effect
noun
influence
That man had a great *effect* on my life. He taught me many things.

effective
adjective
having influence
He is a very *effective* speaker. People listen to him very carefully.

effort
noun
energy, power, strength
He puts a lot of *effort* in his work. He works very hard.

egg
noun
the white or brown ball that hens and other birds lay
I had two *eggs* for breakfast.

eight
noun
a number: 8
Four and four make *eight.*
adjective
a number: 8
There are *eight* children in that family: four boys and four girls.

eighteen
noun
a number: 18
If we add ten and eight, we get *eighteen.*
adjective
a number: 18
We have *eighteen* students in our class.

eighth
adjective
a number showing an order: 8th
He is eight years old. His *eighth* birthday was last week.

eighty
noun
a number: 80
Forty and forty make *eighty.*
adjective
a number: 80
They paid *eighty* dollars and a half ($80.50) for their dinner.

either
pronoun
one or the other
Either of the boys can help us. Both of them are good.

elbow

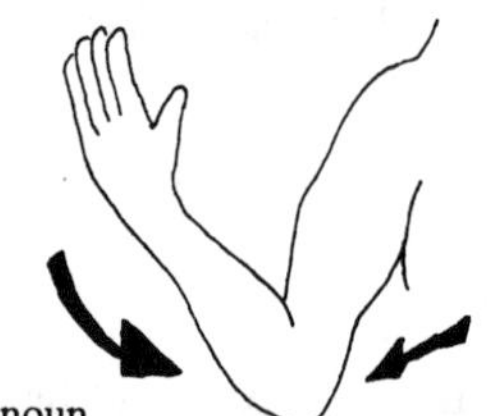

noun
the joint in the middle of the arm
He fell and hurt his *elbow.*

elder
noun
the one who is older
Of the two sisters, Mary is the *elder.* She is one year older than her sister.

elect
verb
vote for (someone) and make him or her win
The team *elected* the tallest player as their captain.

election
noun
the act of electing
The players are meeting now for the *election* of their captain.

electric
adjective
related to electricity
The lights went out as the *electric* wires broke.

electrician
noun
a person who works in electricity
When the electric wires broke, we asked our *electrician* to fix them.

electricity
noun
a kind of energy that comes from a current (an electric current)
Our stove and our refrigerator at home work on *electricity*.

element
noun
1. *a part*
His plan was made up of three *elements*.
2. *a single substance*
Oxygen and hydrogen are *elements*.

elephant

noun
an animal with a trunk
Elephants have very big ears and long trunks.

eleven
noun
a number: 11
Six and five make *eleven*.

eleventh
adjective
a number showing order: 11th
She was the *eleventh* child in the family. Ten children were born before her.

else
adjective
other
He told us everything he knew. What *else* could he tell us?

embrace
noun
holding (someone) with the arms
She gave her son a big *embrace* when she met him at the airport.
verb: embracing, embraced, embraced
hold with the arms
She *embraced* her son when she met him at the airport.

emotion
noun
a strong feeling
They showed their *emotion* when they met after an absence of three years.

emotional
adjective
having strong feelings
They had an *emotional* meeting after an absence of three years.

employ
verb
1. *use*
They *employed* a new method in solving their mathematics problems.
2. *take someone for work*
The company *employed* two new secretaries in the main office.

empty
verb: emptying, emptied, emptied
take everything out of (something)
She *emptied* the cupboards in order to clean them. She left nothing in them. After she cleaned them, she put everything back.
adjective

with nothing in it, opposite of full
This drawer is *empty*. There is nothing in it.

enable
verb: enabling, enabled, enabled
make (someone) able
He couldn't buy the book because he had no money. The money I gave him *enabled* him to buy it.

encounter
verb
meet
The climbers *encountered* some dangers on the mountain. The snow was very deep and the wind was very strong.

encourage
verb: encouraging, encouraged, encouraged
give (someone) the will to do something
She was afraid to take the new job. I *encouraged* her to do so, and she did. Now she likes it very much.

encouragement
noun
giving (someone) the will to do something
She needed *encouragement* to take the new job. When I told her it was a good job, she felt happier.

end
noun
the last part, the finish
There is always some light at the *end* of a tunnel.
verb
finish
He started his work in the morning and *ended* it in the evening.

endeavor
noun
try
His hobby was collecting stamps. Now he wants to move to a new *endeavor*. He wants to try collecting coins.

endure
verb: enduring, endured, endured
1. *last*
If you buy good clothes, they will *endure* for a long time.
2. *bear in hard times*
They *endured* many hardships during the war. They had little food and money.

enemy
noun: enemies
a foe, one who fights against
Our *enemies* wanted to take our city, but our army stopped them.

energy
noun: energies
power and action
She is full of *energy*; she can't stay still; she has to do something all the time.

engage
verb: engaging, engaged, engaged
1. *keep one's attention*
The interesting film *engaged* the children's minds for an hour.
2. *employ*
The company *engaged* a new secretary in the main office.

engaged
See **engage** also.
adjective
planning to get married
Their daughter is *engaged* to a doctor. They are getting married next month.

engagement
noun
1. *a plan to be married*
Henry and Alice are getting married next month. We attended their *engagement* party last month.
2. *an appointment*
I am not free. I have an *engagement* to speak to the students.

engine

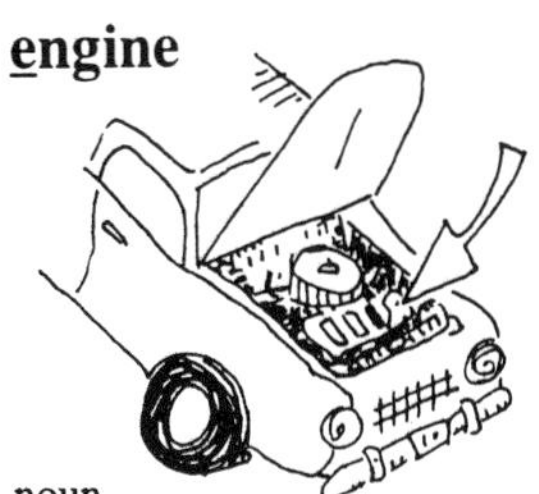

noun
a machine
The *engine* makes a car run.

engineer
noun
1. *a person who designs buildings and other structures*
We asked an *engineer* to draw plans for our office building.
2. *a person who runs an engine*
The train *engineer* stopped the train at the bridge.

engineering
noun
the study of designing buildings and other structures
He wants to build bridges. He is now studying *engineering* in the university.

English
noun
the language spoken in America, England, Australia, and other places
They don't speak *English* very well, but they know French.
adjective
relative to England
There are two German students and three *English* students in our school.

enjoy
verb
1. *have pleasure in*
I like tennis, and I *enjoyed* the game I played yesterday.
2. *have fun*
We *enjoyed* ourselves at the party. We had a nice time.

enjoyable
adjective
giving pleasure
The play we saw was very *enjoyable*; it was nice and interesting.

enormous
adjective
big, great in size
They asked for an *enormous* amount of money for their car. It was too much for me to pay.

enough
adjective
sufficient
He can't buy a train ticket; he doesn't have *enough* money for it.

enter
verb
1. *go into*
The singer was waiting outside. When she *entered* the hall, all the people stood up for her.
2. *join*
My cousin is a good speaker. When he heard that there was a speaking competition, he *entered* the competition.

entertain
verb
1. *have one or more guests*
We *entertained* four guests for dinner last night.
2. *make (someone) joyful, amuse*
She *entertained* us with her funny stories.

entire
adjective
all
The store owner sold his *entire* stock of shirts. He had no more shirts left.

entirely
adverb
completely, fully
I am *entirely* satisfied with my new bicycle. It is very good.

entrance

noun
a place where one can go in

We couldn't go into the hall because the *entrance* was blocked.
2. *going into*
When she took a test, she was allowed *entrance* to the school.

envelope

noun
a paper bag for letters and other papers
I wrote three letters today. I addressed the *envelopes*, and I mailed them at the post office.

equal

adjective
having the same quantity or quality as another
He and his brother are *equal* in weight; they weigh 150 pounds each.

equally

adverb
of the same quantity or quality
He and his brother are *equally* tall; both are five feet and 10 inches tall.

equator

noun
a line that divides the world into two halves: north and south

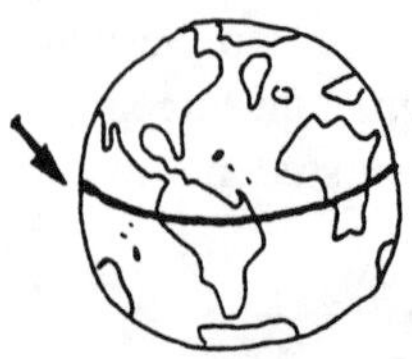

We crossed the *equator* when we sailed from Mexico to Chile.

equipment

noun
the objects one needs to do things
They couldn't get his car fixed because they didn't have the necessary *equipment*; one of their machines was not working.

erase

verb: erasing, erased, erased
wipe off
The student helped the teacher *erase* the blackboard. There was a lot of writing on it.

eraser

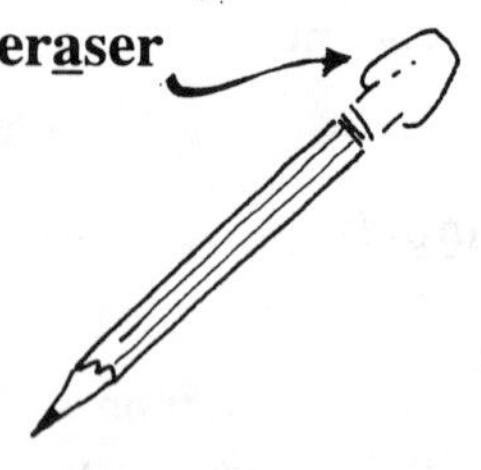

noun
the instrument used to wipe off something
I used an *eraser* to erase a mistake I made when I was writing.

erect

verb
build
The company *erected* a wall around the store.

error

noun
mistake, something wrong
She had five questions on the test. She had only one *error*; she answered four questions correctly.

escape

noun
a flight away from something
The police were looking for the thief after his *escape* from prison.
verb: escaping, escaped, escaped
run away
The thief *escaped* from prison. The police are now trying to catch him.

especially

adverb
specially, particularly
He wanted to save his money *especially* because he was planning to buy a new car.

essential

adjective
very important
If you want to pass your tests, it is *essential* for you to study hard.

establish
verb
start an institution or organization
Some teachers decided to *establish* a new school.

estate
noun
1. *all a person owns*
When he died, his *estate* was divided among his children.
2. *a piece of land*
He built a home and a farm on his *estate* in the valley.

estimate
noun
a guess, an idea
I didn't know how much the car really cost, but my *estimate* was very near the exact price.
verb: estimating, estimated, estimated
guess, calculate
I *estimated* the price of the house. I was almost right.

etc.
short for et cetera, and others
In my bag I have books, pens, pencils, *etc.*

eternal
adjective
lasting for ever
Spirits are *eternal.*

eternally
adverb
for ever
He never stops talking. He talks *eternally.*

Europe
noun
one of the world's continents
France and Germany are in *Europe*.

European
noun
a person from Europe
An Italian is a *European.*
adjective
related to Europe
Belgium is a *European* country.

even
adjective
1. *equal*
I won one game; then he won one game. Now we are *even.*
2. *related to a number that can be divided by two*
Two, four and ten are *even* numbers.
adverb
1. *though*
I'd like to go for a walk *even* if it is raining.
2. *as a matter of fact, indeed*
John is very tall, and his brother is *even* taller.

eve
noun
the night before
On her birthday *eve* she prepared her dress to wear the following day.

evening
noun
the time at the end of the day and early night
We spent the *evening* with our friends and had dinner together.

event
noun
a happening
The year 1492 marked an important *event*: the discovery of America.

eventful
adjective
full of happenings
Last year was very *eventful;* many important things happened.

ever
adverb
at any time
Will he *ever* finish his homework? He seems to be studying all the time.

every
adjective
each
Every student in this school comes to school by bus.

everybody
noun
each person, all persons

His voice is very loud; *everybody* can hear him.

everyone
noun
each person, all persons
Everyone in class has a book.
Nobody is without a book.

everything
noun
each thing, all things
Everything I bought was new. I bought nothing old.

everywhere
adverb
in all places
In our city, *everywhere* you go you find restaurants.

evidence
noun
proof
There was *evidence* that the thief stole a watch. Somebody saw him do it.

evident
adjective
clear
It is *evident* that he doesn't like the food; he is not eating it, and we know he is hungry.

evidently
adverb
clearly
He is not eating his food. *Evidently*, he does not like it.

evil
adjective
bad
He hurts people and he tells lies; he is an *evil* man.

exact
adjective
very correct
She gave me the *exact* time when I asked for it: 5:32 p.m.

exactly
adverb
completely correct
I plan to meet them at the station. I want to know *exactly* when they are coming.

examination (exam)
noun
test
She went to her doctor for a medical *examination*. We have an *exam* in English tomorrow.

examine
verb: examining, examined,examined
study, test
She *examined* the ring before she bought it. She wanted to be sure it was the correct size.

example
noun
one (of a kind)
We saw an *example* of their art work.

excellent
adjective
very good, superior
His work is *excellent;* it is the best I've seen.

except
preposition
not including, but not
Everyone was in class *except* Bill. We don't know where he was.

exception
noun
a situation in which one person or thing is left out
Traffic rules apply to all. No *exceptions* are allowed.

exchange
noun
taking something in return for something given
There is an *exchange* in buying and selling. One person pays money and receives what another person sells.
verb: exchanging, exchanged, exchanged
give something in return for something else
My friend and I *exchanged* bicycles. I rode his and he rode mine.

excite
verb: exciting, excited, excited
move or stir the feelings
The music *excited* the people in the hall. They began to sing and clap.

excitement
noun
stirring the feelings
His words caused some *excitement*; some people stood and shouted.

exciting
See **excite** also.
adjective
causing strong feelings
We watched an *exciting* film on television. We jumped with happiness several times.

exclamation
noun
surprise
She gave me a look of *exclamation* when I told her the story. She didn't know whether to believe it or not.

excuse
noun
explanation
There was no reason for him to be late. He had no *excuse* for that.
verb: excusing, excused, excused
forgive, pardon
The teacher *excused* me for being late. The traffic was very heavy.

exercise
noun
practice
He does some grammar *exercises* every day. He wants to learn English fast. Riding a bicycle is good *exercise* for the whole body.
verb: exercising, exercised, exercised
practice, put into action
He *exercises* every day; he wants to become strong.

exist
verb
be, be present
Many forests *exist* in Africa. Wild animals live in them.

existence
noun
being
The *existence* of forests in Africa helps some animals live there.

exit

noun
a way out
We could not leave the hall fast because there were only two *exits.*
verb
go out
When the film was over, we *exited* through two doors.

expect
verb
believe that something will be happening
We *expected* it to rain yesterday, and it did for a short time.

expedition
noun
a journey with a purpose
The captain joined an *expedition* around the island to see how big it was.

expense
noun
money paid
He could save some money; his *expenses* were not so high.

expensive
adjective
costing much
I didn't have enough money to buy the bicycle; it was very *expensive*.

experience
noun
knowing something from practice

He knows what he is talking about; he has *experience* in it.

experiment
noun
trying something in practice
In the laboratory, we did many *experiments* with weights.

expert
noun
a person who knows something very well
If you want a good mechanic to fix your car, go to Sam; he's an *expert.*

explain
verb
make clear, make understood
The student could not understand the science lesson. The teacher then *explained* it in an easy way.

explanation
noun
making (something) clear
The teacher's *explanation* of the science lesson made all the students understand it well.

expose
verb: exposing, exposed, exposed
leave (something) open without cover or protection
Don't *expose* yourself to cold weather. Protect yourself.

express
verb
give an opinion or feeling through language, music, or art work
He *expressed* his ideas clearly in his talk. She *expressed* her feelings in a poem and a painting.

expression
noun
giving an opinion or feeling in some way
The beautiful music we heard was an *expression* of the musician's happiness.

extend
verb
stretch out
His land *extends* beyond the river. I *extended* my hand to reach the pen.

extension
noun
making (something) longer
They gave us two days to finish the work. We asked for an *extension* of time. We needed three days to finish it.

extent
noun
1. *size*
I cannot walk the full *extent* of his property. It is too big.
2. *level, degree*
We could not understand the *extent* of his sadness. He was very unhappy.

external
adjective
related to the outside
He fell and had an *external* wound. He had a cut on his hand.

extra
noun
something in addition to the usual thing
In this restaurant, a pizza comes with cheese. Olives and other things are *extras.*
adjective
additional
One student wrote very slowly. The teacher always gave him *extra* time to do his work.

extraordinary
adjective
unusual
It never rains there during this month. The rain they had yesterday was *extraordinary.*

extremely
adverb
very
He is not only a good player; he is *extremely* good. He's the best.

eye

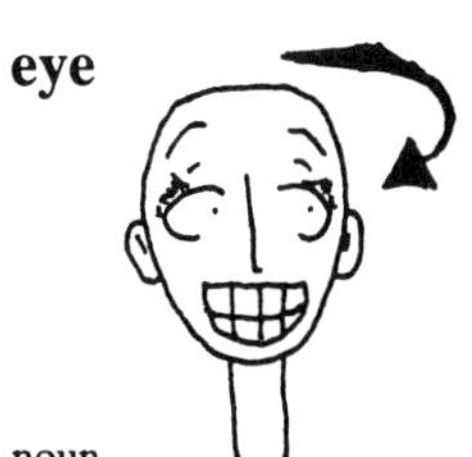

noun
the part of the body that we see with
We hear with our ears and we see with our *eyes.*
verb: eying or eyeing, eyed, eyed
look with interest
When they brought the fruits to the table, I *eyed* the strawberries until I had some.

Ff

fable
noun
an old story
She likes to read famous Indian *fables.*

fabric
noun
cloth or material like cloth
She bought new soft *fabric* for her curtains.

fabricate
verb: fabricating, fabricated, fabricated
create, invent
Don't believe his story; he *fabricated* it himself.

fabulous
adjective
great, wonderful
We saw a *fabulous* film last week; it was extremely interesting.

face

noun
the front part of the head
The mouth and eyes are parts of the *face.*
verb: facing, faced, faced
meet and oppose
Our soldiers *faced* the enemy very bravely.

fact
noun
a truth
We were not sure what happened exactly, but he was there, and he gave us all the *facts.*

factor
noun
1. *an element that contributes towards something*
We were not sure if we wanted to go on a picnic, but the bright sun was the *factor* that decided the matter.
2. *a number that another bigger number can be divided into*
Four is a *factor* of twelve and twenty.

factory
noun: factories
a place (building) where things are manufactured or made
There are many toy *factories* in the U.S.

fade
verb: fading, faded, faded
lose color
After washing the shirts a few times, their colors *faded.* After being dark blue, they became light blue.

fail
verb
1. *not pass, opposite of pass*
Because he was very lazy, he *failed* his school tests.
2. *not to do something*
I expected to see her at the meeting, but she *failed* to come.

failure
noun
1. *no success*
His *failure* in the test was a result of his laziness.
2. *not doing something*
Her *failure* to attend the meeting made us decide to meet at a later date.

faint
adjective
weak
After his illness, he felt *faint*; he couldn't walk easily.

fair
noun
a sale
We bought some nice glasses at the country *fair.*
adjective
1. *just and correct*
Our teacher is very *fair* with us; our grades are exactly what we deserve.
2. *clear, not rainy*
Our picnic was on a day of *fair* weather. The sun was out and the sky was blue.
3. *light-colored*
Because she has such *fair* skin, the sun can hurt her.

fairly
adverb
quite (a bit)
He bought a *fairly* expensive car; he wanted a good one.

faith
noun
belief
He has strong *faith* that his business will be a success. He knows that he is a good manager.

faithful
adjective
sincere
Dogs are very *faithful* friends; they stay with their masters.

fall
noun
1. *defeat, surrender*
In our history class we learned about the *fall* of Rome.
2. *a drop*
The *fall* in the price of fruits made everybody want to buy them.
3. *the act of falling*
The football player hurt his knee when he took a big *fall.*
verb: falling, fell, fallen
1. *surrender*
The city *fell* to the enemy after a brave struggle
2. *drop*
When the farmers brought all their fruits to market, the prices *fell.*
Some sold their fruit for half the regular price.
3. *go down*
The football player hurt his knee when he *fell* on it.

fallen
See **fall.**

false
adjective
not true
If you say that three and three make seven, your answer is *false.* The correct answer is six.

fame
noun
public regard
After he discovered America, the *fame* of Columbus spread around the world.

familiar
adjective
1. *known*
That store is *familiar* to me; I've been there several times.
2. *happening frequently*
Monkeys are a *familiar* sight on many roads in India.
3. *very informal*
The manager doesn't like his workers to become *familiar* with him.

family
noun: families
a group of persons who are related and who may be living together
Their *family* consists of the father, the mother, and two children.

famous
adjective
well known

Harvard is a very *famous* university.

fan

noun
an instrument used to blow air
She uses her Japanese *fan* when she feels warm.
verb: fanning, fanned, fanned
use an instrument to blow air
She *fanned* herself when she felt warm.

fancy
noun: fancies
1. *like*
She does what suits her *fancy.*
2. *imagination*
Cows can fly, according to his *fancy.*
verb: fancying, fancied, fancied
1. *like*
He *fancies* eating chocolates.
2. *imagine*
Can you *fancy* an animal flying?

fantastic
adjective
very great, unreal
We saw a *fantastic* show; it was excellent.

far
adverb: farther/further, farthest/furthest
opposite of near
I can't walk to the station; it is too *far* from here.

fare
noun
the price for travel
Air *fares* are usually higher than train *fares.*

farewell
noun
good-bye
We went to the station to wish our friends *farewell* before they left.

farm

noun
a piece of land where crops are grown or animals raised
They had ten cows and thirty sheep on their *farm.*

farmer
noun
a person who owns or works on a farm
The *farmer* sold his milk and eggs in the city.

farther
See **far.**

farthest
See **far.**

fashion
noun
1. *way*
This doctor treats people in a *fashion* that makes them trust him.
2. *the latest style*
Wearing hats used to be the *fashion* in this place.

fast
adjective
quick
The *fast* train will get you there in half the time.
adverb
quickly
He worked very *fast* to finish his job early.

fasten
verb
attach
I *fastened* the papers with a pin.

fat
noun
animal oil and grease
Fried foods contain a lot of *fat.*

adjective: fatter, fattest
opposite of thin
She wants to lose some weight; she thinks she is too *fat*.

fatal
adjective
deadly
He was in a *fatal* accident; he died in it.

fate
noun
luck, fortune
It was his *fate* to meet that lovely lady. They are married now.

father
noun
a male parent
These children have a very good *father* and mother.

fault
noun
1. *a mistake, an error*
They considered it a *fault* when the ball went out in the game.
2. *a weakness, something wrong*
She bought the dress at half price because there was a *fault* in it: one sleeve was longer than the other.

favor
noun
1. *a kindness*
She did me a *favor* by opening the door for me early.
2. *acceptance, approval*
The teacher nodded in *favor* of my idea.
verb
prefer
He *favored* me over my cousin for the job; he knew I would do a better job.

favorite
adjective
preferred
Chocolate is my *favorite* sweet; I love it.

fear
noun
a state of being afraid
We are planning a picnic. Our *fear* is that it might rain.
verb
be afraid of
The driver *feared* the rain, because rain slows him down.

feast
noun
a very big meal
We had a *feast* on her birthday. She prepared many kinds of delicious foods.
verb
enjoy something very much
We *feasted* over the turkey at her birthday dinner party.

feather

noun
a piece of a bird's outer parts
The lady had a *feather* in her hat.

feature
noun
1. *the look and shape of a face*
She and her brother have very similar *features.*
2. *an important quality or characteristic*
This car has two main features: its price and strength.
verb: featuring, featured, featured
give (something) an important position
The newspaper *featured* the president's speech on the front page.

February
noun
the second month of the year
February comes after January and before March.

fed
See **feed.**

federal
adjective
related to a group of political states
Each state in the U.S. has a state government, but the *federal* government is located in Washington, D.C.

feed
noun
food
I bought some bird *feed* for the birds that come to my garden.
verb: feeding, fed, fed

give food to
I bought some seeds to *feed* the birds.

feel
verb: feeling, felt, felt
1. *have a sensation*
I *feel* hungry; I need to eat.
2. *touch*
I *felt* the material; it was rough.

feeling
See **feel.**
noun
sensation
She has kind *feelings* towards her family.

feet
See **foot.**

fell
See **fall.**

fellow
noun
1. *a male person*
My uncle is a nice *fellow.*
2. *a member of a society*
He is a *fellow* of the Royal Society.
2. *a colleague*
My *fellow* students and I are studying hard for our examinations.

felt
See **feel.**

female
noun
opposite of male
Women and lionesses are *females.* Men and lions are males.

fence

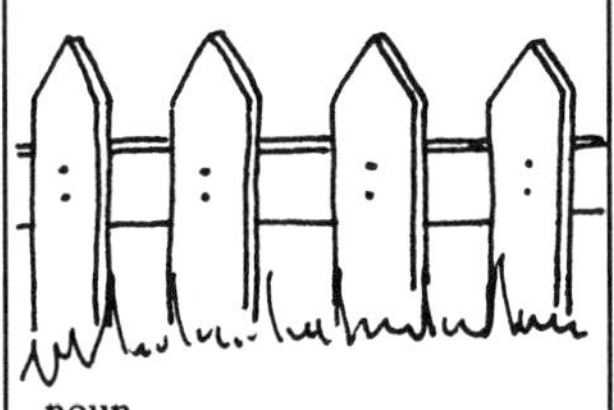

noun
a border or wall that separates two areas
The castle has a high stone *fence* around it.
verb: fencing, fenced, fenced
fight with a sword
In the past, soldiers *fenced* to protect their cities.

fender

noun
metal cover of a car's wheels
The driver's *fender* was bent in the accident.

ferry

noun: ferries
a boat that transports people, cars, or other things
We took our car on the *ferry* to the island.
verb: ferrying, ferried, ferried
transport people, cars, or other things across on a boat
We *ferried* our car to the island.

fetch
verb
bring
My friend forgot his book at home. His teacher asked him to go back home and *fetch* it.

fever
noun
high temperature of the body
The doctor told her to stay in bed because she had a *fever*.

few
adjective
not many
Few students in our school are very tall or very short.

(a few)
noun
some
A few of us in class wanted to go on a field trip. The teacher said he couldn't have a field trip for five or six students.

fiction
noun
the product of imagination
She likes to read *fiction*; she read a good novel last week.

field
noun
1. *land used for planting crops*
We drove through wide corn *fields*.
2. *a place of battle*
The battle*field* was full of broken guns and tanks.
3. *an area of work or specialization*
He is interested in the *field* of philosophy.

fierce
adjective
very strong
The firemen could not enter the burning house; the heat was too *fierce*.

fifteen
noun
a number: 15
Ten and five make *fifteen*.

fifth
noun
1. *a number showing order: 5th*
I was *fifth* to enter the plane. Four people entered before me.
2. *one of five equal parts*
Five of us wanted to taste the pie. Each one of us had one *fifth* of it.

fifty
noun
a number: 50
Five tens make *fifty*.

fig

noun
a soft fruit with very small seeds in it
I like to eat grapes and *figs* in summer.

fight
noun
a struggle
The children had a little *fight* over the toys. Their mother broke up the *fight* and gave each child a toy.
verb: fighting, fought, fought
use force against somebody
The children *fought* with each other over the toys.

figure
noun
1. *a number*
The number 457 has three *figures* in it: 4, 5, and 7.
2. *a shape*
She drew a few lines on a piece of paper. Her drawing was a *figure* of a cat.
verb: figuring, figured, figured
consider
When they didn't come to the meeting, I *figured* they were not interested.

file
noun

1. *a drawer or folder to keep papers*
She has all her important notes and letters in *files.*

2. *a tool with a rough surface*
After she cut her nails, she used a *file* to make them smooth.
verb: filing, filed, filed
1. *put in a drawer or folder*
She *files* all her letters in the office.
2. *make smooth*
She *filed* her nails after cutting them.

fill
verb
put in to make full
He *filled* his closet with his toys and clothes.

filling
noun
something used to fill a hole
The dentist told her that one of her teeth needed a *filling.*

film
noun
movie
We saw an interesting *film* yesterday. The actors were excellent.
verb
make a movie of
The parents *filmed* the wedding. Now we can see it again.

final
noun
a last examination
My cousin is in college. He has his *finals* next month.
adjective
last
We had a big dinner last night. The *final* course was chocolate cake.

finally
adverb
at last, in the end
He tried to jump over the wall. He tried it many times without success. *Finally*, he jumped over it.

finance
noun
money to pay for things
They couldn't build a new home because they didn't have the *finances* for it.
verb: financing, financed, financed
pay for something
They borrowed some money to *finance* their new business.

financial
adjective
related to finance
When they lost their business, they had serious *financial* problems.

find
verb: finding, found, found
1. *learn, discover*
I worked on the problem and *found* the right answer.
2. *discover, come across*
I *found* a watch in school, and I took it to the office.

fine
noun
money paid for doing something wrong
If you park your car in the wrong place, you will have to pay a *fine.*
verb: fining, fined, fined
ask someone to pay for doing a wrong
The police *fined* the driver fifty dollars for driving too fast.
adjective
good
She feels *fine* now after resting a bit. The speech he gave was *fine.*
adverb
well

He was sick, but now he is *fine*.

finger

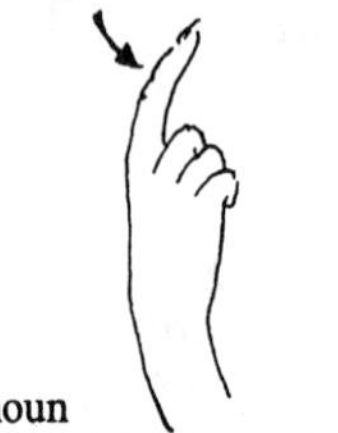

noun
one of the five ends of the hand
Hands have *fingers*; feet have toes.

finish
verb
end
He started writing at 8:00 and he *finished* at 11:00.

finished
adjective
done, ended
My work is *finished*; I have nothing more to do today.

fire
noun
a burning flame
We cooked the meat on a coal *fire* in the yard.
verb: firing, fired, fired
1. *shoot*
The soldiers *fired* their guns at once.
2. *let go from work*
The manager *fired* two workers because they were always late and lazy.

firm
noun
a company
He is the manager of a *firm* that has twenty-five lawyers.
adjective
strong, steady
Their house has a *firm* foundation.

first
noun
number one in order
I was the *first* to arrive. There was nobody there when I arrived.
adverb
in the beginning
When you have a test, *first* study hard; then think and write carefully.

fish

noun: fish (sometimes fishes)
a creature that lives in the water
The *fish* in this bowl are red.
verb
1. *catch fish*
I like to *fish* with a net.
2. *look (for)*
A person who is not honest is *fishing* for trouble.

fisherman

noun: fishermen
a man who catches fish
We bought fresh fish from the *fishermen* on the coast.

fishing
noun
going to catch fish
They go *fishing* in their own boat.

fit
noun
1. *a match*
I tried my new jacket, and it was a perfect *fit*. It was just the right size.
2. *an attack*
She was in a *fit* of anger when her children were late from school.
verb: fitting, fitted, fitted
be right for
The prize *fitted* the champion; he won the car race, and his prize was a new car.
adjective
able and healthy
He can work hard when he feels *fit*.

five
noun
a number: 5
Three and two make *five*.

fix
noun
a difficult situation
He was in a *fix*: he had no money and no place to go.
verb
1. *mend*
Our door was not closing properly; then I *fixed* it; now it is working well.
2. *make firm*
The heel of her shoe came off, and the shoemaker *fixed* it in place.

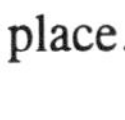

flag

noun
a piece of cloth with a nation's colors and designs
The *flag* of the U.S. has 50 stars.
verb: flagging, flagged, flagged
wave or give a sign with a flag
The workers on the road *flagged* the drivers to slow down.

flame

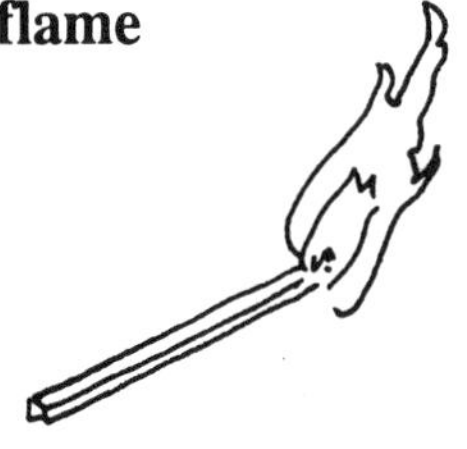

noun
the shining part of a fire
The little boy burned his finger in the *flame* of the candle.

flash
noun: flashes
a quick glow of light
From our house we saw a *flash* of light from a passing car.
verb
make a quick show of light
We *flashed* our light to see our way in the dark.

flat
adjective: flatter, flattest
level
The road was very *flat*; it was very easy to walk on it.

flavor
noun
taste
The cake she made had a strong chocolate *flavor*.
verb
add some taste or flavor
She *flavored* the cake with a bit of lemon.

fled
See **flee.**

flee
verb: fleeing, fled, fled
escape, run away
The thief *fled* from the police station. Now they are trying to catch him again.

fleet
noun
a united group of warships
Strong nations have good armies, good air forces, and good *fleets*.

flesh
noun
the soft part of any body
The *flesh* of this little lamb is very tender. I like the *flesh* of a mango.

flew
See **fly.**

flies
See **fly.**

flight
noun
1. *the act of flying*
On our *flight* to New York, we saw many beautiful clouds under us.
2. *running away*
He was followed by the police after his *flight* from prison.

float

noun

something that stays on top of the water

The new swimmer had a *float* to help him swim across the pool.

verb

stay on top of the water

Wood *floats* easily on the water.

flock

noun

a group of birds or other animals

The shepherd took his *flock* of sheep to the fields to eat.

verb

gather

All the neighbors *flocked* together when the storm hit.

flood

noun

water from a river or sea covering land

There was a big *flood* last year; many roads were covered with water.

verb

cover land with water

The river *flooded* the city. People used boats to go from place to place.

floor

noun

1. *the flat bottom part of a house or room*

They covered the *floor* with a beautiful rug.

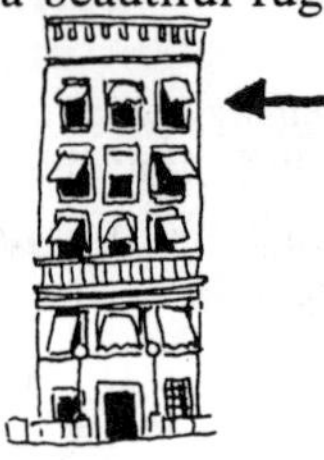

2. *a level or story of a building*

We live on the third *floor* of our building. There are two *floors* below us.

flour

noun

ground grain used for bread or cakes

She put *flour*, eggs, sugar, and milk in her cake.

flow

noun

a steady movement

I had a *flow* of letters from my friends when I got my new job.

verb

move steadily

The water *flowed* down the roads after the heavy rain.

flower

noun

the pretty part of a plant

She had some beautiful *flowers* in a vase on the table.

verb

produce flowers

Trees usually *flower* in the spring.

flown

See **fly**.

fly

noun: flies

an insect

I don't like it when *flies* come on the food.

verb: flying, flew, flown

go up and travel in the air

We *flew* from New York to Boston. It took about one hour.

fold

noun

a double, one thing on top of another

Her blouse had many *folds* in it in the front.

verb

lay one side on top of another
I *folded* the paper in half to put it in the envelope.

folk
noun
the people of a nation or group
They visited an African country and found the *folk* very kind.

follow

verb
1. *go or move after*
The players *followed* their captain to the field.
2. *listen and obey*
He *followed* his doctor's orders and stayed in bed.
3. *come after*
May *follows* April.

follower
noun
a person who follows
The new leader had many *followers* who liked him very much.

following
adjective
coming after
I like the *following* fruits: apples, oranges, and bananas.

fond
adjective
liking very much
I am very *fond* of chocolate cake. I eat it whenever I can.

food
noun
things to eat
We need *food* and drink to live.

fool
noun
a person who has little sense
I told him not to drive without lights. He was a *fool* to do so.

foolish
adjective
without much sense
A *foolish* person acts before thinking.

foot

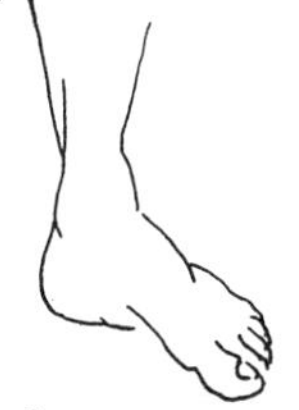

noun: feet
the end (bottom) part of the leg
We stand on our *feet.*
verb: footing, footed, footed
pay (for)
Five of us had dinner in a restaurant, and my uncle *footed* the bill.

football
noun
a ball game with eleven players on each side
My cousin plays *football;* he is a back.

for
preposition
1. *(showing length of time)*
I studied in the library *for* three hours.
2. *(showing amount paid)*
That book is *for* ten dollars.
3. *(showing action towards)*
She made a cake *for* me. What can I do *for* you?
conjunction
because
She wore a coat, *for* she was cold.

force
noun
strength
His car has a lot of *force*; he can pull another car behind him.
verb: forcing, forced, forced
use strength to do something
The room was full of people, but he *forced* his way in.

forceful
adjective
having a lot of strength

His speech was *forceful*; he affected everyone.

forehead

noun
the top part of the face
This girl lets her hair cover her *forehead.*

foreign

adjective
belonging to another place or country
He speaks a *foreign* language; he speaks Japanese.

foreigner

noun
a person from another country
Many *foreigners* visit Washington, D.C. They come from many parts of the world.

forest

noun
a place with a lot of trees
Many animals live in the *forests* of Africa.

forever

adverb
till the end of time
This man can work *forever;* he never stops.

forget

verb: forgetting, forgot, forgotten
lose memory of, opposite of remember
My friend could not write his composition. He *forgot* his pen at home.

forgive

verb: forgiving, forgave, forgiven
pardon
He hurt his sister with his rough words, but she *forgave* him.

forgot

See **forget.**

forgotten

See **forget.**

fork

noun
1. *an instrument used for eating*
We use a spoon with our soup. We cut our meat with a knife, and we eat it with a *fork.*
2. *a division*
We didn't know which way to take when we reached a *fork* in the road.

form

noun
1. *shape*
Water takes the *form* of the glass it is in.
2. *a paper to be filled out*
She wrote her name and address on the school *form.*
verb
make, establish
The businessman *formed* a new company with his friends.

formal

adjective
according to certain rules
The two leaders had a very *formal* meeting. Everything they said and did was correct and proper.

former

adjective
earlier
On my second visit to the museum, I saw some things I had not seen on my *former* visit.

formerly
adverb
before (in time)
She has been a doctor for two years. *Formerly*, she was a nurse.

fortunate
adjective
lucky
We had planned for a whole week to go on a picnic last Saturday. We were very *fortunate* with the weather. It didn't rain.

fortunately
adverb
luckily
We wanted good weather for our picnic. *Fortunately*, it didn't rain.

fortune
noun
luck
It was our good *fortune* to have a sunny day for our picnic.

forty
noun
a number: 40
She bought a book for $25 and another for $15. She paid *forty* for both.

forward
verb
send onward
He was in Paris when a letter arrived for him in Boston. His sister *forwarded* the letter to him.
adjective
near the front
I like one of the *forward* seats when I see a play.
adverb
towards the front
The soldier kept walking *forward* until he reached the front of the line.

fought
See **fight**.

found
See **find.**

foundation
noun
1. *basis, base*
This building is very strong; it has a good *foundation*.
2. *organization*
I met the president of an art *foundation*.

fountain

noun
1. *a place where water comes out, a spring*
We came across a natural water *fountain* in the mountains.
2. *a source*
My wise uncle is a *fountain* of knowledge.

four
noun
a number: 4
Two and two make *four*.
adjective
a number: 4
They have *four* children.

fourteen
noun
a number: 14
Ten and four make *fourteen*.
adjective
a number: 14
They were away for *fourteen* days.

fourth
noun
1. *a number showing order: 4th*
They have four children. The first three were boys. The *fourth* was a girl.
2. *one of four equal parts*
We divided the apple in four. Each one of us had a *fourth*.
adjective
a number showing order: 4th
April is the *fourth* month of the year.

frame

noun
a border that holds things
I put my pictures in glass *frames* so that they can stand on a table.
verb: framing, framed, framed
put in a border that holds things
I *framed* my pictures in wood and glass frames.

frank

adjective
open and free in expressing oneself
She was very *frank* with us; she told us what she liked and what she didn't like about our house.

free

adjective
1. *not in prison, not tied*
After spending two years in prison, he became a *free* man.
2. *not busy*
The principal will be *free* to see us at three o'clock.
3. *not costing anything, without paying anything*
In that store, if you buy two shirts, you get one *free*.

freedom

noun
the state of being free
Many countries have fought for their *freedom*.

freeze

verb: freezing, froze, frozen
1. *make cold at or below 32°F*
We *froze* the water to make ice.
2. *feel cold*
It was so cold outside, we *froze*.

freight

noun
cargo, goods transported
Their train does not carry passengers; it is a *freight* train.

frequent

verb
go to or be in very often
Students *frequent* this restaurant; it has good food at low prices.
adjective
occurring often
Students like that restaurant and make *frequent* visits to it.

frequently

adverb
often
Students go to that restaurant *frequently* because they like the food there.

fresh

adjective
1. *not cooked or canned*
I like to eat *fresh* fruits and vegetables straight from my own garden.
2. *without salt*
We swam in a *fresh* water lake.
3. *newly made*
All the cakes we have are *fresh;* they have just come out of the oven.

Friday

noun
a day of the week
Friday comes after Thursday and before Saturday.

fried

See **fry.**

friend

noun
a person who likes another and has the same interests
I have two very good *friends* in school; we study and play together.

friendly

adjective: friendlier, friendliest
acting like a friend
We met very fine people on our trip; they were

very kind and *friendly*.

friendship
noun
the state of being friendly
My neighbor and I have been friends for many years. I treasure his *friendship*.

fries
See **fry.**
noun
fried food (usually potatoes)
He likes *fries* with his steak.

fright
noun
the condition of being afraid
The child screamed in *fright* when he saw the big dog.

frighten
verb
make (someone) afraid
The big dog *frightened* the child when he barked.

frog

noun
an animal that lives on land and in water
I always know there is some water around when I hear *frogs*.

from
preposition
1. *(showing a starting point)*
We walked *from* the library to our class.
2. *(showing a source)*
I took ten dollars *from* my father.

front
noun
1. *not a true appearance*
He is not a good man; he uses nice words only to put on a *front*.
2. *a forward position*
I was sitting in the back, but my brother was sitting in the *front* of the bus.

(in front of)
adverb
facing
The girl is standing *in front of* a mirror.

frost
noun
a thin ice cover
Early in the morning we can see the *frost* on the grass.

frozen
See **freeze.**

fruit
noun

a plant food that is usually sweet
Strawberries are her favorite *fruit*.

fry

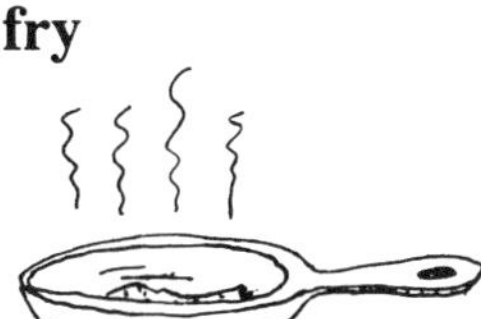

verb: frying, fried, fried
cook in a pan with oil or butter
Sometimes we *fry* our chickens and sometimes we barbecue them.

full

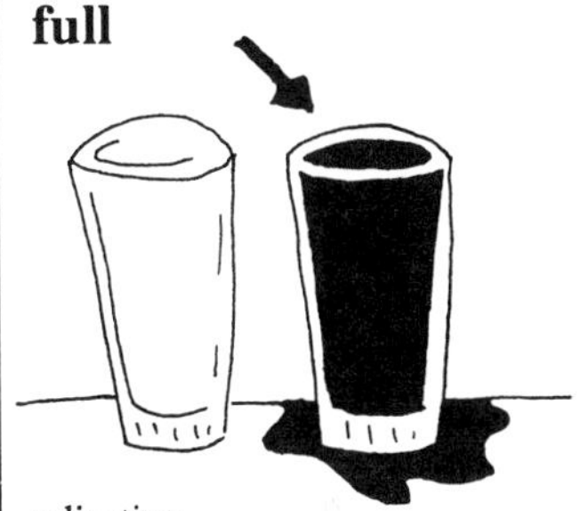

adjective
opposite of empty
I can't put any more clothes in my suitcase; it is *full* now.

fully
adverb
completely
We must understand and know the rules *fully*; if we don't, we might make mistakes.

fun
noun
enjoyment
We had a lot of *fun* at the party; we sang and danced and ate.

function
noun
purpose
The *function* of a car is to take you to different places.
verb
serve
A car *functions* as a means of transportation.

fund
noun
a source of money or capital
The parents of this child have a special *fund* for his education.
verb
provide a source of money or capital
His parents *funded* his education.

fundamental
adjective
important and necessary
There are some *fundamental* principles in life. One of them is honesty.

funeral
noun
a formal program or act for a dead person
He was a very kind man. When he died, many people attended his *funeral*.

funny
adjective: funnier, funniest
producing fun and laughter
He is a *funny* man with *funny* stories; whatever he does or says makes us laugh.

fur

noun
material made from the skin and hair of some animals
She bought a beautiful *fur* coat for herself.

furnish
verb
1. *provide, give*
The school *furnished* each classroom with enough chalk.
2. *fill with or provide furniture*
They bought a new home and *furnished* every room.

furniture

noun
the items (equipment) in a house or office
We bought two pieces of *furniture* last week: a desk and a chair.

further
See **far** also.
adjective
a longer distance away (from)
Boston is *further* than New York City from Washington, D.C.

furthest
See **far** also.
adjective
the longest distance away (from)
The fastest runner ran to the *furthest* point in the time we were given.

fuss
noun
a useless act of anger
Just because the train was one minute late, he created a *fuss*. He was very angry.

futile
adjective
useless
He wanted to jump over the wall. He tried several times, but everything he did was

futile.

future
noun
the time that is coming (after now)
My cousin has good plans for the *future*: he wants to become a doctor.

Gg

gain
noun
a profit, opposite of loss
He bought the bicycle for $50 and sold it for $53. He made a *gain* of $3.
verb
win, get
He is working well and *gaining* confidence in himself.

game
noun
1. *a sport*
Football is a *game* we like to watch on television.
2. *something to play with another person or more*
I like to play board and card *games* with my brother and sister.

garage, garage
noun
a place to keep a car
Their *garage* holds two cars.

garden

noun
a small piece of land for growing flowers and some fruits and vegetables
She grows roses in the *garden* behind her house.
verb
work in and take care of a garden
In his free time, he likes to *garden*; he plants flowers and waters them.

gardening
noun
working in a garden
In his free time, he does some *gardening*. He plants flowers.

garlic

noun
a vegetable with a strong taste and used in cooking
She likes onions and *garlic* in her salad.

garment
noun
something to wear
She buys all her *garments* (coats and dresses) from that store.

gas
noun
1. *a physical substance like oxygen and air*
Boiling water changes to a *gas*.
2. *a substance (liquid) that is used in cars and machines*
He filled his car with *gas* before he drove away.

gate

noun
a door to an outside area like a garden or a school
The wall around their house has two *gates*.

gather
verb
1. *collect*
I *gathered* all the leaves in the garden and threw them away.
2. *group together*
All the students *gathered* in the field to watch the game.

gathering
noun

a meeting
My friends and I had a little *gathering* in my home. We talked and played games.

gave
See **give.**

gaze
verb: gazing, gazed, gazed
look straight for a long time
That child couldn't turn his head away from the television. He *gazed* at those pictures without moving.

geese
See **goose.**

gem

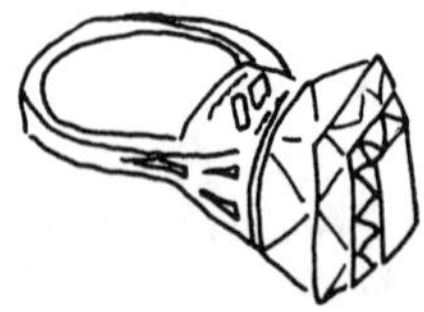

noun
a jewel
All her rings have beautiful *gems* on them.

general
noun
a high rank in the armed forces
The *general* gave his orders to the troops to advance.

adjective
1. *common*
We have a *general* rule in the library: everybody must work quietly.
2. *relating to the whole*
I did not want all the details; I only asked for a *general* picture of what happened.

generally
adverb
in general, as a whole
He is seldom angry; he is *generally* very happy.

generation
noun
1. *the time it takes for people to have their own children*
The customs we have in our country have been passed from one *generation* to the next.
2. *production*
This engine is used for the *generation* of electricity.

generous
adjective
kind and giving
He is very *generous* with his time and money. He helps others in every way he can.

genius
noun
a person with remarkable ability
He is a *genius* in mathematics; he can solve problems quickly and easily.

gentle
adjective
kind and tender
That nurse is very *gentle* with her patients; she treats them kindly.

gentleman
noun: gentlemen
a man with very fine manners
He treats everybody with respect; he is a real *gentleman.*

gently
adverb
in a gentle way
She treats little children very *gently*; she is kind and nice to them.

geography
noun
The study of the natural elements of the earth: mountains, rivers, plains, etc.
We studied about the mountains of the world in our *geography* class.

get
verb: getting, got, got or gotten
1. *bring*

She forgot her book at home; she went back to *get* it.
2. *reach*
We *got* to school at eight o'clock.
3. *become*
They *got* hungry after a day without food.
4. *have to*
I've *got* to study for my test.
5. *receive*
I *got* a telephone call in my room.

get along
verb
deal nicely (with)
I *get along* very well with my neighbors. We are good friends.

get by
verb
manage
His money is not much, but he *gets by.*

get up
verb
rise
He goes to bed at nine o'clock and *gets up* at six.

ghost
noun
spirit
She dreamed that she saw her grandmother as a *ghost*.

giant
noun
a very big person
Stories and pictures of *giants* frighten the little girl.

gift
noun
1. *a present*
She received many *gifts* on her birthday.
2. *an ability*
Singing is one of her *gifts*.

girl

noun
a young female person
They have four children: one boy and three *girls*.

give
verb: giving, gave, given
1. *present, offer*
He didn't have a pencil; so I *gave* him one of mine.
2. *present in public*
She *gave* a very good talk on health.

given

See **give.**

glad
adjective: gladder, gladdest
happy
They wanted very much to see us, and they were *glad* when we arrived.

glance
noun
a quick look
She couldn't tell us who was there; she only saw them at a *glance.*
verb: glancing, glanced, glanced
give a quick look
She *glanced* at them, but she didn't see them very well.

glare
noun
a strong and bright light
I couldn't read in the sun because of the *glare*.

glass
noun
1. *a hard substance that one can usually see through*
We put new curtains on our *glass* windows.

2. *a container to drink from*
I had a *glass* of water with lunch.

glasses
noun
spectacles, eye-glasses

She needs her *glasses* to read.

gleam
noun
1. *a light*
A *gleam* shone through her bedroom windows.
2. *a ray*
The good news he heard gave him a *gleam* of hope for the future.

glimpse
noun
a quick look
We took a *glimpse* of the people in the street from our window.

glitter
noun
a shine
Gold gives a nice *glitter* in the sun.
verb
shine
Gold *glitters* in the sun.

global
adjective
all over the world
Pollution is a *global* problem.

globe
noun
a ball with the map of the world
I like to spot the places we have visited on our *globe.*

glorious
adjective
excellent, magnificent
We had our picnic on a *glorious* day; it was warm and sunny.

glove

noun
a cover for the hand
She wears wool *gloves* in winter. He wears leather *gloves* to drive.

glow
noun
a shine
Her ring gave a nice *glow* when she held it near the light.
verb
shine
Her ring *glowed* in the light. She is *glowing* with happiness.

glue
noun
material that sticks things together
She used *glue* to stick the pictures on the board.
verb
stick
If you want these papers to stay together, *glue* them to each other.

go
verb: going, went, gone
1. *leave*
They arrived last week. Yesterday they *went* to a museum.
2. *reach*
The elevator *goes* to the fifth floor.
3. *move*
They *went* slow in the snow.
4. *sell*
That old car *went* for $1,000.
5. *be accepted*
Those old coins won't *go* here.
6. *happen*
I don't know what is *going* on there.

go back
verb: going back, went back, gone back
return
They arrived last week, and they *went back* yesterday.

go on
verb: going on, went on, gone on
continue
She started working on her dress an hour ago,

and she is still *going on* with it now.

goal

noun

1. *purpose, end*

He and his sister are studying very hard. His *goal* is to become a doctor, and her *goal* is to become a lawyer.

2. *the area towards which players go to score*

We scored three *goals* and they scored two *goals* in the hockey game.

goat

noun

an animal like a sheep

Goats are very clever in climbing mountains.

God

noun

the being that people worship

They believe in *God* and pray to Him.

goes

See **go**.

going

See **go**.

going to

verb

showing future action

She hasn't written her letter yet, but she is *going to* write it soon.

gold

noun

a precious metal (yellow or white in color)

She wears a lot of *gold* and silver on her arms.

golden

adjective

1. *made of gold*

She bought a *golden* ring.

2. *favorable*

When it stopped raining, we felt it was a *golden* opportunity for us to leave.

gone

See **go**.

good

adjective: better, best

1. *kind and nice*

My aunt is a very *good* lady; she is kind to people, and she helps them.

2. *fit, suitable*

That car is *good* for them; it is big enough to hold the whole family.

3. *useful*

Exercise is *good* for you; it keeps you well.

4. *right*

The teacher asked me four questions, and I gave four *good* answers.

good-bye

noun

farewell

We went to the station to say *good-bye* to our friends who were leaving.

goodness

noun

the act of being good

We could sense that man's *goodness*; he was always kind and helpful.

go off

verb: going off, went off, gone off

explode

A bomb *went off* on the field when the soldiers were practicing. Nobody was hurt.

goose

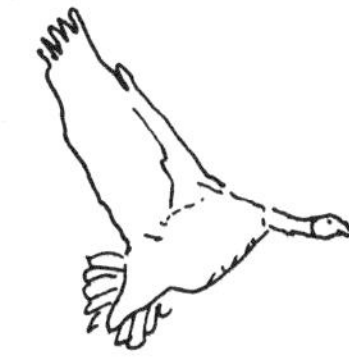

noun: geese

a bird with a long neck that swims
Children like to feed the ducks and the *geese* by the river.

gorgeous
adjective
very nice and beautiful
Yesterday was a *gorgeous* day; the sun was out, and it was warm. We went for a drive and saw some *gorgeous* views of the mountains.

governor
noun
a person who governs or rules
Every state in the U.S. elects its own *governor*. He or she is the head of the state government.

gown

noun
1. *an official robe*
All the graduates and the teachers wore their caps and *gowns* at graduation.
2. *a loose garment worn at home*
She wore her morning *gown* to breakfast.

grace
noun
1. *a prayer said before a meal*
We usually say *grace* before we eat.
2. *style and charm*
Everything she does is done with *grace*. She is very refined.

grade
noun
1. *a mark*
She received a *grade* of A on her test.
2. *a quality level*
The eggs we bought were *grade* A. They were big and fresh.

gradual
adjective
moving step by step
The change in temperature was very *gradual*. It became cooler and cooler very slowly.

gradually
adverb
step by step
He was very ill and weak. Then as he began to eat, he *gradually* became well and strong.

grain
noun
1. *a seed of a cereal*
We make bread from flour which comes from wheat *grains*.
2. *a tiny particle*
The beach is full of *grains* of sand.

gram
noun
a small measure of weight
She used two *grams* of salt in her cooking.

grand
adjective
1. *very nice*
We had a *grand* time on the beach.
2. *of high quality*
I met some *grand* people at dinner. They came from good families and behaved very well.

grandchild
noun: grandchildren
the son or daughter of a son or daughter
This man and his wife have two children and seven *grandchildren*.

granddaughter
noun
the daughter of a son or daughter
This old lady attended her *granddaughter's* third birthday.

grandfather
noun
the father of a father or mother
I did not know my *grandfather*, but my

father has told me a lot about him.

grandma
Same as **grandmother**.

grandmother
noun
the mother of a father or mother
I loved my two *grandmothers.* My father and mother loved them too.

grandpa
Same as **grandfather**.

grandparent
noun
the father or mother of a father or mother
I loved my four *grandparents.*

grandson
noun
the son of a son or daughter
They have two grandchildren: one *grandson* and one granddaughter.

grant
verb
give
The school *granted* us permission to go home early.

grape
noun
a fruit that comes from a vine

I like to eat *grapes* and figs in summer. Red *grapes* are my favorite.

grapefruit

noun: grapefruit
a fruit that looks like an orange
I like to eat half a *grapefruit* for breakfast.

grass

noun
thin green leaves
Their lawn is very green; they take good care of their *grass.* Sheep and goats love to eat *grass.*

grateful
adjective
thankful
We were very *grateful* to them; they helped us very much when we moved.

grave
noun
a place where dead people are laid to rest
They visited their parents' *grave* and put flowers on it.
adjective
serious
They faced a *grave* situation; their money was limited and they didn't know what to do.

gray
noun
a color (between black and white)
I like *gray* for suits.
adjective
a color
She wears a red rose on her *gray* dress.

great
adjective
1. *grand*
We saw a *great* play. It was well acted.
2. *big, huge*
The bookstore sold a *great* number of books last year.

greatly
adverb
in a big way
Drivers are *greatly* affected by weather conditions.

greed
noun
great selfishness, wanting things for oneself

People don't like him because of his *greed*; he always wants things for himself.

greedy
adjective: greedier, greediest
wanting things for oneself
People know that he is *greedy* because he takes everything for himself and leaves nothing for others.

green
noun
a color, a mix of blue and yellow
I like *green*; it is the color of tree leaves.
adjective
a color
She wore a beautiful *green* dress.

greet
verb
meet and receive with kindness
I *greeted* the guests at the door when they arrived for tea.

grew
See **grow.**

grief
noun
sadness
They met the news of their uncle's death with *grief*.

grieve
verb: grieving, grieved, grieved
be sad
They *grieved* over their uncle's death.

grip
noun
a tight hold with the hand
He gave me a tight *grip* when he shook my hand.
verb: gripping, gripped, gripped
hold tightly
He *gripped* my hand and would not let me go.

grind
verb: grinding, ground, ground
break into bits by pressing hard
We *grind* our wheat to make flour.

groan
noun
a loud sound from pain or unhappiness
We could hear the sick man's *groans* in the hospital.
verb
give a loud sound from pain
The sick man *groaned* all night. He was uncomfortable and in pain.

ground
See **grind** also.
noun
1. *reason, basis*
His disagreement with the manager is *grounds* for him to leave the company.
2. *the top of the earth*
An apple fell from the tree to the *ground*.

group
noun
1. *a number of people*
My friends and I were a small *group* in school interested in butterflies.
2. *a number of things*
As we went up the road, we saw a *group* of trees on one side.
verb
get together in a group
We *grouped* the children according to their heights. The tall ones were in our group.

grove
noun
a small number of trees together
She likes to sit and read on a bench in the middle of the *grove* in her garden.

grow
verb: growing, grew, grown
1. *increase in size or age*
The baby is *growing* very fast. He now weighs twenty pounds.
2. *plant and care for*
She *grows* roses in her garden.

grow old
become old in age
My grandfather is *growing old.* He is now seventy-five years old.

grown
See **grow.**

grown-up
noun
a person who is old enough to take care of himself
The children stayed at home; the *grown-ups* went out to dinner.

growth
noun
increase in size or number
The *growth* of our city has been fast. This year we had 3,000 more people in it.

guard
noun
a person who watches an entrance
When you drive to the school, ask the *guard* at the gate where you can park.
verb
watch
The policemen *guarded* the palace. They didn't let any strangers go in.

guess
noun
an opinion which may or may not be true
He asked me how many pennies he had in his hand; I made a *guess*; I said three. He had four.
verb
give an opinion which may or may not be true
"I *guess* you have three pennies in your hand," I said. He had four.

guest
noun
1. a *person (who is invited and) who comes to other people*
We had four *guests* at our dinner table last night.
2. *a person who eats in a restaurant or stays in a hotel or motel*
This hotel treats its *guests* very well. *Guests* always feel happy there.

guide
noun
a person who leads
Our *guide* told us many interesting things when we visited the museum.
verb: guiding, guided, guided
lead
We didn't know the way to the museum, but a kind man *guided* us to it. He walked with us all the way.

guilty
adjective: guiltier, guiltiest
having done something wrong
He is *guilty* of lying to his teacher. He did not tell the truth.

guitar
noun
a string instrument
He played lovely tunes on his *guitar* and we sang.

gulf
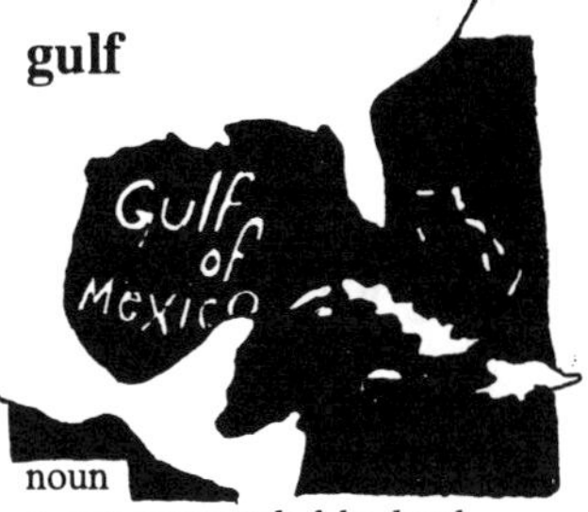

noun
a sea surrounded by land but not fully
We visited a number of cities in the *Gulf* of Mexico last winter.

gumbo
noun
a thick soup
One of my favorite soups is a shrimp *gumbo.*

gun
noun
1. *a hand weapon which is fired*

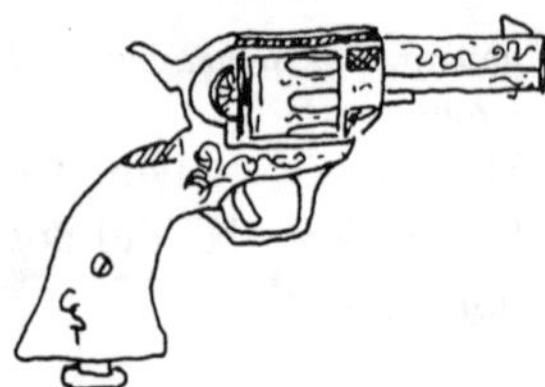

Policemen carry *guns* on their sides.
2. *a field weapon which is fired*
The army used big shells when they fired their *guns.*

guy
noun
boy or man
My uncle is a very tall *guy.*

gym
noun
1. *physical exercise*
He's doing some *gym* now to keep fit.
2. *gymnasium*
We are going to the *gym* to lift some weights.

gymnasium
See **gym** also.
a place where people do physical exercise
Our school built a new *gymnasium;* now we can do lots of exercise there.

Hh

habit
noun
custom, the usual way of acting
She has a *habit* of playing with her hair; she does it all the time.

had
See **have**.

hadn't
negative of had, had not
See **had**.

hail
noun
small balls of ice coming down from the clouds
It was very cold and stormy. The *hail* came down with force.
interjection
greeting
Hail to the champion.

hair

noun
a thin thing growing on the head and on skin
She has beautiful long *hair* and she wears it in a nice style.

half
noun: halves
one of two equal parts of something
My brother and I had one apple. Each of us had a *half.* The two *halves* were equal.

hall
noun
1. *a narrow way in a building*
We have a long *hall* leading to the bedrooms in our house.
2. *a school or public building*
The meeting was held in Johnson *Hall.*

halves
See **half.**

hamburger
noun
fried or barbecued ground meat
She likes her *hamburgers* with fries.

hammer

noun
a tool used to drive nails in by pounding
He needed a *hammer* and nails before he could hang his pictures.

hand
noun
1. *the end part of the arm*

that has the fingers

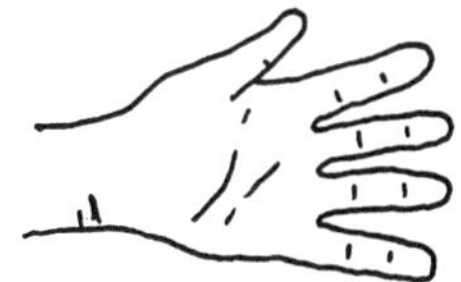

We use our *hands* to eat and write with.
2. *help*
I couldn't carry the bag alone; so he gave me a *hand*.
3. *one of two or three metal pointers on a clock or watch.*
My watch has an hour *hand*, a minute *hand*, and a second *hand*.
verb
give
She *handed* me her bags to put in the car.

handkerchief
noun
a small piece of cloth that one puts in a pocket or handbag and uses to wipe one's hands or face
Our teacher wipes her hands with a *handkerchief* after she uses chalk to write on the blackboard.

handle

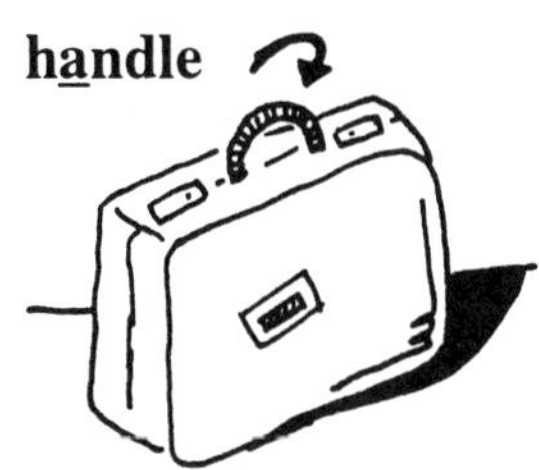

noun
the thing one holds to open or carry something
The *handle* of my suitcase broke; so I couldn't carry it any more.
verb: handling, handled, handled
manage
He *handles* his business and the people who work for him very well.

handout
noun
a paper given out free
Our teacher gave us two *handouts* to help us understand the lesson.

handsome
adjective
nice looking
The main actor in the film was tall and *handsome*; he had brown eyes and brown hair.

hang
verb: hanging, hung, hung
be attached to something high without having support from below
Monkeys like to *hang* from ropes and trees.

hang up
verb: hanging up, hung up, hung up
1. *put up on a rod or rope or nail*
She likes to *hang up* the pictures on the wall herself.
2. *end a telephone conversation*
She was talking with her sister on the phone; then suddenly her sister *hung up*.

happen
verb
occur, take place
I don't know what *happened* there, but my brother was there, and he can tell me.

happily
adverb
1. *in a happy way*
I didn't want them to spend too much time helping me, but they did it *happily*.
2. *fortunately*
We wanted to go on a picnic; *happily*, it didn't rain that day.

happiness
noun
the condition of being happy
When they received the good news about their son, one could see their *happiness* on their faces.

happy
adjective: happier, happiest
feeling glad and pleased
The children are very *happy* playing together in the garden.

harbor

noun
port, a place where ships can stay safely in deep and calm water
We counted the ships in the *harbor*; there were eighteen of them.

hard

adjective
1. *not soft*
It is not comfortable to sit on a rock for a long time because it is *hard*.
2. *difficult*
Of the four questions the teacher asked me, one was *hard* for me to answer; I didn't know the answer.
3. *strong*
There was a *hard* knock on the door; I heard it in the back of the house.

hardly

adverb
barely
I could *hardly* hear the speaker; his voice was very low.

harm

noun
injury, damage
A big rock rolled down the hill, but it caused no *harm*; nobody was hurt.
verb
cause injury or damage
The rock that came down the hill *harmed* nobody; nobody was hurt.

harvest

noun
gathering in the products of a field
The farmers were happy with their *harvest* this year. They had a lot of crops and other products.

has

See **have** also.
She *has* a nice new dress. He *has* given her the dress as a present.

hasn't

negative of has
This is her first visit to this restaurant; she *hasn't* been here before.

has to

See **have to**.

haste

noun
hurry, speed
He made some mistakes, because he did his work in great *haste*. He did not give it enough time.

hasten

verb
be quick
She *hastened* to get back home before it rained.

hasty

adjective: hastier, hastiest
quick
He made some mistakes, because he was rather *hasty* in his work.

hat

noun
head cover
She wears gloves and a *hat* when she goes out.

hate

verb: hating, hated, hated
dislike strongly
He is a very honest person; he *hates* hearing lies.

have

verb: having, had, had
possess
I *have* three books in my school bag.

auxiliary verb
I *have* eaten my lunch; I am not hungry now.

haven't
negative of have
This is the first time I see them; I *haven't* seen them before.

have to
verb: having to, had to, had to
must
We *have to* study hard to pass.

hay
noun
dry grass for animals to eat
The carriage driver gave his horses *hay* to eat and water to drink.

he
pronoun: he, him, his
third person masculine singular
He is a very kind man; I know him very well.

head

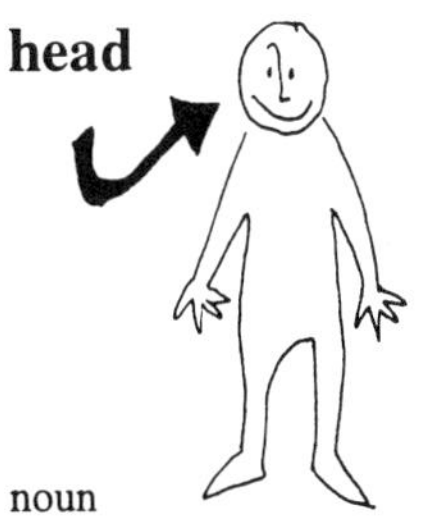

noun
1. *the top part of the body, the part above the neck*
He wore a cap to keep his *head* warm.
2. *chief*
He is the *head* of his company; he has forty people working for him.
3. *top, front*
The captain was at the *head* of the line as the soldiers marched through the city.
verb
be the chief
My uncle *headed* his company for fifteen years.

headache
noun
pain in the head
His head is hurting him; he has a *headache*; he needs to sleep.

health
noun
good condition of the body or mind
The children are in good *health*; they feel well and happy.

healthful
adjective
good for the health
Eating well is a *healthful* practice.

healthy
adjective: healthier, healthiest
having good health
He is well and he works hard; he is very *healthy*.

heap

noun
pile
She couldn't work at the table; there was a *heap* of books on it.
verb
make a pile of
She *heaped* her books on the table; she had ten books on top of each other.

hear
verb: hearing, heard, heard
receive sounds by the ears
He didn't answer my question, because he didn't *hear* it.

heard
See **hear**.

heart

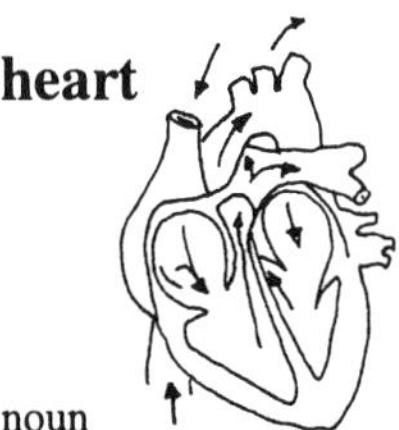

noun
1. *the part of the body that pumps blood*
The doctor examined her and said that her *heart* and lungs were excellent.
2. *courage*

She didn't have the *heart* to visit her sick aunt in the hospital.

heat
noun
warmth, being hot
It was warm in the kitchen; there was a lot of *heat* coming from the oven.
verb
make hot
She *heated* the soup before she gave it to me; it was hot when I had it.

heaven
noun
paradise, the place where angels live
They told us that all good people go to *heaven* when they die.

heavily
adverb
in a difficult way
She walked *heavily*; her foot was hurting her.

heavy

adjective: heavier, heaviest
having great weight
She couldn't carry the box; it was too *heavy* for her.

he'd
pronoun and auxiliary verb
1. *he had*
He did that for the second time; *he'd* done it before.
2. *he would*
He'd like to see the film I saw.

hedge

noun
a wall of plants or trees
The farmer had a *hedge* around his farm.
verb: hedging, hedged, hedged
hesitate
When we asked her to come with us, she *hedged*; she wasn't sure what she wanted to do.

height
noun
a measure of how high or tall someone or something is
He is six feet in *height*.
We could not climb the whole *height* of the mountain.

held
See **hold**.

helicopter

noun
an airplane that has a propeller on top and that can fly straight up
He took a *helicopter* ride to see the city.

he'll
pronoun and auxiliary verb
he will
I know *he'll* be coming tomorrow.

hello
interjection
informal greeting
When I met him, I said, "*Hello*. How are you?"

help
noun
assistance, aid
I couldn't do the job alone; I needed some *help*.
verb
give assistance or aid
When she saw that I couldn't do the job alone, she *helped* me with it.

helpful
adjective
useful, able to help
My neighbor is a very *helpful* person; he likes people and he likes to help them.

helpless
adjective
not able to take care of oneself
When she was sick, she was *helpless*; she needed someone to feed her and take care of her.

hen

noun
a female bird
Their *hen* lays three eggs a week.

hence
adverb
therefore
It is raining now; *hence*, it is difficult for us to leave.

her
pronoun: she, her, hers
third person feminine singular
She is a nice person. I know *her*, and I know *her* parents.

herd

noun
a number of animals together
We saw a *herd* of goats in the field.

here
adverb
in this place
Come *here*; I'd like to ask you a question.

hero
noun: heroes
1. *the leading man in a play or film*
John Wayne was a *hero* in many films.
2. *a brave man*
The president honored all the *heroes* after the war.

heroine
noun
feminine of hero
See **hero.**
The *heroine* in the play acted very well.

hers
pronoun: she, her, hers
third person feminine singular
This is her book; do not take it; it is *hers*.

herself
emphatic pronoun
she alone
She did the work *herself*.
reflexive pronoun
her own self
She hurt *herself* with the kitchen knife.

he's
pronoun and verb
he is
He's a good man.
pronoun and auxiliary verb
1. *he is*
He's doing it again.
2. *he has*
He's gone; he isn't here.

hesitate
verb: hesitating, hesitated, hesitated
wait before doing things
She never gives you a direct and fast answer; she *hesitates* for a time and then answers you.

hid
See **hide**.

hidden
See **hide**.

hide
verb: hiding, hid, hidden
put something where it cannot be seen
She *hid* the presents in the closet; she didn't want the children to see them before the party.

high
adjective
above ground level
The airplane was *high* in the sky. The table is four feet *high*.

highly
adverb
greatly
She is *highly* liked among her friends.

highway
noun
a big main road
We saw many restaurants as we drove down the *highway*.

hill

noun
a small mountain
There is a small forest on the *hill* near our city.

hilly
adjective: hillier, hilliest
has hills
We drove up and down the *hilly* area around our city.

him
pronoun: he, him, his
third person masculine singular
He is a very wonderful person; I know *him* very well.

himself
emphatic pronoun
he alone
He did the job *himself*.
reflexive pronoun
his own self
He hurt *himself* with the kitchen knife.

hip

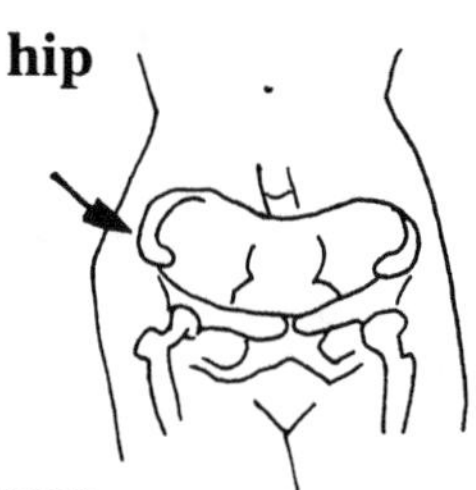

noun
a part of the body, the side above the leg
She cannot sleep very well on her right side, because she has hurt her right *hip*.

hire
verb: hiring, hired, hired
1. *rent*
The boy *hired* a boat to row for an hour.
2. *take someone to work for pay*
The company *hired* five new secretaries.

his
pronoun: he, him, his
third person masculine singular
This is *his* book; don't take it; it is *his*.

history
noun: histories
the study of events according to the time they happened
We learned about Athens and Rome in our *history* class.

hit
noun
1. *something very excellent*
All of us told stories, but his story was a *hit*; it was wonderful.
2. *a strike*
He gave his friend a *hit* on the hand.
verb: hitting, hit, hit
strike
He *hit* his friend in class, but he didn't hurt him.

hobby
noun: hobbies
something one does in one's free time
My *hobby* is collecting stamps.

hockey
noun
a game with five players on each side
Our *hockey* team won the game last night.

hold
verb: holding, held, held
1. *have in the hand*
He *held* his money and would not let anybody take it.
2. *own*

They *hold* some shares in the company.
3. *keep under control*
The policeman *held* a thief in his car.

hole
noun

1. *an opening*
The water went through a *hole* in the bottle.

2. a *hollow area*
The children dug a deep *hole* in the ground to make a small pool.

holiday
noun
1. *a free day*
We had no classes last Monday; we had a *holiday*.
2. *vacation*
We went to Florida for a *holiday*.

hollow
adjective
having a hole or opening
A small part of their garden was quite *hollow*, and it needed to be filled with dirt.

holy
adjective: holier, holiest
sacred
There are many *holy* places in Jerusalem.

home
noun
the place where one lives
He is not in his office today; he is at *home*.
You are always welcome in their *home*.

homework
noun
a school duty to be done after school (at home)
She never goes to bed before she finishes her *homework*.

honest
adjective
truthful
He is a very *honest* man. He never tells lies.

honesty
noun
being honest, being truthful
He is known for his *honesty*; he never tells lies.

honey
noun
the sweet food that comes from bees
Sometimes she uses sugar and sometimes she uses *honey* in her tea.

honor
noun
high respect, a good name
He is a man of *honor*; he is very honest and kind.
verb
1. *stick to and follow agreements*
The store owner told us that he would sell us things at half price. He *honored* his word, and we paid half.
2. *give respect to someone*
The brave soldier was *honored* by the president at a special party.

honorable
adjective
deserving honor
Honesty and kindness are *honorable* qualities.

hook
noun

1. *a device to catch fish*
They use *hooks* to catch fish.

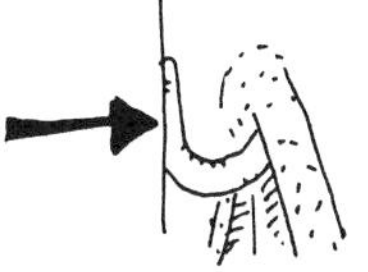

2. *a small device to hang things on*
She hung the towel on a *hook* in the bathroom.

hop
verb: hopping, hopped, hopped
make small jumps
In their free time, some of the children in school *hop* in the field.

hope
noun
a desire to have something happen
His *hope* is to become a doctor.
verb: hoping, hoped, hoped
desire to have something happen
He *hopes* to become a doctor.

hopeful
adjective
feeling that something good will happen
He is *hopeful* about his future; he thinks he will be successful.

horn
noun

1. *a device that makes a noise*
Some drivers blow their car *horns* for no reason; they just make a lot of noise.
2. *the hard parts that stick out of the heads of some animals*

Some deer have long and beautiful *horns.*

horrible
adjective
terrible, very bad
I didn't like the taste of the fish I ate; it was *horrible.*

horror
noun
great fear
There was a look of *horror* on the faces of the children when they saw the fire at home.

horse

noun
an animal used in races and to ride on
The carriage was drawn by two *horses.*

hospital
noun
a place where sick people stay
The nurse took care of her patients in *hospital.*

host
noun
a person who receives guests
We were invited to dinner, and our *hosts* met us at the door and welcomed us warmly.

hostess
noun
a female host
The *hostess* introduced us to the other guests.

hot
adjective: hotter, hottest
high in temperature
She needed some *hot* water for her tea. It was very *hot* yesterday; the temperature was 95°F.

hotel
noun
a building where people can sleep and eat for pay
We stayed in three different *hotels* during our vacation in France last summer.

hour
noun
a period of time: sixty minutes
The film we saw lasted two *hours* and fifteen minutes.

house
noun
a building where people live
Our *house* is on a

corner. From our windows, we can see two streets.

household
noun
the people (a family) who live together in one house
They are so kind that they consider their guests as members of their *household.*

how
question word, adverb
1. *asking about the way things are done*
How did you bake that cake?
2. *asking about the extent*
How far is the library from here?
3. *asking about quantity*
How much money do you have?
4. *asking about numbers*
How many books did you buy?
5. *asking about price*
How much was your watch?
6. *asking about someone's health*
How are you?

however
adverb
1. *to whatever extent*
I want a big car, but I will buy the one you told me about *however* small it is.
2. *in spite of this*
He doesn't study very hard; *however*, he is bright enough to pass.

hug
noun

an embrace, a hold with the arms
She gave her son a warm *hug* when he returned from his travels.
verb: hugging, hugged, hugged
embrace, hold with the arms
She *hugged* her son when he returned from his travels.

huge
adjective
very big
The elephant is a *huge* animal.

human
adjective
relating to men and women
Human language is different from animal language

humble
adjective
modest
The general was very *humble*; he talked with all the soldiers, and he wasn't proud.

humor
noun
the ability to see the funny or pleasant side of a thing
She has a very good sense of *humor*; she enjoys jokes and she tells funny stories.

humorous
adjective
funny
He told us some very *humorous* stories; they were very funny. He is a *humorous* man himself.

hundred
noun
a number: 100
Sixty and forty make one *hundred.*
adjective
a number: 100
There are a *hundred* cents in a dollar.

hundredth
noun
1. *a number showing order: 100th*
The first day of the year falls in January. The *hundredth* falls in April.
2. *one of a hundred equal parts: 1/100*

A cent is worth one *hundredth* of a dollar.

hung
See **hang**.

hunger
noun
the need to eat
They gave her some food to eat when they noticed her *hunger*.

hungry
adjective: hungrier, hungriest
feeling the need to eat
I eat only when I feel *hungry*.

hunt
verb
go after birds or animals to catch them or shoot them
They wanted to eat deer meat; so they *hunted* a deer in the forest.

hunter
noun
a person who hunts birds or animals
Many *hunters* go to the jungles of Africa to hunt wild animals.

hunting
noun
going after birds or animals to catch them or shoot them
My cousin takes his dog with him when he goes *hunting*.

hurry
noun
a rush
She is walking fast because she is in a *hurry*; she needs to get to work soon.
verb: hurrying, hurried, hurried
rush
She *hurries* to school when she thinks she is late.

hurt
verb: hurting, hurt, hurt
1. *feel pain*
His head *hurts*; he has a headache.
2. *cause pain*
He *hurt* his hand when he fell.

husband
noun
the male partner in a marriage
She is a very good wife; she prepares her *husband's* dinner every evening.

hut

noun
a small place to live in
They stay in a wooden *hut* during their vacations.

hygiene
noun
health science
Personal and community *hygiene* are very important.

hygienic
adjective
clean
I like to eat in this restaurant, because I know they are very *hygienic*.

hyphen
noun
a punctuation mark, a small dash used between words or parts of a word
Use a *hyphen* when you cut a word at the end of one line and finish it at the beginning of the next line.

Ii

I
pronoun: me, my, mine
first person singular
My name is Mark; *I* am Mark; *I* live with my parents.

ice
noun
frozen water

He likes a lot of *ice* in his water. There was *ice* on the roads last winter.

ice cream

noun
a frozen dessert
Some of us had apple pie for dessert, and some had *ice cream.*

icy
adjective: icier, iciest
like ice, very cold
His hands were *icy* after he played in the snow.

I'd
pronoun and auxiliary verb
1. *I had*
I felt I could see a film, because *I'd* done my homework.
2. *I would*
I'd like to see a new film tomorrow.

idea
noun
a thought
She wanted to go on a picnic, and we thought it was a good *idea.*

ideal
noun
an excellent example, a perfect model
She is my *ideal* of what a teacher should be.
adjective
perfect
In an *ideal* situation, everyone will be honest and kind.

identical
adjective
the same
These two brothers look exactly the same; they are *identical.*

idle
adjective
not working, not doing anything
Don't be *idle*; always find something to do.

if
conjunction
on condition that, in the event that
If you turn on the radio, we will hear the news.

ill
adjective: worse, worst
not well, sick
He is *ill*; the doctor told him to stay in bed.

I'll
pronoun and auxiliary verb
I will
I'll be here next week if you want to see me.

illness
noun
sickness
Because of his *illness*, he couldn't travel with his friends.

illustrate
verb: illustrating, illustrated, illustrated
1. *show with pictures*
The artist *illustrated* the book; she drew pictures on every page.
2. *show or explain with examples*
Our teacher *illustrated* the lesson by giving us clear examples.

I'm
pronoun and verb
I am
I'm a student; you're a teacher.
pronoun and auxiliary verb
I am
I'm studying English now.

image

noun
picture
I had an *image* of a beautiful sunset in my mind.

imagination
noun
having pictures or ideas in the mind
Very often the work she does is the result of her fine *imagination.*

imagine
verb: imagining, imagined, imagined
picture in the mind
He wants to become a doctor and very often he tries to *imagine* how he will deal with his patients.

immediate
adjective
done right now
He asked me a question and wanted me to give him an *immediate* answer; he was in a great hurry.

immediately
adverb
at once, right now
She had something very important to tell me, and she wanted to see me *immediately.*

importance
noun
significance
We must look after our health because of its *importance*.

important
adjective
significant
It is very *important* for us to look after our health.

impossible
adjective
not possible, not able to happen
It is *impossible* for a horse to fly.

impression
noun
1. *a mark*
When he walked on the sand, his shoes made *impressions* in the sand.
2. *a picture in the mind*
Her manner and her talk left a very good *impression* with everyone.

improve
verb: improving, improved, improved
become better
She was not very well yesterday, but she is *improving*; the medicine she is taking is good.

improvement
noun
the act of getting better
He received a C first, then a B, and then an A in English. The *improvement* is clear.

in
adverb
1. *on the inside, not out*
The principal was *in*; we could see him.
2. *towards the inside*
Walk *in* and sit down.
preposition
1. *(with time)*
They arrived *in* the afternoon. She came here *in* July.
2. *(with areas or fields of activity)*
I am interested *in* history.
3. *(with place)*
He is *in* his office now.
4. *(with method or way)*
She spoke *in* an interesting manner.
5. *(with language)*
She wrote a letter *in* English.

inch

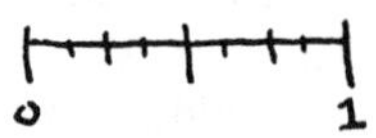

noun: inches
a measure of length: 2.54 centimeters
There are twelve *inches* in a foot.

inclined
adjective
drawn (to think or do something)

When I heard his story, I was *inclined* to believe him.

include
verb: including, included, included
consider (something) as a part of (something else)
They *included* me with the guests; I was one of the guests.

income
noun
money coming from work
They live quite well; their *income* is very high.

increase
verb: increasing, increased, increased
become bigger in number or size
The price of cars *increases* every year. You pay more for them every year.

indeed
adverb
really
She is a very fine person *indeed*; she is kind and helpful.

independence
noun
freedom
Many countries fought for their *independence*. They wanted to be free.

independent
adjective
free
He wants to be *independent*; he doesn't like anyone to control him.

indicate
verb: indicating, indicated, indicated
point out, show
By mentioning the museum, they *indicated* an interest in visiting it.

individual
noun
a person
There are five *individuals* waiting to see the doctor.
adjective
separate
The children had *individual* shares in their father's company.

indoor
adjective
happening inside
They only played *indoor* games, because it was very cold outside.

indoors
adverb
inside
They played all their games *indoors* when the weather was bad.

industrial
adjective
related to industry
Some countries are more *industrial* than agricultural.

industrious
adjective
hard working
My uncle is a very *industrious* person; he is always doing something.

industry
noun: industries
the product of a factory
Cars are one of the *industries* of Michigan.

influence
noun
effect
The weather has a big *influence* on our decision to go on a picnic.
verb
affect
The weather *influences* us in many ways. What we wear and where we go are *influenced* by the weather.

inform
verb
give knowledge to, tell
Our teacher *informed* us about the new school rules.

information
noun
(given or received) knowledge
I knew about his problem from the *information* he gave me on the telephone.

inhabit
verb
live in
They *inhabited* the house until it was sold.

inhabitant
noun
a person who lives somewhere
They were the *inhabitants* of the house until it was sold.

injure
verb: injuring, injured, injured
harm, hurt
She *injured* her hand when she fell.

injury
noun: injuries
harm
They were in a car accident, but they suffered no *injury.* Nobody was hurt.

ink

noun
a blue or black liquid used in writing or printing
Her pen has black *ink* in it.

innocent
adjective
free from doing wrong
The police held three people after the store was robbed. One of them was guilty of stealing; the other two were *innocent.*

inquire
verb: inquiring, inquired, inquired
ask (about)
She *inquired* about the time that trains left the station. She wanted to know if she could leave early.

insect

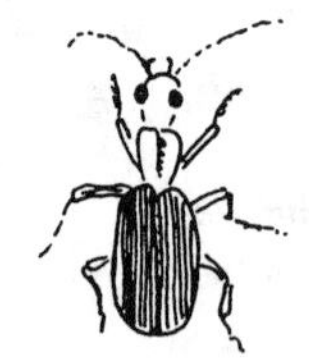

noun
a small creature
Flies and butterflies are two kinds of *insects.*

inside
noun
the inner part of something

The *inside* of the house is warm.
adverb
to the inner part or side
When she felt cold outside, she came *inside.*

insist
verb
take a position and stick to it
I wanted him to pass his test, and I *insisted* that he should study. He did.

inspiration
noun
the act of moving the mind or the feelings
The good example that the football hero gave was an *inspiration* to young children. They wanted to be like him.

inspire
verb: inspiring, inspired, inspired
move the mind or the feelings
The football hero *inspired* the children to work hard and behave well.

instance
noun
example
His kindness to us was an *instance* of his love.

instant
noun
moment, exact time
The *instant* I saw her, I knew who she was.

instantly
adverb
immediately
He had something very important to tell us; he wanted to see us *instantly*.

instead
adverb
as a different choice
He didn't read the book I gave him; *instead*, he read the one he had bought.

instinct
noun
a natural way of doing or feeling things
Hunger is an *instinct*.

instinctive
adjective
related to a natural way of doing or feeling things
Animal language is *instinctive*; human language is learned.

institution
noun
an organization used by the public
Schools and universities are educational *institutions*.

instruct
verb
1. *teach*
She *instructed* her students in English.
2. *tell (someone) what to do*
The general *instructed* his troop to cross the bridge.

instruction
noun
teaching
The students received their *instruction* in English.

instructions
noun
what and how to do things
I built my own desk after reading the *instructions* on the box.

instrument

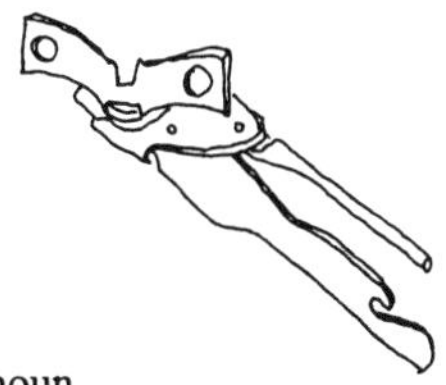

noun
a device used for doing things
A bottle opener is an *instrument* that helps us open bottles easily. A musical *instrument* is one we use to play music.

instrumental
adjective
helpful
Having two cars was *instrumental* in getting us all to school on time.

insurance
noun
the business of protecting (covering) people against things that might happen to them
He bought life *insurance* and health *insurance* for him and his family.

intelligence
noun
the ability of the mind
He is a person of great *intelligence*; he understands things very fast.

intelligent
adjective
having great ability of the mind
She is very *intelligent*; she understands things well and fast.

intend
verb
plan or have in mind to do something
Jack and Mary *intend* to get married next

month. They have made definite plans for that.

intention
noun
a definite plan to do something
It is their *intention* to get married next month. They have plans for that.

intentional
adjective
done by plan or on purpose
His absence was *intentional*; he did not want to be there at all.

interest
noun
1. *the money that money earns*
The bank lent him money at a low rate of *interest*.
2. *attention to or concern in something*
He has great *interest* in sports; he plays and watches many of them.
verb
make (someone) show attention to
Sports *interest* him very much.

interested
adjective
showing concern
She is *interested* in music; she wants to learn how to play the piano.

interesting
adjective
catching the attention
We saw a very *interesting* film last night; the story was good and the acting was good too.

interior
noun
the inside
Their house was not so nice on the outside, but the *interior* was beautiful.
adjective
inside
The *interior* part of their house was well decorated.

internal
adjective
inside
She had *internal* injuries in the accident; some bones were hurt.

international
adjective
related to two or more countries
Many countries were interested in an *international* agreement to control crime.

interrupt
verb
cut into something that is going on
As the father and mother were talking, their son came in and *interrupted* them; he wanted something to eat.

interruption
noun
a cut into something that is going on
When our teacher is explaining something, he doesn't like any *interruptions*; we can ask him questions after he finishes.

interval
noun
a short time between parts of a play or game
We saw an interesting play yesterday; and in the *interval*, we had a chance to go out and eat something.

into
preposition
from the outside in
We stood up for the president when he walked *into* the room. My little brother likes to jump *into* the pool.

introduce
verb: introducing, introduced, introduced
present something or someone

He *introduced* his talk with an interesting story. They *introduced* us to the new principal.

introduction
noun
1. *an opening part*
The purpose of the book was explained in the *introduction.*
2. *a presentation of someone to someone else*
We wanted an *introduction* to the new principal; we wanted to meet him.

invent
verb
create something new
He *invents* his stories; they are not real. Do you know who *invented* the radio?

invention
noun
the creation of something new
That story is not true; it is nothing but his own *invention.* The radio is a very useful *invention.*

inventive
adjective
able to create something new
He has a very *inventive* mind; he is always thinking of something new.

inventor
noun
a person who creates something new
Who is the *inventor* of the radio?

invitation
noun
asking someone to join you for something
They accepted our *invitation*; they came to our home and had dinner with us.

invite
verb: inviting, invited, invited
ask someone to join you for something
We *invited* them to dinner, and they accepted our invitation.

involve
verb: involving, involved, involved
draw in as a part of something
Playing football *involves* a lot of practice.

iron
noun

1. *a metal*
My hammer is made of wood and *iron.*

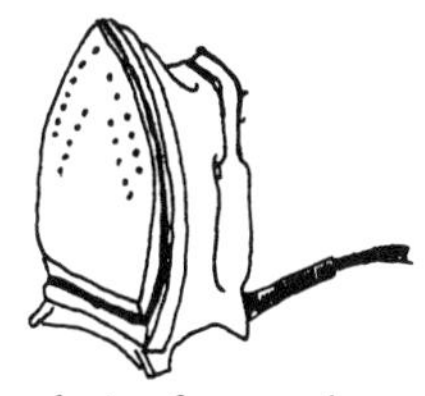

2. *a device for pressing clothes or other material*
She used an *iron* to press my shirts.
verb
press
She *irons* my shirts very well.

irresponsible
adjective
not responsible
He is very *irresponsible* with his money; he spends it without thinking.

is
verb: be, am, is, are
She *is* a good teacher.
auxiliary verb
She *is* coming to see us tomorrow.

island 

noun
a piece of land surrounded by water
We went to the *island*

in a small boat.

isn't
is not
She *isn't* a teacher; she's a student.

issue
noun
a point of differing views
Who cleans the house is an *issue* between the two sisters.
verb: issuing, issued, issued
produce in print
Our school *issues* a newsletter once a month.

it
pronoun: its
third person singular (for things and animals)
My book is interesting; *it* has good stories; I like *it*.

it'll
pronoun and auxiliary verb
it will
She says *it'll* rain tomorrow.

its
pronoun
third person singular
I have a cat; *its* name is Brownie.

it's
pronoun and verb
it is
This is an animal. It isn't a cat; *it's* a dog.
pronoun and auxiliary verb
it has
It's been raining for an hour.

itself
emphatic pronoun
it alone
The cat caught the mice *itself.*
reflexive pronoun
its own self
Our cat hurt *itself* when it jumped through the window.

I've
pronoun and auxiliary verb
I have
I've been studying English for a long time.

ivory
noun
a white or yellow material that comes from the tusks of elephants
Her ring is made of *ivory*. She bought it in Africa.

Jj

jack

noun
a device used to raise heavy objects
Before he changes his tires, he raises his car on a *jack.*

jacket

noun
a short coat
He bought a new *jacket* to go with his trousers, and his wife bought a *jacket* to go with her skirt.

jail
noun
prison
The police put the thief in *jail.*
verb
put (someone) in prison
The police *jailed* the thief.

jam
noun
1. *a sweet food made of fruits and sugar*
She likes butter and *jam* sandwiches.
2. *a crowd of people or cars*
We couldn't move very fast because of the traffic *jam* in the city.
verb: jamming, jammed,

jammed
fill, crowd
The students *jammed* the hall; there were too many of them in that small place.

janitor
noun
a person who takes care of a building
We didn't know on which floor our friends lived. The *janitor* told us it was the fourth floor.

January
noun
the first month of the year
She was born in *January*. *January* comes before February.

jar

noun
a container with a big opening
They offered us some candy from a candy *jar*.

jaw
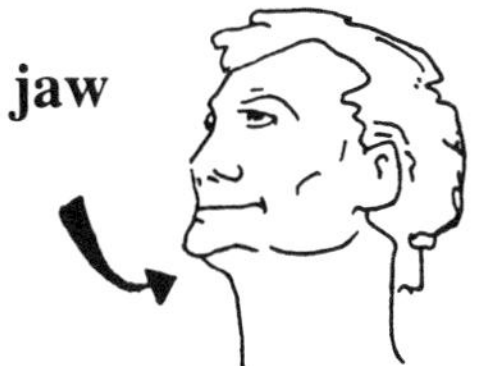
noun
one of the two bone parts of the face that hold the teeth
When we eat or talk, we move our lower *jaw*.

jazz
noun
a kind of American music with a fast beat
She likes to listen to *jazz*; it makes her feel like moving and dancing.

jealous
adjective
wanting full attention and loyalty
He is a very *jealous* husband; he doesn't want his wife to even talk with other people.

jeans

noun
a pair of blue cotton pants
He wore his *jeans* to class yesterday.

jewel
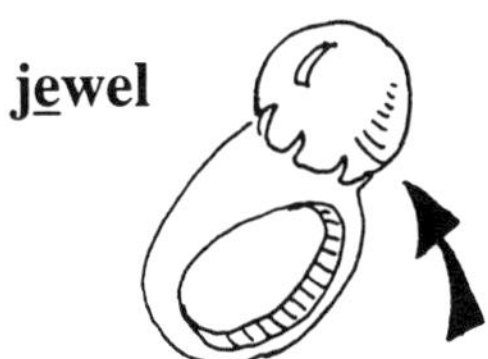
noun
a precious stone
She has a green *jewel* in her ring.

job
noun
work
He has just finished his studies; now he is looking for a *job*.

jobless
adjective
without work
They made him leave his work; now he is *jobless*.

join
verb
1. *become a part of*
They *joined* the tennis club; they are now members of the club.
2. *put together*
The cup broke into two pieces, and she *joined* them together with a special kind of glue.

joint
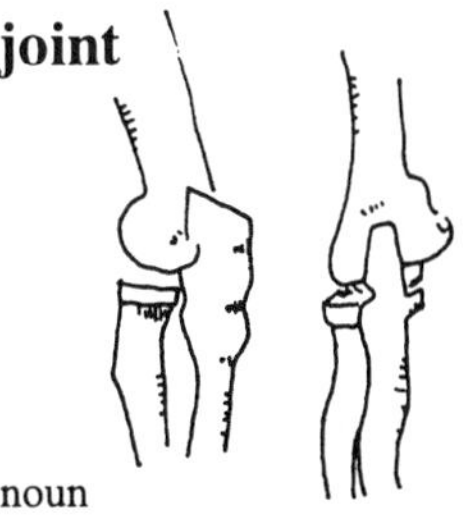
noun
the place where two bones meet
The knee is one of our *joints*.
adjective

united
The teachers of both schools had a *joint* meeting to talk about a common library.

joke
noun
a funny statement or story
Everybody told funny stories last night, but my father's *jokes* were the best.
verb: joking, joked, joked
1. *tell funny things*
They *joked* about school all day; they told funny stories about it.
2. *not be serious*
Did you say you were leaving? You must be *joking*; I don't believe it.

journal
noun
a periodical
She read an article on diets in a medical *journal*.

journey
noun
a long trip, a travel
They went on a *journey* to Australia. Sometimes they flew, and sometimes they sailed.

joy
noun
happiness
Their moment of *joy* came when they won the basketball game. They were very happy then.

judge
noun
a person who decides on legal matters
The *judge* ruled in court that the thief should go to prison for two years.

judgement, judgment
noun
a decision
The judge sent the thief to prison for two years. That was his final *judgement*.

judicial
adjective
related to legal matters
All decisions made in a court of law are *judicial* decisions.

jug

noun
a large container that has a handle and a small opening on top
Many people keep their oil in *jugs*.

juice
noun
the liquid that comes from fruits or vegetables
She drinks orange *juice* in the morning; her husband likes grapefruit *juice*.

juicy
adjective: juicier, juiciest
full of juice
I bought some *juicy* oranges. I can get a lot of juice from them.

July
noun
the seventh month of the year
July comes after June and before August.

jump
noun
1. *a rise*
There was a *jump* in the price of fresh fruits this week. We are paying more for them now.
2. *a spring using the legs*
He could reach the branch of the tree with a high *jump*.
verb
1. *rise*
The price of fresh fruits has *jumped* this week.
2. *spring*
She *jumped* to catch the ball.

June
noun
the sixth month of the year
June comes after May and before July.

junior
noun
1. *a person in the year before last in high school or college*
She is a *junior* in high school and her brother is a *junior* in the university.
2. *a person who is younger in age or lower in position*
The manager had an assistant; the assistant was his *junior* in age and position.
adjective
1. *lower in position*
The new assistant was a *junior* member of the company.
2. *younger in age*
The children were *junior* members of the family.

junk
noun
things of little value
All the *junk* from the city was put in one place far away from where people live.

juror
noun
a member of a jury
The judge asked the twelve *jurors* to meet and give the court their decision.

jury
noun: juries
a group of people who are asked by a court of law to decide on a legal matter
My uncle was asked to serve on a *jury*, and he did. He and the other jurors gave their decision to the judge.

just
adjective
1. *deserved*
She did very fine work, and she received a *just* reward.
2. *fair*
The judge made *just* decisions; everybody was happy with them.
adverb
1. *only*
I waited *just* two minutes for the train to arrive.
2. *a very short time ago*
He has *just* gone out of his office; he'll be back again soon.
3. *directly*
Their school is *just* across the river from their home.
4. *exactly*
She had 75 cents with her; that was *just* enough for a cup of coffee.

justice
noun
1. *fairness*
Giving everyone his or her right share is a matter of *justice*.
2. *the administration of law*
Every country has a department of *justice* to see that the laws of the land are followed.

justify
verb: justifying, justified, justified
show that something is just or right
The big old tree in the garden was dead and dangerous; that *justified* cutting it down.

Kk

keen
adjective
1. *quick and alert*
He has a very *keen* mind; he thinks and understands fast.
2. *sharp*
She used a *keen* knife to cut the meat with.
3. *showing great interest*
He is very *keen* about football; he plays it and watches the games on television.

keep
verb: keeping, kept, kept
1. *hold in one's possession*

They *keep* a dog and a cat at home.
3. *fulfill*
He is very honest; he *keeps* his promises; he does what he promises to do.
3. *stay*
Our teacher asked us to *keep* quiet in the library.

kept
See **keep.**

kettle

noun
a vessel for boiling water
She put the *kettle* on the fire to prepare the tea.

key

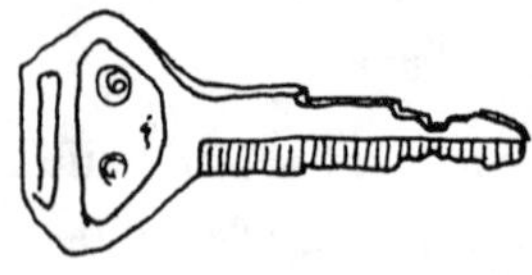

noun
1. *a device to open doors and locks*
She locks and opens her drawer with a *key*.
2. *solution*
We did our mathematics problems first; then we checked the *key* at the end of the book to see if we were right.

keyboard

noun
a number of keys on a surface
If you want to know how to type or use a computer, you must learn to use their *keyboards.*

kick

noun
a strike with the foot
He gave the ball a hard *kick* and sent it up in the air.
verb
strike with the foot
Soccer players learn how to *kick* the ball well.

kid
noun
1. *a child*
Don't expect them to be very wise; they are still *kids*.
2. *a little goat*
We saw sheep, goats, and *kids* in the field eating grass.
verb: kidding, kidded, kidded
joke
He did not mean what he said; he was only *kidding*.

kill
verb
take the life of
The tiger caught the deer and *killed* it for something to eat.

kilogram
noun
a measure of weight: 1000 grams
He weighs 75 *kilograms.*

kilometer
noun
a measure of length: 1000 meters
We drove three hundred *kilometers* in one day.

kimono

noun
a robe

She wore a nice *kimono* for breakfast. It was long and had roses on it.

kin
noun
relatives
Their *kin* came to live with them; an uncle, an aunt, and two cousins came.

kind
noun
type, variety
That restaurant offers many *kinds* of food.
adjective
polite
She is very *kind* with children; she treats them softly and nicely.

kindly
See **kind** also.
adverb
please
Kindly close the window. Thank you.

kindness
noun
the act of being kind, politeness
She shows her *kindness* in everything she says and does; she is very good and polite.

king
noun
a male monarch

Queen Elizabeth II is the queen of England now; her father, King George VI, was the *king* before her.

kingdom
noun
a country that has a king or a queen
Morocco is a *kingdom*.

kiss
noun
a loving touch with the lips
She gave her daughter a *kiss* on her cheek when she returned from school.
verb
give a loving touch with the lips
She *kissed* her daughter when she returned from school.

kitchen
noun
the room in the house where food is cooked
My mother baked a chocolate cake in the *kitchen*. Our stove and our refrigerator are in the *kitchen*.

kite

noun
a paper plane with a string
Their children like to fly *kites*; their father makes the *kites* for them.

kitten

noun
a baby cat
Our cat had five *kittens* at the same time.

knack
noun
cleverness in doing things
He has a *knack* for fixing clocks; he fixes people's clocks everywhere.

knee
noun
the place where our legs bend

The football player hurt his *knee* when he fell on it.

knew
See **know**.

knife

noun: knives
an instrument that we cut with
We use forks, *knives*, and spoons when we eat. We cut things with a *knife.*

knit

verb: knitting, knitted, knitted
use needles to make a fabric
My mother *knitted* me a warm scarf.

knob
noun
a round handle

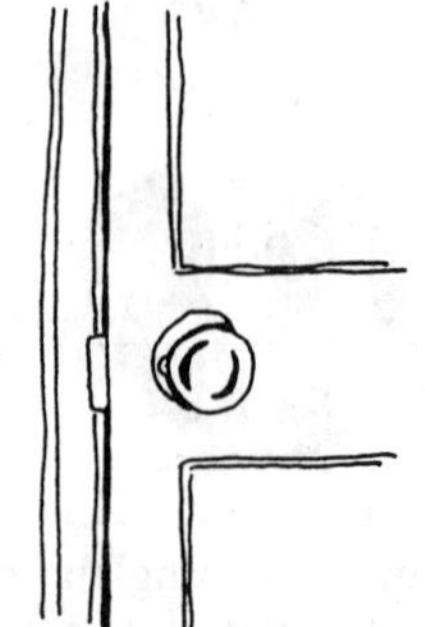

I could not open the door, because the door *knob* was broken.

knock
noun
a bang, a strike
She opened the door when she heard a *knock* on it.
verb
strike
We always *knock* on doors before we open them.

knot
noun
a tie
She couldn't undo the *knot* in the ribbon, because it was too tight. So she cut the ribbon to open her present.

know
verb: knowing, knew, known
have in the mind, recognize
I *know* the people who are here; I've met them before. She *knows* English and Spanish.

known
See know.

Ll

lab
noun
laboratory
The scientist is working in the *lab.*

label

noun
a slip of paper on something saying what it is or who owns it
The *label* on the jar said JAM.
verb
put a slip of paper on something saying what it is or who owns it
When you travel, it is good to *label* your bags and suitcases.

laboratory
noun: laboratories
a place where experiments are done
All our science classes have *laboratories.*

labor
noun
effort

Moving the bed to the other bedroom took a lot of *labor*.
verb
work
We *labored* hard to move the car up the hill when the motor stopped.

lack
noun
need
There is a *lack* of fresh air in the room. Let us open the window.
verb
need
We *lack* fresh air here. Let us open the window.

lad
noun
a young male person
Two *lads* drove up to the station and bought train tickets.

ladder

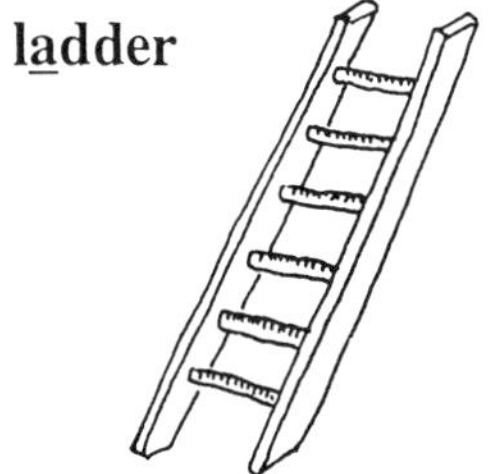

noun
a device for climbing with wood or metal steps that can be moved easily
He climbed on a *ladder* to paint the ceiling and the walls.

lady
noun: ladies
1. *a woman of fine qualities*
She is a real *lady*; she is grand, and she speaks softly.
2. *a woman*
There were fifteen people in the restaurant: eight *ladies* and seven gentlemen.

ladle

noun
a deep spoon with a long handle
She served the soup with a *ladle*.

laid
See **lay.**

lain
See **lie.**

lake

noun
a body of water surrounded by land
My friends like to swim and fish in a *lake* near their home. It is called Silver *Lake*.

lamb

noun
1. *a young sheep*
We saw sheep, *lambs*, goats, and kids eating grass in the field.
2. *the meat of sheep*
Their favorite meat is *lamb*. They like *lamb* chops and *lamb* roasts.

lamp

noun
a device that gives light
People used oil *lamps* before they had electricity.

land
noun
the hard part of the earth
One quarter of the world is *land*; the rest is water. They have a big piece of *land* in the valley.
verb
get down to earth

The plane *landed* in the airport after flying for six hours.

la̲nding
noun
1. *coming down to earth*
The plan was late, but it made a smooth *landing* in the airport; we didn't feel it when it landed.
2. *the flat area between parts of a staircase*
The old man rested on the *landing* before he continued up the stairs.

lane
noun

1. *a small street*
Their house is at the end of a *lane* near the main street.

2. *a part of a road marked by lines for cars to drive in*
Drivers must be very careful when they change *lanes*.
3. *a narrow way in the fields*

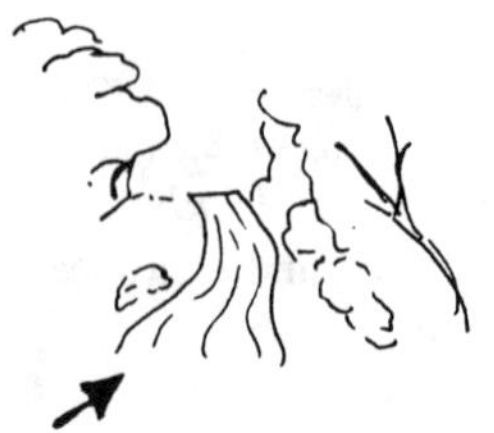

We took several *lanes* to cross from one farm to another.

la̲nguage
noun
the oral or written form that people use to communicate with each other
She knows two *languages* well: English and Spanish.

lap
noun
1. *a turn*
The driver made three *laps* around the field.
2. *the upper part of the legs when one is sitting*

She put her child on her *lap* to feed him.

large
adjective
big
They have a *large* bedroom in their house; it holds four beds.

la̲rgely
adverb
mainly
The book is *largely* pictures; the writing in it is very little.

last
verb
take the time
The play *lasted* one hour and a half; it was ninety minutes long.
adjective
coming at the end
The first train in the morning leaves at six; the *last* train in the evening leaves at ten.
adverb (**at last**)
finally
We wanted to go out, but it rained for a long time. At *last* it stopped raining, and we could leave.

late
adjective
happening after the proper time
The bus was *late* today; it didn't come at 8:00; it came at 8:15.
adverb
beyond the usual or expected time
We didn't have enough sleep, because our guests stayed *late* last night; they didn't leave till 11:00.

latter
adjective
the second of two things or persons
John and Mary are brother and sister. The former is three years old; the *latter* is two.

laugh
noun
a sound of joy with a smile
I heard his *laugh* when I told a joke.
verb
make a sound of joy with a smile
They *laughed* when they heard my joke.

laughter
noun
sounds of joy with smiles
I heard their *laughter* when I told them funny stories.

launch
verb
1. *start*
They *launched* a new program in school; it had never been tried before.
2. *send or shoot off*
They *launched* a space rocket from Florida last month; it went straight up in the air.

laundry
noun: laundries
a place where clothes are cleaned and pressed
He sends his dirty shirts to the *laundry*; he gets them clean and ready to wear.

law
noun
1. *a rule*
One of the *laws* for drivers is to stop at red lights.
2. *the study of the legal system*
That family has two sons. One of them is studying medicine; he wants to become a doctor. The second one is studying *law*; he wants to become a lawyer.

lawn

noun
a piece of land with short green grass
They water the *lawn* around their house every day in the summer.

lawyer
noun
a person who practices law
If you have a problem with the law, you take your problem to a *lawyer*.

lay
See **lie** also.
verb: laying, laid, laid
1. *put or place*
She *laid* her baby on the bed to change her clothes.
2. *produce (eggs)*
Their hen *lays* three eggs a week.
3. *spread*
She asked her daughter to *lay* the table for dinner.

lazy
adjective: lazier, laziest
not active, not hard working
He is a very *lazy* boy; he doesn't study, and he doesn't do much.

lead
noun
a front position
For half the race he was the second runner; then he took the *lead* and won the race.
verb: leading, led, led
direct
He *led* the discussion very nicely; he kept everybody talking in order.

lead
noun
a metal
Lead is a heavy metal.

leader
noun
a person who directs
The *leader* told his men where to go and what to do.

leading
adjective
main, most important
I read the *leading* newspaper of our town; most people read it too.

leaf
noun: leaves

1. *a green part of a plant*
Many trees drop their *leaves* in the fall.

2. *a paper in a book or notebook*
He turned the *leaves* of the book to see if there were any pictures in it.

league
noun
a group of people, clubs, or countries that work together on something
The women in the city formed a *league* to discuss the problems of the city and try to help the mayor.

lean
verb: leaning, leaned or leant, leaned or leant
put one's weight on one side of something
The worker *leaned* against the wall to get some rest.
adjective
without fat
She likes to eat *lean* meat; she doesn't want to put on weight.

leap
verb: leaping, leaped or leapt, leaped or leapt
jump
He *leaped* over the wall to go to his neighbor's house.

learn
verb: learning, learned or learnt, learned or learnt
get to know and understand
The little girl *learned* to ride a bicycle. We are *learning* English now.

least
See **less** also.
adverb
smallest
The red bicycle costs \$100; the blue one costs \$130; and the green one costs \$150. The red bicycle is the *least* expensive, and the green one is the most expensive.

leather
noun
the material from the skin of animals
Her coat, gloves and shoes are made of the best *leather*.

leave
noun
a break from work
The soldier asked for a *leave* to see his sick mother. They gave him a ten-day *leave*.
verb: leaving, left, left
1. *go away, move from a place*
The train arrived at the station at 9:05 and *left* at 9:15 a.m.
2. *keep*
They told us to *leave* our things in the bus when we went down to take pictures.

led
See **lead**.

left
See **leave** also.
noun
one of two sides: left and right
I stood in the middle; my brother stood on my *left* and my sister stood on my right.
adjective
left side

My right hand is stronger than my *left* hand.
adverb
to or on the left side
When we reached the light, they went *left* and we went right.

leg
noun

1. *a limb used for walking*
Our feet are at the end of our *legs*.

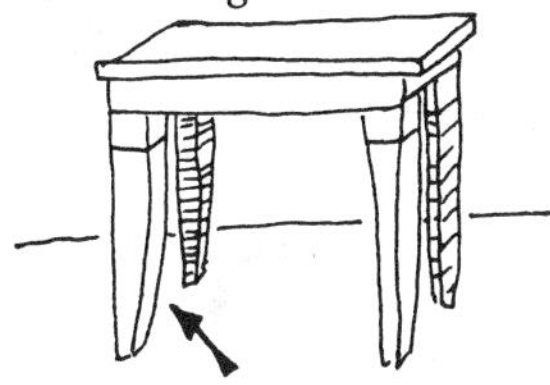

2. *something that things stand on*
Chairs and tables stand on *legs*.
3. *part of a trip or journey*
The first *leg* of our journey around the world was from New York to London.

legal
adjective
related to law
Judges and courts decide *legal* matters.

legend
noun
an old story
Our story books are full of *legends* that people have known for a very long time.

lemon

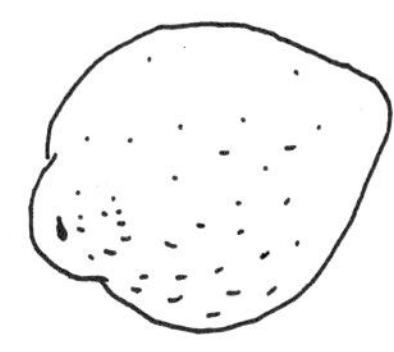

noun
a bitter fruit
She used oil and *lemon* in the salad.

lemonade
noun
a drink with lemon
Some had tea, some had coffee, and some had *lemonade* at lunch.

lend
verb: lending, lent, lent
give for a time
When I knew he needed money, I *lent* him some; he returned it in a week.

length
noun
1. *a measure of distance*
The *length* of the road was six miles.
2. *the longest side of an area*
His land was 70 yards in *length* and 50 yards in width.

lengthen
verb
make longer
Her dress was too short for her. Her mother *lengthened* the dress to make it right for her.

lengthy
adjective: lengthier, lengthiest
long
He told us a very *lengthy* story. He kept talking for a long time.

lenient
adjective
easy, not strict
Our teacher is *lenient* with us; he lets us do what we like at times.

lent
See **lend.**

less
See **little** also.
adjective
smaller in quantity or size
I have $10; he has $12; I have *less* money than he has.

lessen
verb
make less, make smaller
Because people thought the prices were high, one merchant *lessened* his prices to encourage

people to buy things from him.

lesson
noun
1. *the time for a class*
Our *lesson* started at 9:00 and ended at 9:50 a.m.
2. *something learned*
We had a good history *lesson* today; we learned many interesting facts.

lest
conjunction
so that (someone or something) might not
We wrote a little note about the party, *lest* we forget it.

let
verb: letting, let, let
1. *rent*
They *let* their house to a friend while they were away.
2. *allow*
They *let* us play in their garden.

let's
verb and pronoun
let us
Let's go now before it rains.

letter
noun
1. *a mark or symbol used in writing languages*
The word child has five *letters* in it: *c*, *h*, *i*, *l*, and *d*.
2. *a written message*
When I was studying in the university, I wrote my mother a *letter* every week.

lettuce

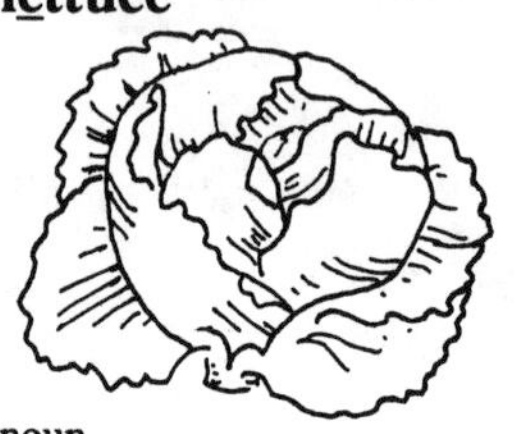

noun
a vegetable with large green leaves
She put *lettuce* and tomatoes in the salad.

level
adjective
straight and flat
They made the garden *level* for the children not to fall. The road is very *level*; it is easy to drive on it.

liberty
noun: liberties
freedom
We had the *liberty* to do what we wanted in the afternoon; some studied and some played games. Many countries have fought for their *liberty*.

library
noun: libraries
a place where one can read and take books out
Our school *library* has many interesting books.

lick
verb

1. *pass the tongue over or into (something)*
Animals *lick* their wounds.
2. *defeat, win over*
We *licked* them in basketball; we won the game last night.

lid

noun
a cover
All our pans and kettles have *lids*.

lie
noun
something which is not true
The thief told a *lie* in court; the judge knew it was not true.
verb: lying, lied, lied
say something which is not true

The thief *lied* to the judge; the judge knew that he was not telling the truth.

lie
verb: lying, lay, lain
be in a flat position, rest
She *lay* in bed to rest a bit.

life
noun: lives
the quality of being alive
He helped people all his *life*. We studied the *life* of a bee in school.

lift
verb
raise something to a higher level
She could not *lift* the box; it was too heavy for her.

light
noun
the thing around us that makes us able to see
I cannot read very well if there is no *light* in the room. The sun gives us a lot of *light*.
verb: lighting, lit, lit
start (something) to burn
She *lit* the fire for the barbecue.
adjective
1. *not heavy in weight*
She can carry this box; it is *light*.
2. *not dark in color*
The sky today is a *light* blue.

lightly
adverb
with little attention or interest
He thought he had a good idea for his friends, but they took it *lightly*.

lightning

noun
short bright lights made by clouds
When they had a strong storm, they could see the *lightning* and hear the thunder.

like
verb: liking, liked, liked
find (something or someone) to have good qualities
I *like* my friends and I *like* to play games with them.
preposition
1. *the same as*
He wanted his son to be *like* him.
2. *as an example*
One student, *like* my friend, wants to go home now.

likely
adverb: likelier, likeliest
probably, expected to happen
It is *likely* to rain tomorrow; let us not plan a picnic for tomorrow.

lily

noun: lilies
a plant with wide leaves and big white flowers
Their garden is beautiful; they have red roses and white *lilies* in it.

limb
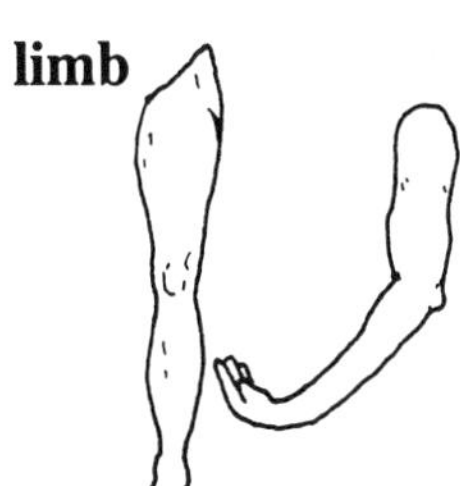
noun
one of the arms or legs
Snakes have no *limbs*.

limit
noun
1. *a boundary*
The fence marked the *limits* of the playground.
2. *a top or bottom point*
There is a *limit* to what they can do; they don't have much time or

money.
verb
set a top or bottom point
The teacher *limited* the questions we could ask to five each.

limp
noun
difficulty in walking
After she hurt her knee, she walked with a *limp.*
verb
walk with difficulty
She *limped* after she hurt her knee.

line
noun
1. *a long mark drawn*
The teacher drew *lines* under the important words.
2. *a wire or rope for hanging clothes*
After they washed the shirts, they hung them on a *line* to dry.
3. *the straight order of people or things*
The students stood in five *lines* in front of the school.

lined

adjective
with lines
It is easier to write on *lined* paper.

linen
noun
cloth made from flax
All their bed sheets are made of *linen.*

lion

noun
a male animal, the king of animals
The hunter took a picture of a *lion*, a lioness, and two cubs.

lioness

noun
a female animal, the female of a lion
The *lioness* fed her cubs.

lip

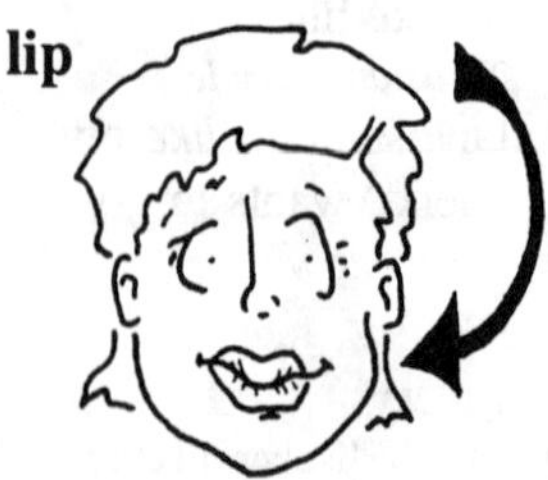

noun
one of two parts in the front of the mouth
The mother kissed her child on his check with her *lips.*

liquid
noun
a substance like water or oil
We eat solids and drink *liquids.*

list
noun
a series of names, words, or numbers
The office sent our teacher a *list* of the names of the students in our class.
verb
put in a series or order
Our teacher *listed* the names of the students who were going to visit the museum.

listen
verb
1. *pay attention in order to hear*
We *listened* carefully to what our teacher was saying.
2. *follow or obey*
Children must *listen* to their parents.

lit
See **light.**

liter
noun

a measure of liquid volume
A *liter* of water weighs one kilogram.

literally
adverb
really
She was *literally* great; she talked and sang beautifully.

literary
adjective
related to literature
My friend in school wrote a very good story. The teacher told him that his story was very *literary*.

literature
noun
very good written material
Shakespeare's plays and Poe's poems are a part of English and American *literature*.

little
adjective
small
She gave the child a *little* ball to play with.
adjective: less, least
not much
She has *little* money in her bag; it is not enough for her to buy a book.

live
verb: living, lived, lived
1. *have life*
All they want is to *live* happily.
2. *reside*
They *lived* in that house for two years.

live
adjective
alive, having life
The soldier who was shot was *live* and well in the hospital.

lively
adjective
active, full of life
That child is very *lively*; he is doing something all the time.

load
noun
1. *a weight that is to be moved*
My brother gave me a *load* to take in my car to my sister.
2. *a lot*
They have *loads* of money; they are quite rich.
verb
to put a weight of things on what will move it
We *loaded* our car with boxes of books and took them to school.

loaf

noun: loaves
a shape of a food like bread
I had a piece of bread from the *loaf* we bought at the bakery.

loan
noun
something (like money) borrowed or lent
He took a *loan* of $2,000 from the bank. He returned it in six months.
verb
lend
The bank *loaned* him $2,000. He returned it in six months.

local
adjective
related to a specific place or area
I made two telephone calls: a *local* call in the city and an international call.

locate
verb: locating, located, located
place, find
We were looking for our teacher; then we *located* her in the library. The students *located* London and Paris on the map.

lock
noun
a device used to keep things

closed

We have a big *lock* on our front door.
verb
use a lock to close
We *lock* our front door before we go to bed.

lodge
noun
a place to live for a time
We spent three nights in a *lodge* on our way south.

log

noun
1. *a part of a tree trunk*
They used *logs* to build their summer cabin.
2. *a record of activities*
She kept a *log* of everything they did daily on their trip.

lonely
adjective: lonelier, loneliest
a feeling of being alone
Whenever her husband left on business, she felt *lonely*.

long
adjective
1. *going for some distance*
The piece of land they bought is quite *long*, but it isn't very wide.
2. *a measure of length (distance or time)*
Their land is 63 yards *long*. Our lesson is 50 minutes *long*.

look
noun
the act of looking
I gave the man I met a good *look* and I knew that he was our old neighbor.
verb
see, use the eyes
Look. Here is your friend.

look after
verb
take care of
When the mother went to see her parents, her husband *looked after* the children.

look at
verb
see
Look at that building; it is our school.

look for
verb
try to find
I lost my pen; I *looked for* it at home and found it.

look up to
verb
think highly of
We *looked up to* our teacher and wanted to be like him.

loose
adjective
not tight
His necktie was *loose* around his neck; his wife fixed it for him.

lose
verb: losing, lost, lost
1. *miss, not find*
I *lost* my pen; I looked for it and found it under my book.
2. *opposite of gain*
They *lost* some money in their business last year.
3. *shed*
She *lost* some weight by exercising every day.

loss
noun
opposite of gain
She lost $1000 and he lost $2000 in their businesses. His *loss* was greater than her *loss*.

lost
See **lose**.

lot
noun

1. *share*
Three of my friends and I picked some flowers from the garden. Then we came home and divided them. Each of us got an equal *lot*.
2. *a piece of land*
They bought a *lot* to build a small house on.
3. *a big quantity*
He puts a *lot* of sugar and milk in his coffee; he likes his coffee white and sweet.

lots
noun
a big quantity
They have *lots* of problems at work; they need help. We have *lots* of books in the library.

loud
adjective
high in sound
They heard *loud* noises in the field; many children were playing.

lounge
noun
a room with easy and comfortable chairs
Our school has a *lounge* for visitors; they can sit there and read or meet with teachers.

lousy
adjective: lousier, lousiest
bad, poor
We thought it was going to be an interesting film, but it was really *lousy*; don't waste your time seeing it.

love
noun
1. *a strong affection for someone*
A mother shows great *love* for her children.
2. *a strong liking*
She has a *love* for painting; she does it all the time.
verb
1. *have a strong affection for someone*
She *loves* her children.
2. *have a strong liking for something*
She *loves* painting.

lovely
adjective: lovelier, loveliest
nice, beautiful, pretty, good
Today is a *lovely* day; the sun is out; it is warm, and the sky is blue. She is a *lovely* person; she is beautiful and she helps others.

low
adjective
not high
She can reach the book on the shelf; the shelf is *low*; it isn't too high for her.

loyal
adjective
faithful, sincere
The captain was very *loyal* to his country; he fought well and served his country courageously.

lucid
adjective
easy to understand
Her talk was very *lucid*; we understood it quickly.

luck
noun
chance, fortune
He had very good *luck* on his test; he answered all the questions correctly.

luckily
adverb
fortunately
We wanted to go on a picnic; *luckily*, the weather was good.

lucky
adjective: luckier, luckiest
fortunate
She was very *lucky*; she wanted that job and she got it.

lucrative
adjective
profitable
He went into a

lucrative business; he is making a lot of money.

luggage
noun
bags and suitcases for travel
She couldn't carry her *luggage* to the train; she had two suitcases and three bags.

lump
noun
a solid quantity of something
He put his books in a *lump* on the table. She put two *lumps* of sugar in her tea.

lunch
noun
1. *a light meal at noon*
We had *lunch* at noon today.
2. *a light meal at any time.*
We had a little *lunch* before we went to bed.

luxurious
adjective
very good and expensive
They bought a very *luxurious* car; it is very comfortable, big, and powerful.

luxury
noun: luxuries
1. *having lots of expensive things and enjoying them*
She lived in *luxury*; she had a big house, a lovely car, and beautiful clothes; she was very rich.
2. *an expensive thing which is not really needed*
They did not buy the big car, because they thought it would be a *luxury* for them.

lying
See **lie** and **lie**.

Mm

machine
noun
an instrument that makes work easier
In his office, he has a *machine* that makes copies fast.

mad
adjective
1. *crazy*
He is *mad* if he thinks he can do the work alone. It takes three people together to do it.
2. *nervous, angry*
She got *mad* when her son didn't come home on time.

made
See **make.**

magazine
noun
a weekly or monthly publication
The National Geographic *magazine* gives very interesting information.

magic
noun
a trick that is hard to catch
The children enjoyed the *magic* he did at the party.

magnificent
adjective
lovely, excellent, wonderful
We heard a *magnificent* piece of music last night. Everybody thought it was excellent.

maid

noun
a woman servant
The princess had four *maids* to help her and serve her in the palace.

mail

noun

the letters and other packages sent or received by post
We received our *mail* in our post office box.
verb
send by post
They *mailed* me a card from Paris when they visited there.

main
adjective
principal, major
All the stores in that village are in the *main* square.

major
noun
a rank in the armed forces
He is a *major* in the air force.
adjective
main, principal
The *major* part of her time is spent at home. She goes out a few times a week only.

majority
noun: majorities
most people, more than half
The *majority* of students in our school are from this state. Fifty-five percent are local students.

make
noun
product
This car is a good *make*. It is an excellent car.
verb: making, made, made
do, create, put together
They *make* cars in Michigan. My sister *made* a new dress for herself.

male
noun
a masculine creature, opposite of female
Our cat had four kittens; two *males* and two females.

man
noun: men
an adult male human being
There were twelve people at the party: six *men* and six women.
verb: manning, manned, manned
have a person work somewhere
The director *manned* his office very quickly. He had two people working for him the first week.

manage
verb: managing, managed, managed
direct, run
He *manages* his business very well. He is a good organizer.

management
noun
direction
He is known for his good *management*. He runs his business very well.

manager
noun
director, a person who manages
He rose fast in the company. He was a salesman first. Now he is the *manager*. He directs the company.

manufacture
verb
make by using machines
They *manufacture* cars in Detroit.

many
adjective: more, most
quite a number, not few
If you need a pencil, take one of mine. I have *many* pencils in the drawer.

map

noun
a picture showing countries, cities, roads, or seas
We studied our road *map* well before we drove south.

march
noun
walk in an organized way
The soldiers went on a *march* through the city.
verb
walk in an organized way
The soldiers formed lines and *marched* through the city.

March
noun
the third month of the year
They couldn't come in *March*; so they came the following month; they came in April.

mark

noun
a sign
I put a *mark* in the book to know where I had reached.
verb
put a sign
I *marked* the important parts of my lesson with a yellow pen.

market
noun
a place where things are sold and bought
We bought fresh tomatoes from the vegetable *market*.
verb
sell
The farmer *marketed* his fruits in the city.

marriage
noun
being related as husband and wife
Jack and Alice got married eight years ago. Their *marriage* is eight years old.

married
See **marry** also.
adjective
related as husband and wife
We had eight guests for dinner: three *married* couples and two singles.

marry
verb: marrying, married, married
take as a husband or wife
The couple plan to *marry* next June.

marvelous
adjective
wonderful, excellent
She wrote a *marvelous* poem; the words were good and the feelings were tender.

mass
noun
a body of matter
The workers left a *mass* of iron on the side of the road.

master
noun
a person who does something very well
He is an excellent tennis player; he is a *master* at that.
verb
do or know something very well
He has *mastered* the game of tennis. She is *mastering* her cooking skills.

match

noun
1. *a small stick that one strikes to light a fire*
He used half a box of *matches* to light the fire in the wind.
2. *something that goes or fits with something else*
He and his wife make a good *match*.
verb
make something go or fit with something else
She bought a new blouse to *match* her skirt. He wore a tie that didn't *match* his suit.

mate
noun
friend, colleague

All my *mates* and I in class like our teacher. And the teacher likes me and my *classmates.*

material
noun
1. *cloth*
She bought *material* for a new dress.
2. *substance*
The book I bought has very good *material* in it for artists.
adjective
made of matter
Her friends are rich people. She likes people with *material* wealth.

mathematics
noun
the study of subjects like arithmetic, algebra, calculus, and geometry
She is very clever in English and history, but she is not doing very well in *mathematics*; her grades in algebra and geometry are not very high.

matter
noun
physical substance
Everything we can touch is made of *matter*.
verb
concern
What he does in school *matters* a lot. What is the *matter* with you? You don't look very happy.

maximum
noun
most, opposite of minimum
I don't have very much free time. The *maximum* I can give you is half an hour.

may
auxiliary verb: might
1. *(showing permission)*
You *may* enter now.
2. *(showing ability)*
He *may* or *may* not know the answer, but let us ask him the question anyway.

May
noun
the fifth month of the year
They couldn't come in April, but we saw them in *May*.

maybe
adverb
perhaps
I'm looking for my brother. *Maybe* he's here; *maybe* he isn't.

mayor
noun
the elected head of a city or town
Every city in America has a *mayor*, and every state has a governor.

me
pronoun: I, me, my, mine
first person singular
He came to *me* to see my book. I showed it to him.

meadow
noun
a piece of land with green grass
We saw lots of cows and sheep in the *meadow* outside the city.

meal
noun
the food we eat at different times of the day
Breakfast is a *meal* I enjoy very much.

mean
verb: meaning, meant, meant
give a sense
Large *means* big. By not coming, he *meant* to tell us that he is not interested.

meaning
See **mean** also.
noun
sense
When I don't know the *meaning* of a word, I look it up in a dictionary.

meant
See **mean**.

measure

verb: measuring, measured, measured
find out the size of a thing
The farmer *measured* his farm; it was six acres in area.

measurement
noun
finding out the size of a thing
She used a ruler for the *measurement* of the room. The room was 15 feet long and 12 feet wide.

meat

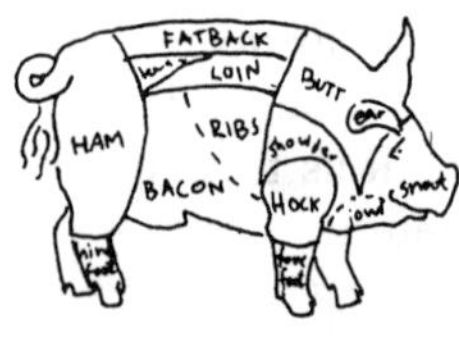

noun
the flesh of animals
They barbecue their *meat* and eat it with potatoes and corn.

mechanical
adjective
1. *automatic, working by machine*
A motor is a *mechanical* instrument to do things more easily.
2. *related to machines*
She does not have a *mechanical* mind; she likes to do things by hand.

medical
adjective
related to medicine
He was not feeling well; he needed *medical* care from his doctor.

medicine
noun
1. *the medical field*
She is studying *medicine*; she wants to become a doctor.
2. *a drug one takes to get well*
She was not feeling well, but the *medicine* her doctor gave her made her feel much better.

medium
adjective
in the middle, average
They have one son, who is of *medium* height; he is neither tall nor short.

meet
verb: meeting, met, met
1. *be together*
We wanted to discuss things with each other, and we decided to *meet* in the library.
2. *face*
Everything is going well with him; I don't think he will *meet* any difficult problems.

meeting
See **meet** also.
noun
getting together, a gathering
The captain called for a *meeting* of all the football players. We met in the field.

melon

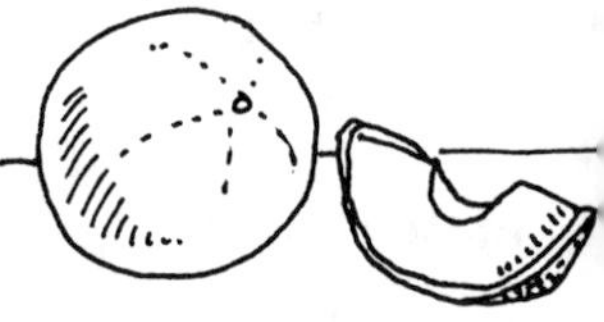

noun
a fruit
I like yellow *melons* in summer.

melt
verb
change to liquid form
When the sun came out, all the snow and ice *melted*.

member
noun
one of a group in a club or society or team
Sam is a *member* of our football team; he is a half back.

memory
noun: memories
the ability to remember or keep things in mind
Her *memory* is excellent; she never forgets people's names.

men
See **man.**

mend
verb
fix, repair
One of her coat buttons came off, and she *mended* it.

mental
adjective
related to the mind
I gave him a *mental* problem to solve. He did it; he is very intelligent.

menu
noun
a list of the foods in a restaurant
I looked at the *menu* and picked a salad and a sandwich for lunch.

mention
verb
bring up a subject in conversation
They were happy talking about a picnic until I *mentioned* the weather; it was cold and rainy.

merchant
noun
a person who buys and sells
All the *merchants* in town tried to lower their prices.

mercy
noun: mercies
kindness
The rich had *mercy* on the poor in that city; they gave them food and shelter.

mere
adjective
only, not more than
All he had was a *mere* handful of food; he didn't have enough to eat.

merely
adverb
only
He is *merely* a soldier in the army; he is not an officer.

merit
noun
worth
He is respected in the city because of his *merit*.
verb
deserve
His good work in the country *merited* a medal from the president.

merry
adjective: merrier, merriest
happy
We saw how *merry* the children were at the party.

message
noun
a note sent to or received by someone
When I didn't find her in her office, I left her a *message* on her desk.

messenger
noun
a person who takes news somewhere
The secret documents were delivered to the king by a *messenger*.

met
See **meet.**

metal
noun
a mineral matter
Iron and lead are *metals*.

meter
noun
1. *a measure: 100 centimeters*
The field was 80 *meters* long and 45 *meters* wide.
2. *a device that controls things*
When we parked our car near the store, we

put some coins in the parking *meter*.

method
noun
way
Our teacher has a successful *method* of teaching; she uses many examples to make her points clear.

midday
noun
noon, the middle of the day
We have breakfast in the morning, lunch at *midday*, and dinner in the evening.

middle

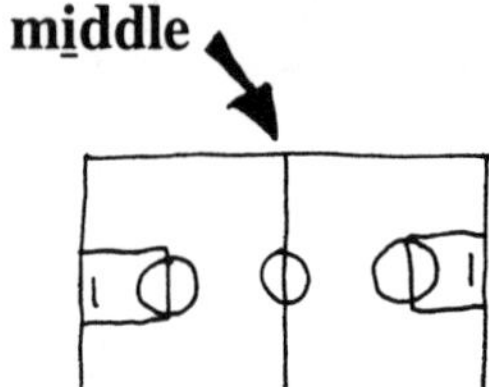

noun
center
A basketball game starts in the *middle* of the court.

midnight
noun
the middle of the night
When she woke up, she knew it was *midnight*; it was 12:00 o'clock.

midst
noun
middle
We stood in the *midst* of the crowd; there were people all around us.

might
See **may** also.
noun
strength
He got his way because of his *might*; he is a very strong person.
auxiliary verb
(showing probability)
He said he *might* come tomorrow.

mighty
adjective: mightier, mightiest
strong
He is a very *mighty* person; he usually gets what he wants.

mild
adjective
gentle, not strong
The weather is very *mild* today; it is neither hot nor cold. Her manner is very *mild*; she is kind with people and her voice is soft.

mile
noun
a measure of length: 1,760 yards
They run a distance of three *miles* every day.

military
adjective
related to the armed forces
He led the soldiers into battle; he is a *military* officer.

milk

noun
the liquid we drink that comes from cows or goats
She drinks a glass of *milk* with her breakfast every morning.

mill
noun
a place where flour is made from wheat or some other grain
We buy our flour straight from the *mill*.

millimeter
noun
a small measure of length
Ten *millimeters* make a centimeter, and 100 centimeters make a meter.

million
noun
a number: 1,000,000
It takes a long time to count to one *million*.
adjective
a number; 1,000,000

Over 250 *million* people live in the U.S.A.

mind

noun

the power that makes us think

She has a good *mind*; she thinks very clearly.

verb

look after, take care of

She *minds* her own business and does not worry about other people's business.

mine

noun

1. *a place where we get coal or other minerals*

The workers went deep into the *mine* to find gold.

2. *an explosive device*

The ship did not sail out of the harbor, because there were many *mines* in the sea near the harbor.

pronoun

related to first person singular: I, me, my, mine

This is *my* book: it is *mine*; it is not yours.

miner

noun

a person who works in a mine

Her husband is a *miner*; he works in a coal mine.

mineral

noun

a substance like iron and lead found in the earth

Coal is a *mineral*.

adjective

related to such substances

England has many *mineral* products.

minimum

noun

least, opposite of maximum

Three dollars won't be enough for this lunch; the *minimum* I will need is six dollars.

minister

noun

1. *a pastor*

The *minister* gave a good sermon last Sunday.

2. *the head of a government department*

The *minister* of education visited our school last month.

verb

help, care for

The nurse *ministered* to the patient's needs all night.

minority

noun: minorities

fewer than half

A *minority* of students in our school come from Europe; 15% are European students.

minus

preposition

less

Ten *minus* six leaves four. (10-6=4)

below zero

The temperature outside is *minus* five degrees centigrade (-5°C).

minute

noun

a period of time: 60 seconds

There are sixty seconds in a *minute* and sixty *minutes* in an hour.

mirror

noun

a looking glass

She likes to comb her hair in front of a *mirror*.

verb

reflect

His ideas *mirror* what his parents think.

miss

verb

1. *go without*

I *missed* the party last week, because I was out of town.
2. *feel unhappy not to be with*
When she left for college, she *missed* her family very much.

Miss
noun
an unmarried female person
Mr. Brown is getting engaged to *Miss* White. When they get married, she may become Mrs. Brown.

missing
adjective
lost, not found
I counted my books in school. One was *missing*. I must have forgotten it at home.

mistake
noun
an error
I solved six problems. I had only one *mistake*. Everything else was correct.
verb: mistaking, mistook, mistaken
consider something for something else
Because this man looks like my uncle, I *mistook* him for my uncle.

mistaken
See **mistake** also.
adjective
wrong
You are *mistaken* about the time; it isn't 5:10; it is 6:10.

mix

noun
combination, mixture
I like the tea you offered me; it is a *mix* of Indian and Chinese teas.
verb
combine
She *mixed* five vegetables together to make her salad.

mixture
noun
combination, mix
She had a *mixture* of three kinds of apples in her pie.

moan
noun
a sound of pain or discomfort
I heard a *moan* coming from the patient's room. He was in pain.

mob
noun
a large group of people making a lot of noise
The city had many problems. The police worked very hard to control the *mobs*.

mock
verb
laugh at
The boy *mocked* at the way his sister sang, although she sang quite well.

model
noun
1. *a good illustration*
The older brother is a very fine person, and he can act as a *model* for his younger brother.
2. *a small example*
She has a *model* of a sailing ship in her room.
verb
show
Two girls *modeled* dresses in front of the ladies.

moderate
adjective
medium
The climate here is quite *moderate*; it is neither hot nor cold.

modern
adjective
related to the present
Using computers is a *modern* way of teaching in class.

moment
noun
a very short period of time
Please wait for me; I'll be back in a *moment*.

Monday
noun
a day of the week
Monday comes after Sunday and before Tuesday. He arrived on *Monday*.

money

noun
the paper or coins we use to buy things with
She has enough *money* to buy a new dress.

monkey

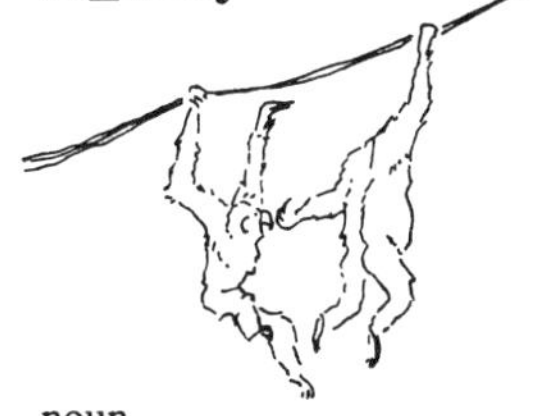

noun
an animal that likes to eat bananas and hang from trees
Our favorite animals in the zoo are the *monkeys*; we like to see them swinging on branches.

month
noun
a period of time
There are twelve *months* in a year. January is the first *month* of the year.

monument
noun
a structure built in memory of someone
A stone *monument* was built in memory of those who died in the war.

monumental
adjective
very big
The artist drew a *monumental* picture of the city on the side of the building.

moon

noun
a planet, the closest planet to earth
We can see our way around when the *moon* is out, especially when it is a full *moon*.

moral
noun
a lesson
There was a *moral* behind the story he told. The *moral* was: be honest always.
adjective
related to good and evil
Honesty is a *moral* concern everywhere.

morale
noun
the way people think and feel about themselves and their actions
They lost a lot during the war, but their *morale* was always high.

more
adjective
opposite of less
I have *more* money than you; you have two dollars, and I have five.
adverb or function word
opposite of less and used with adjectives and adverbs
She is very talented, but her sister is even *more* talented.

moreover
adverb
in addition
She wanted to marry him; he was tall and strong; *moreover*, he was clever and rich.

morning
noun
the early part of the day

He doesn't sleep very long; he sleeps late at night and wakes up early in the *morning*.

mortal
noun
a person (whose life has an end)
All *mortals* are like guests on the face of this earth.
adjective
bringing the end of life
Two soldiers received *mortal* shots to the head in the battle. They died immediately.

mosque
noun
the building where Muslims pray
They prayed in the new *mosque* last Friday.

most
adjective
majority, more than half
Most people want to live in peace.
adverb or function word
opposite of least and used with adjectives and adverbs
Of the three sisters, the youngest was the *most* talented.

mostly
adverb
mainly, generally
Sometimes they take the bus to school, but *mostly* they walk there.

moth
noun
an insect with wings
When we turn the lights on in the garden in summer, hundreds of *moths* come towards them.

mother
noun
a female parent
The children had a fine father and a wonderful *mother*.

motion
noun
movement
Don't put your head or arms out of a car when it is in *motion*.
verb
make a sign by moving
He *motioned* to me with his hand that he was leaving.

motor

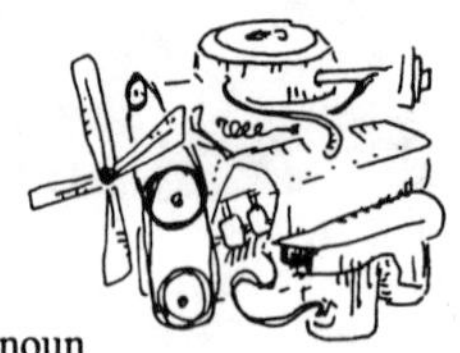

noun
a machine that makes things work
His old car has a new *motor* in it; now he drives easily.

motorbike
noun
small motorcycle

A few students go to school on their *motorbikes*.

motorcycle

noun
a big bicycle that runs on a motor
He went to work on a *motorcycle* before he bought a car.

mount
noun
a mountain
Beyond the plains, we saw a few *mounts* covered with snow.
verb
ride
He *mounted* his horse and went away.

mountain

noun

a high hill or piece of land
The *mountains* are always cooler in summer than the plains.

mouse

noun: mice
an animal, a small rat
Mice are afraid of cats, because cats can catch them.

moustache

noun
the hair between the upper lip and the nose
He likes to grow a long *moustache*.

mouth

noun
the part of the face through which we eat
The dentist asked her to open her *mouth* wide to work on her teeth.

move
verb: moving, moved, moved
1. *change position*
They *moved* their television from the bedroom to the living room.
2. *change residence*
They used to live here, but they have *moved*.

movement
noun
activity
There was a lot of *movement* in school on the first day of classes.

movie
noun
film
The *movie* I saw last night had excellent actors.

Mr.
noun
a title for a male person
Mr. Jones teaches English; he is a good teacher.

Mrs.
noun
a title for a married woman
Mrs. Jones is a teacher like her husband.

Ms.
noun
a title for a female person
Ms. Brown is baking a cake for her party.

much
adjective: more, most
showing quantity of things that cannot be counted
He has *much* money; he is rich.

mud
noun
wet soil
After it rained, we had to step in the *mud* to cross the field.

muddy
adjective: muddier, muddiest
full of mud
The field became *muddy* after the heavy rain.

multiply
verb: multiplying, multiplied, multiplied
make (so many times) more
If you *multiply* six by four, you get twenty-four.

mum
adjective
quiet
I asked him a question, but he remained *mum*; he said nothing.

murder
verb
kill
The thief *murdered* the man in the street to take his money.

murmur
verb
make sounds and say things not very clearly
The sick man *murmured* a few words, but we did not understand them.

muscle

noun
a part of the body that makes us able to move parts of our body
If you do a lot of exercises, you will have strong *muscles*.

museum
noun
a building that has art work, valuable things, old things or other things for people to see
One of the *museums* we saw in Washington, D.C. has wonderful paintings.

music
noun
sounds and tones that come from voices or instruments
We turned the radio on to listen to some *music*; we heard songs and pieces played on the piano.

musical
adjective
1. *related to music*
The violin is a *musical* instrument.
2. *has ability in music*
My young brother is very *musical*; he catches a tune and plays it easily.

musician
noun
a person who sings or plays a musical instrument
Three *musicians* played some music for us; one played the piano; one played the violin; and one played the drums.

must
auxiliary verb
(showing that one is obliged to do something)
I *must* go; it is quite late.

mustn't
auxiliary verb (negative)
must not
I *mustn't* eat too much; it's bad for me.

my
pronoun: I, me, my, mine
first person singular
I have a sister; *my* sister is two years younger than I.

myself
emphatic pronoun
I, nobody else
I did the work *myself*; nobody helped me.
reflexive pronoun
me, my own self
I hurt *myself* when I fell down.

mysterious
adjective
not well known
She is a *mysterious* person; nobody knows what she likes or wants to do.

mystery
noun: mysteries
something that has a secret in it
I don't know how she wrote such a fine story; that will remain a *mystery*. I'm reading an interesting *mystery*; I still don't know who stole the treasure or how he or she was caught.

Nn

nail
noun

1. *the hard part at the end of toes and fingers*
My sister paints her *nails* red.

2. *a thin and long metal piece that is driven into wood or walls to hold things together or to hang things on*
I drove a *nail* into the wall in the living room; now I can hang a picture on it.

naked
adjective

without clothes
The child walked around *naked* at home; he didn't know how to dress himself.

name
noun
a word or words by which we know people or things
My friend's *name* is Sam. The *name* of our bank is First National Bank.
verb: naming, named, named
give a name to
Mr. and Mrs. Smith had a baby girl; they *named* her Alice.

narrow
adjective
not wide
That street is very *narrow*; it doesn't hold more than one car at a time.

nasty
adjective: nastier, nastiest
1. *bad, doing things that hurt*
There was a *nasty* smell coming from their kitchen. I didn't like it.
2. *harmful*
The children don't like Jim; he's *nasty*; he hits them sometimes.

nation
noun
a country
Over 150 *nations* are members of the United *Nations*.

national
adjective
related to a nation
The spread of disease has became a *national* problem.

nationality
noun: nationalities
the condition of belonging to a nation
She was born in Greece, and she has Greek *nationality*. In our school, we have students of many different *nationalities*.

native
noun
a person who was born in a particular place
She is a *native* of India; now she is studying in the United States.
adjective
related to someone's country or place of birth
She speaks English very well, but her *native* language is Spanish.

natural
adjective
related to nature
Mountains, plants, and animals are parts of our *natural* world.

nature
noun
1. *the world as it was created*
They raised their children to love *nature*: the sun, the moon, the stars, the rivers, the birds, the animals, and the fish.
2. *the quality and characteristics of things*
A carpenter must know the *nature* of wood before he can work on

it well.

naughty
adjective: naughtier, naughtiest
a bit bad, not following instructions
Their son was quite *naughty* at home; he didn't listen to his father and mother, and he did things that made them angry.

navy
noun: navies
the sea power of a nation
He wanted to become a sailor by joining the *navy*. The *navy* fought a sea battle.

near
adverb
close (to), not far (from)
His office is *near*; it is only half a mile away.

nearly
adverb
almost
He is *nearly* 20 years old; he will be 20 in two months.

necessary
adjective
needed, important
It is *necessary* to know how to call for help if you need it.

necessity
noun: necessities
a need
Having enough money before you travel is a *necessity*; you need to have it.

neck

noun
the part of the body between the shoulders and the head
She wore a beautiful necklace on her *neck*.

necklace

noun
something worn on the neck as a chain or string of jewels or beads
She bought a gold chain with a blue jewel to wear as a *necklace*.

need
noun
something that is necessary to have, a lack
He has almost everything; his only *need* is a good job.
verb
lack
I *need* some help; I can't do the work alone.

needle

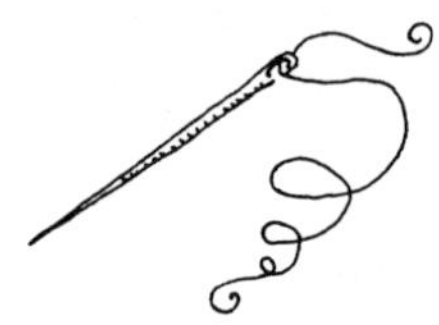

noun
a thin metal piece with a hole in it for a thread to go through it to sew something
She bought a *needle* and colored thread to sew a new dress.

neglect
verb
not give attention to
He *neglected* his business for a long time; now he will have to close it down.

neighbor
noun
a person who is or lives near
We had dinner with our *neighbors* across the street last night.

neighborhood
noun
the area where people live near and around one's house
My *neighborhood* is very clean and safe; all the people who live there are good and friendly.

neighboring
adjective
near, next to
The U.S. has two *neighboring* countries: Canada and Mexico.

neither
pronoun
not the one or the other of two persons or things
I asked my brother and my sister to go to the movies with me; *neither* of them wanted to go.
adverb
and not
She said she didn't speak Japanese; well, *neither* did I.
conjunction
not (and not)
I liked *neither* the meat nor the vegetables in that restaurant; both were bad.

nephew
noun
a son of a brother or sister
My sister has two boys; both of them are my *nephews*.

nerve
noun
a part of the body that sends feelings to the brain
The war and the hard times he had were bad for his *nerves*.

nervous
adjective
anxious and not calm
Being in a crowd all day and hearing loud noises made him very *nervous*; we tried to give him some rest in a quiet place.

nest

noun
a small place where birds lay their eggs
The mother bird brought food to its babies in the *nest*.

net
noun
a piece of material made from thread or string with many holes
Tennis and ping pong players must get the balls over the *net*. Some people use *nets* to catch fish.

never
adverb
not at any time, at no time
He *never* arrives on time; he is always late.

nevertheless
adverb
yet
The weather is very bad; *nevertheless*, we will have to go to work.

new
adjective
not old
I bought a used car; it was two years old; my friend bought a *new* car; nobody had driven it before.

news
noun
recent information about events
We heard the *news* on the radio and we read the same *news* about the war in the newspaper.

newspaper

noun
a paper that prints the news
We get a daily *newspaper* for local and international news.

next
adjective
immediately following
The first person to enter the school today was the principal; the *next* one was a teacher;

these were the first two persons in school today.
adverb
near
She sat *next* to me in class; and both of us sat *next* to the windows.

nice
adjective
1. *good, pleasant*
I saw a *nice* film last night; I liked it very much.
2. *kind, polite*
She is a *nice* lady; she is kind and helpful.

niece
noun
a daughter of a brother or sister
My brother has a boy and a girl; the boy is my nephew; the girl is my *niece*.

night
noun
the dark part of a 24-hour day
A loud noise woke me up at *night*; it was 1:00 a.m.

nine
noun
a number: 9
Nine is one less than ten.
adjective
a number: 9
She has four brothers and four sisters; there are *nine* children in that family.

nineteen
noun
a number: 19
Twelve and seven make *nineteen*.
adjective
a number: 19
Eighteen friends of mine and I are in the same class; our class has *nineteen* students.

ninety
noun
a number: 90
Forty-five and 45 make *ninety*.
adjective
a number: 90
There are *ninety* students in the library now: fifty girls and forty boys.

ninth
noun
1. *a number showing order: 9th*
The *ninth* to arrive will sit in chair number 9.
2. *one of nine equal parts*
The nine children shared their parents' money; each got a *ninth*.
adjective
a number showing order: 9th
Ten people ran in the race; the first five received prizes; the sixth, seventh, eighth, *ninth*, and tenth runners got nothing.

no
adverb
opposite of yes
Is your name Sally? *No*, it isn't; it's Marion.
(like an article)
not any
I have *no* money to spend on travel this year.

noble
adjective
of a very high class and quality
He is a *noble* person with *noble* ideas; he is good and honest, and all his ideas are for the good of the people.

nobody
pronoun
no person
Nobody is at the door; I looked; I saw *nobody*.

nod
verb: nodding, nodded, nodded
1. *bend the head down*
He was so sleepy that he *nodded* his head while sitting on the chair.
2. *bend the head to mean yes*
I asked if she was hungry, and she

nodded; she wanted to eat.

noise
noun
a sound
There was a lot of *noise* in the field; the motors were running and there were many people working.

noisy
adjective: noisier, noisiest
making a lot of noise
I couldn't study in the living room; there were too many people in it, and it was *noisy*.

none
pronoun
1. *no one*
I invited three people to eat with me; *none* came; I ate alone.
2. *nothing*
I tried different parts of the meal; *none* of it was good; I threw it away.

nonsense
noun
something that has little or no meaning
Everything he said was wrong and no good; it was *nonsense*.

noon
noun
the middle of the day: 12:00 a.m.
We had a light lunch at *noon*.

no one
pronoun
no person
I thought I heard the door bell, but when I opened the door, I saw *no one*.

nor
adverb
and not
I didn't eat any of the apples; *nor* did my brother.
conjunction
(not) and not
I liked neither the meat *nor* the vegetables in that restaurant; both of them were bad.

normal
adjective
common, expected, usual
The *normal* thing to do when you receive a letter is to answer it.

north
noun
the part nearer the North Pole
The *north* is cooler than the south in the U.S.
adverb
towards the north
They drove *north* from Miami to New York.

northern
adjective
from the north
There is a *northern* gentleman here now; he is visiting the south for a week.

nose

noun
a part of the face, the part we breathe through when our mouth is shut
She put her *nose* close to the flowers to smell them.

not
adverb
a negative word
He is *not* a student; he is a teacher.

note

noun
1. *a message*
I left her a *note* on her desk when I didn't find her in her office.
2. *a musical sound*
He played a few *notes* on the piano.
verb: noting, noted, noted
notice

We *noted* that they were in a hurry; so we let them go.

nothing
pronoun
not a thing
There is *nothing* on the table now; it is empty.

notice
noun
a message for the public
I read a *notice* in school about a change in class time.
verb: noticing, noticed, noticed
see
I *noticed* somebody running across our garden; I couldn't tell who it was.

notion
noun
idea
He has the *notion* that he is the tallest boy in class; he's wrong.

noun
noun
a part of speech that may have a plural form
Mary, Florida, and table are examples of *nouns*.

novel
noun
a long story
She read a *novel* last week; she read *All Quiet on the Western Front.*
adjective
new
Everyone had a different idea, but her idea was really *novel*; it was new and interesting.

November
noun
the eleventh month of the year
November comes after October and before December.

now
adverb
at this time, at the present time
I can't wait for your answer; I want it *now*.

nowhere
adverb
in no place
He is *nowhere* in the house; he is either in the garden or with the neighbor.

number
noun
1. *a figure*
Three is a *number*.
2. *some*
A *number* of people came to the game.
verb
give numbers *in order*
The teachers *numbered* the students as they entered the building; there were 50 students; I was number 12.

numerous

adjective
many
He has written *numerous* books: between six and ten.

nurse

noun
a person who takes care of patients and helps doctors
She works in a hospital; she is a *nurse*.

nut

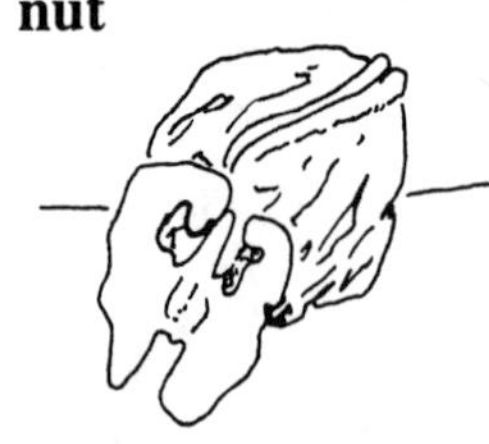

noun
a fruit with a hard shell
My mother put some *nuts* in the cake she baked.

nylon
noun
a kind of material used as thread or as a piece of cloth
Her new dress is made of *nylon.*

Oo

oar

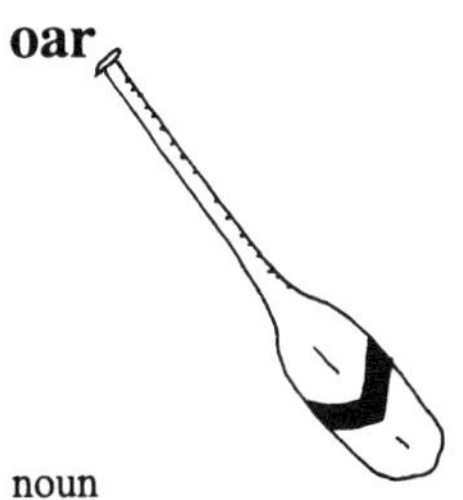

noun
a long piece (of wood) with a broad end used to row a boat
We rowed the boat across the lake with two *oars.*

obey
verb
do what somebody has asked
The parents asked their children not to play outside that day; the children *obeyed* their parents; they didn't play outside.

object
noun
a thing
I have two *objects* in my hand: a pencil and a coin.

object
verb
say that one is against (something)
My friends wanted me to pay for something I didn't eat. I *objected* to that; I said that it was not right.

oblige
verb: obliging, obliged, obliged
let someone feel that he or she has to do something
They feel *obliged* to come to our party, because we went to theirs.

observe
verb: observing, observed, observed
1. *notice*
I *observed* that few students walked into the library today.
2. *say (something)*
"This is a good museum," he *observed.*

obtain
verb
get
We couldn't find the book in the library; so we *obtained* one from the bookstore.

occasion
noun
1. *a special time when something happens*
The party they had was an *occasion* for people to meet.

occasionally
adverb
sometimes
He doesn't go to the library very often, but we see him there *occasionally.*

occupation
noun
field of work
Teaching is her *occupation*; she is a teacher.

occupied
See **occupy** also.
adjective
busy
Don't go into the principal's office now; he is *occupied* with some teachers.

occupy
verb: occupying, occupied, occupied
1. *fill and use (a place)*
My class *occupies* Room 20 at 10:00 o'clock.
2. *take and hold*
The army *occupied* the city for a month.
3. *use*
I *occupy* my free time reading books.

occur
verb: occurring, occurred, occurred
happen
The accident *occurred* at 3:15 in the afternoon.

ocean
noun
a very big sea
The Atlantic *Ocean* lies between Europe and America.

o'clock
adverb
of the clock (showing time)
They are coming at 4:00 *o'clock* in the afternoon.

October
noun
the tenth month of the year
October comes after September and before November.

odd
adjective
1. *a number that cannot be divided by 2.*
One, three, and fifteen are *odd* numbers.
2. *strange*
He is a very *odd* person; he does things in a very funny and different way.

of
preposition
1. *(showing that something is a part of something else)*
Three *of* the people here are teachers.
2. *(showing possession)*
The name *of* the book is *My English.*
3. *(showing kind)*
He bought three bags *of* oranges.
4. *(after the word afraid)*
She is afraid *of* big dogs.
5. *(showing relations)*
He is a teacher *of* history. The president *of* the U.S. lives in the White House.

off
adverb
1. *away*
The handle of the bag was too loose; it came *off* easily.
2. *not on*
She turned the lights *off* before she went to bed.
preposition
not on
He took *off* his shoes and wore his slippers.

offer
verb
present
She *offered* me a piece of cake; I took it and ate it.

office
noun
a place where a person sits and works (and where there may be a telephone and a typewriter)
The principal left his *office* to walk around the school.

officer
noun

1. *a commander in the army, air force or navy*
The *officer* gave his soldiers orders to move forward.
2. *a person who has a position in an organization*
She is an *officer* of the club; she is the secretary.

official
noun
a person who works for the government
He needed a passport to travel; he went to three *officials* and got it.
adjective
related to an office, formal
She received an *official* letter from the school saying that she has passed all her courses.

often
adverb
frequently
He goes to the library quite *often*; he is there

three or four times a week.

oh

interjection
(showing surprise)
Oh! Is he really in the hospital? I didn't know that.

oil

noun
1. *a black liquid that comes out of the earth or the sea*
Venezuela is very rich in *oil.*
2. *the liquid (fat) that comes from vegetables*
She cooked the food in olive *oil* yesterday; today she is using corn *oil.*
verb
put oil on or in
When his machine didn't work very well, he *oiled* it.

OK

adjective
fine, good
The letter she wrote had many mistakes; now it is *OK.*
adverb
very well
OK. I'll go with you.

old

adjective
1. *not new*
He couldn't buy a new car; so he bought an *old* one.
2. *not young*
He is an *old* man; he is 92.
3. *(showing age)*
He is 92 years *old.*

olive

noun
a vegetable that gives oil and has a pit in it
She likes to put *olives* in her salad. We like black and green *olives.*

on

preposition
1. *(with days)*
She arrived *on* Wednesday.
2. *(showing place)*
I put the book *on* the table.
3. *(with radio and television)*
I heard the news *on* the radio and watched a game *on* television.

once

adverb
one time
She didn't remember the story very well, as she heard it only *once.*

one

noun
a number: 1
If you take two out of three, you are left with *one.*
adjective
a number: 1
We have only *one* car; it is enough for us.

onion

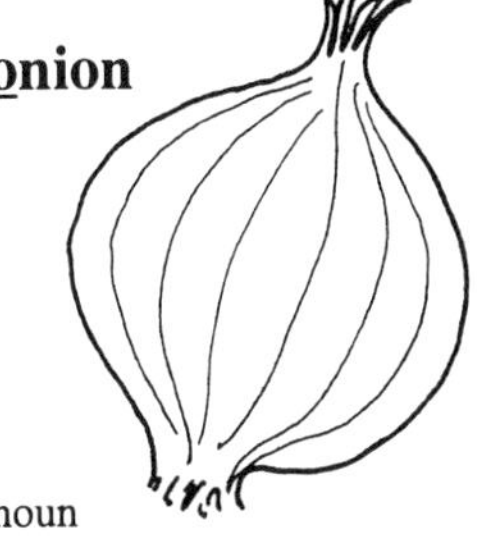

noun
a vegetable with a sharp taste
She likes to add green *onions* to her salad.

only

adjective
no other (than)
They have an *only* child; they care for her a lot.
adverb
and no other
His doctor told him to eat once a day *only.*
conjunction
but
He can go to the cinema with us; *only* he must buy his own ticket.

open

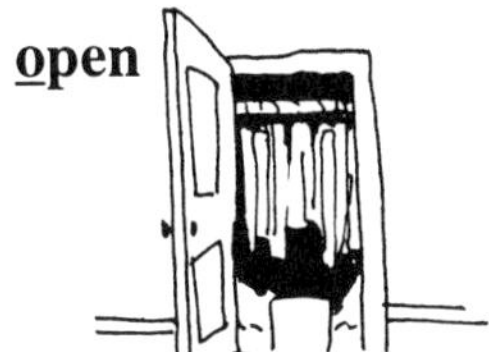

verb
opposite of close
We *opened* the door when we heard the bell; a man was standing there.
adjective
not closed
The door is *open*; you can walk in.

opening

noun
a place where someone or something can go in or out
The thief ran out of prison through an *opening* in the wall.

operate

verb: operating, operated, operated
1. *run or work (something)*
I couldn't use the machine, because I didn't know how to *operate* it.
2. *cut open a part of a person or animal for medical reasons*
The doctor *operated* on my friend; he removed a piece of metal from his leg.

operation

noun
1. *the act of running or working (something)*
The *operation* of this new machine is difficult for her; she never had one like it.
2. *the act of opening up a part of a person or animal for medical reasons*
The doctor removed a metal piece from my friend's leg; the *operation* was successful.

opinion

noun
a person's idea
She wanted the picnic on any day. I had a different *opinion*; I wanted the picnic only on a sunny day.

opportunity

noun: opportunities
a good chance
The teacher asked the students for ideas about our class trip. This gave us an *opportunity* to tell him exactly what we thought.

oppose

verb: opposing, opposed, opposed
go against
She wanted to ride her bicycle to school. Her parents *opposed* that idea because the streets were not safe with so much traffic on them.

opposite

noun
the one that is very different, the one that is contrary
The *opposite* of tall is short; the opposite of heavy is light.

or

conjunction
1. *(showing choice)*
You can eat here; *or* you can eat in a restaurant today.
2. *(with either and showing choice)*
You can either eat here *or* in a restaurant.

orange

noun
1. *a fruit with a lot of juice*
She likes to eat bananas and *oranges* in winter; she likes watermelon in summer.
2. *a color*
If you mix red and yellow, you get *orange*.
adjective
a color
She has an *orange* bag to go with her *orange* dress.

order

noun
1. *command*

The captain gave his men an *order* to move forward.
2. *an organized arrangement*
Everything in his room was in *order*. There was peace and *order* in the city when the army arrived.
verb
give a command
The captain *ordered* his men to move forward.

ordinary
adjective
usual
Helping people was a very *ordinary* thing for him to do; he does it all the time.

organ
noun

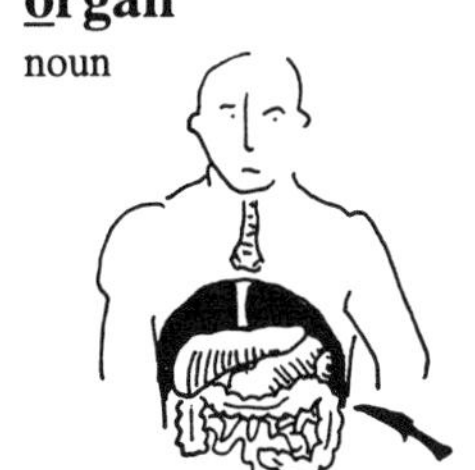

1. *a part of the body*
The brain and the heart are two important *organs* in our bodies.

2. *a musical instrument*
He played the *organ* and his wife sang at the party.

organization
noun
1. *a firm, an institution, a business*
The lawyers formed a new *organization* in the city.
2. *order, the way one does his or her work*
She is known for her *organization* of her papers and business.

organize
verb: organizing, organized, organized
put things in order
He is successful in his work because he *organizes* it very well.

original
adjective
1. *new*
She always has *original* ideas; her ideas are new and fresh.
2. *real, first*
He kept the *original* copy of the letter; we received machine copies.

ornament

noun
something used to make a place beautiful
She uses her own pictures as *ornaments* in her living room.

other
noun
not this
I have two pens; this one is blue; the *other* is green.
adjective
not the one mentioned
You have three books with you; I have read one of them; I'd like to borrow one of the *other* two books, please.

ought
auxiliary verb
(showing duty or necessity)
I *ought* to leave now; I don't want to be late.

our
pronoun: we, us, our, ours
first person plural
This is *our* car; it is ours; it is not theirs.

ours
pronoun: we, us, our, ours
first person plural
This is our car; it is *ours*; it is not theirs.

ourselves
emphatic pronoun
we, nobody else
We did the work *ourselves*; nobody

helped us.
reflexive pronoun
us, our own selves
We hurt *ourselves* when we fell running down the hill.

out
adverb
not in
We can't see the principal in his office now; he is *out*.

outdoor
adjective
outside
The weather was good; so we had an *outdoor* party.

outdoors
adverb
outside
The weather was good; so we held our party *outdoors*.

outside
adjective
the side which is not in
The *outside* wall of my room is wet from the rain.

outside
adverb
out, not inside
They played *outside*; we didn't want them to play in the house.

oven

noun
a place where food is cooked
My mother baked a cake in the *oven*.

over
adjective
finished
The class started at 8:00, and it was *over* at 9:00.
adverb
again
He couldn't understand the story very well; so he read it *over* many times.
preposition
on top of
I couldn't see the wood on the table; they had a cover *over* it.

overcame
See **overcome**.

overcome
verb: overcoming, overcame, overcome
defeat
Our army *overcame* the enemy and took the city.

owe
verb: owing, owed, owed
be in debt to
I lent him ten dollars; he gave me four dollars back; he still *owes* me six dollars.

owing
See **owe** also.
preposition
because of
Owing to the rain, we couldn't go on our trip.

owl

noun
a bird that flies at night
The only real *owl* I have seen was in the zoo.

own
pronoun
(showing strong possession)
This pen is my *own*; I bought it myself.
verb
possess
They *own* one house in the city and a cottage by the sea.

owner
noun
a person who possesses
He is the *owner* of the house I live in; I pay him my rent every month.

ox

noun: oxen

a strong male animal

The farmer had one *ox* and six cows on his farm.

oxen

See **ox**.

oyster

noun

a shell fish

He likes to eat raw *oysters*.

Pp

pace

noun

walking speed

He walked at a faster *pace* than his sister; he got to school before her.

pack

noun

a number of things of the same kind put together

He plays card games with his friends; he has two *packs* of cards.

The hunters saw a *pack* of wolves in the forest.

verb

put together (to move or travel)

We *packed* our suitcases for the trip; we took the clothes we needed.

package

noun

a container of things put together

I received a *package* in the mail from my friend; he sent me two books and a game.

packet

noun

a container of things put together

The *packet* I received in the mail had some books and some sweets; my father sent them to me.

page

noun

one side of a sheet of paper in a notebook, a book, a magazine, or newspaper

The book I read had 275 *pages* in it. On *page* 16 there was a picture.

paid

See **pay**.

pain

noun

a hurt, an ache

He felt some *pain* in his left leg when he fell.

verb

hurt

It *pains* me to see people doing wrong things.

paint

noun

a liquid material used for coloring

They bought blue *paint* for the walls of their

son's bedroom.
verb
color with a liquid material
They *painted* the walls blue. She *painted* a beautiful picture.

painter

noun
a person who paints
The picture we have in the living room was done by a very famous *painter*.

painting
noun
a picture that was painted
We bought one of the *paintings* from the art museum.

pair
noun
two of a kind
He is wearing a brown *pair* of trousers and a brown *pair* of shoes. He and his wife make an interesting *pair*.

pajamas

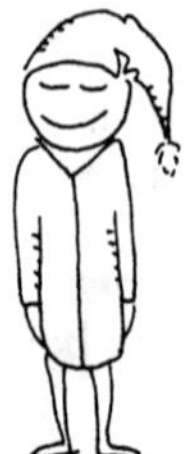

noun
a suit worn in bed or at home
She bought new wool *pajamas* to keep her warm at night.

palace

noun
a very big house, a house where kings and queens live
The tourists visited the summer *palace* of the queen.

pale
adjective
1. *not having enough color*
He was ill; now he is better, but he looks *pale*.
2. *light in color*
The sky today is *pale* blue.

palm
noun

1. *the inside of the hand*
She held the money in the *palm* of her hand.

2. *a tall tree that gives fruit*
We get dates from *palm* trees.

pan

noun
a container used for frying or cooking food
She cooked the rice in a *pan* and fried the potatoes in a frying *pan*.

paper
noun
1. *a newspaper*
We read the daily *paper* when we get it in the morning.
2. *the material that pages in a book are made of, the material that we write on*
The teacher gave us some *paper* to write our names on.

parachute

noun

a very big "umbrella" used for dropping from airplanes to the ground
The soldiers used *parachutes* to land behind the enemy lines.

paragraph

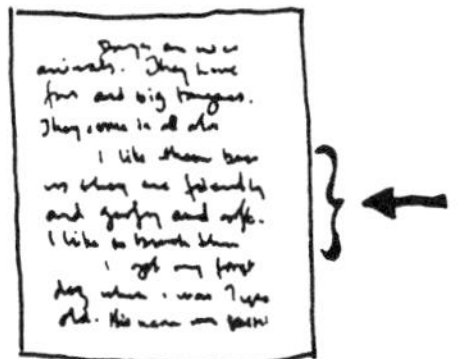

noun
a number of sentences that form one group and one main idea in writing
The teacher asked us to write a story in three or four *paragraphs*.

parcel

noun

a package
I received a *parcel* in the mail; in it there were three books and a dictionary.

pardon

verb
forgive, excuse
The teacher *pardoned* the student for coming late; the school buses were late. "*Pardon* me; may I pass through here?"

parent

noun
a father or a mother
The principal of the school said that she would like to see at least one *parent* of every student at the school meeting. She has very good *parents*; her father and mother are wonderful people.

park

noun
1. *a public place where people can walk and sit*
I saw some old people sitting in the sun in the *park*.
2. *a place where cars or vehicles are put for a time*
We left our cars in the garage *park* when we went shopping.
verb
put a car or vehicle for a time
The drivers *parked* their cars in front of the building.

part

noun
1. *a role in a play*
My cousin took the *part* of a policeman in the play; he acted very well.
2. *a section (of something), a piece*
We only saw a *part* of the house; we did not see it all.
verb
separate
When we saw the two boys fighting, we *parted* them.

particular

adjective
exact, special
She didn't just want any dress to buy; she wanted a *particular* kind with a *particular* color.

particularly

adverb
especially
Wear warm clothes, *particularly* if it is snowing.

partly

adverb
in part, not completely
The door was *partly* open; the dog tried to leave through it.

partner

noun
a person who shares in owning something
Three brothers started a business together; they were *partners*; they were equal *partners*; each of them owned one third of the business.

party

noun: parties
1. *a political group*
In the U.S., there are two main political parties: the Democratic

Party and the Republican *Party*.
2. *a social occasion*
I was invited to her birthday *party*; we had cakes and sandwiches, and we sang some songs.

pass
noun
a permit
She has a *pass* to enter the palace; you can't go in without a *pass*.
verb
1. *go beyond*
We *passed* the school on the way to the market.
2. *succeed in a test or course*
She *passed* all her courses.

passage

noun
a way to go through
This little path is a *passage* to the corn field.

passenger
noun
a person who travels on a plane, train, ship, bus, or car
The plane had 156 *passengers* on it. In his small car, he can take one *passenger* only.

passion
noun
a very strong feeling
He has great *passion* for his family. She has a *passion* for chocolate.

passionate
adjective
showing strong feelings
She is a very *passionate* person; she loves her family and friends and does all she can for them.

passport

noun
a small book with the picture of a citizen that is used for travel to other countries
We show our *passports* at the border when we enter another country.

past
noun
the time before now
In the *past*, people didn't have cars or electricity.
adjective
the time before (this)
It is colder this year than in *past* years.
adverb
to and further than
Many cars drove *past* as we were walking down the road.

pasture
noun
a piece of land with green grass where animals can eat
The shepherd took his sheep to *pasture*.

pat
noun
a light touch or stroke
She gave her dog a few *pats* on the back.
verb: patting, patted, patted
touch or stroke lightly
She *patted* her dog when he was sitting near her.

path

noun
a narrow way
There is a *path* that the farmer took to get to his neighbor's farm. We took a *path* down the hill to the main road.

patience
noun
the act or ability to wait for something to happen without getting anxious

I have never seen anyone with my father's *patience*; he can wait a very long time for anything or anyone.

patient
noun
a sick person
The hospital received four new *patients* yesterday.
adjective
able to wait without getting anxious
She is very *patient* with her students; they can take all the time they need to do or learn things.

pattern
noun
the way things are arranged
Look at the two following sentences; their *patterns* are different:
1. *He is a nice man.*
2. *Is he a nice man?*

pause
noun
a short stop
He made a *pause* in his speech and drank some water.
verb: pausing, paused, paused
make a short stop
They *paused* for an hour to eat on their way south.

pay
noun
money given for work done
He has a good job; he gets a high *pay* in it.
verb: paying, paid, paid
give money for something
I *paid* one dollar for this pen.

payment
noun
giving or receiving money for something
The merchant sold a car yesterday; he is now waiting for *payment* to be made.

P.E.
physical education
In the *P.E.* class, I run; my friends swim.

pea

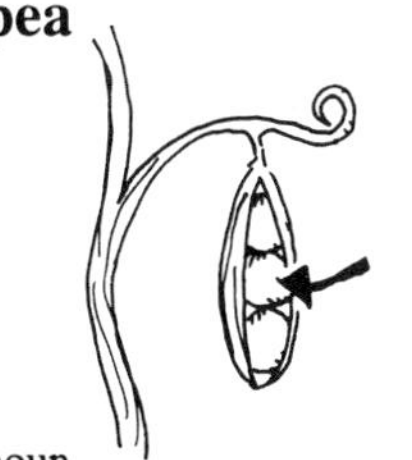

noun
a vegetable (small, round, and green)
We had steak, potatoes, and *peas* for dinner.

peace
noun
a time of no war or fighting
People enjoyed the *peace* between the two wars.

peach
noun: peaches
a fruit

In summer she likes to put ice-cream on her *peaches*.

peanut

noun
a nut in a shell that monkeys like to eat
He likes *peanuts* on his ice-cream. He also likes *peanut* butter sandwiches.

pear

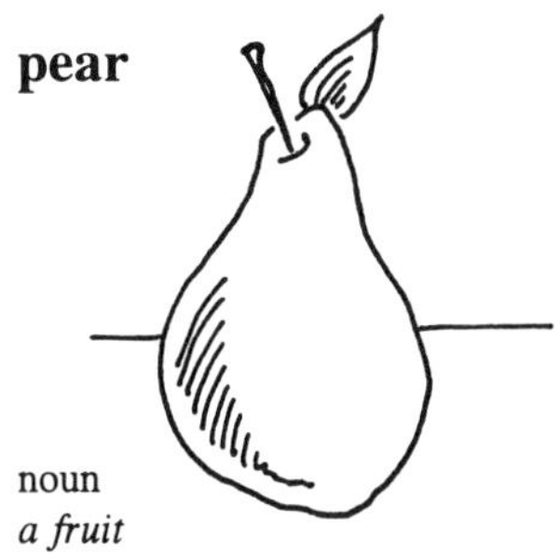

noun
a fruit
My brother likes apples; I prefer *pears*.

pearl

noun
a jewel that comes from the shell of a sea animal
She wore a ring with a big white *pearl* on it.

peculiar
adjective
strange
He walks in a very *peculiar* manner; he moves his whole body when he walks.

peel

noun
the outer layer or skin of a fruit or vegetable
Many people make jam from orange *peel.*
verb
remove the skin of a fruit or vegetable
I *peel* apples before I eat them; my friend eats the peel.

pen

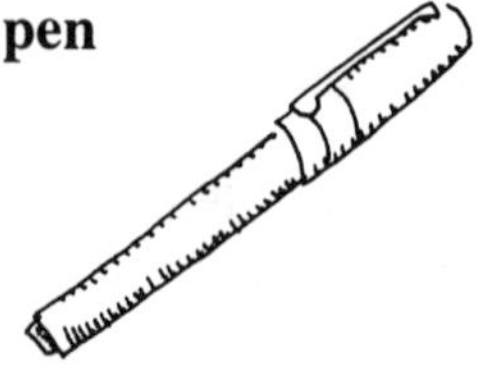

noun
something to write with in ink
The teacher asked us to use *pens* and write in ink.

pencil

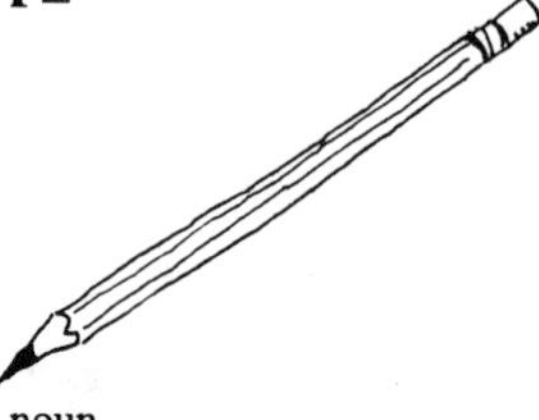

noun
something to write with that has lead
We used our *pencils* to draw in class; the teacher wanted us to draw in *pencil.*

penny
noun: pennies
a cent
One hundred *pennies* make a dollar.

people
noun
persons
There were twenty *people* in the room: ten men and ten women.

pepper
noun
1. *a hot spice that is red or black*
He likes a lot of *pepper* on his steak; his wife adds only a bit of salt.

2. *a red, green, or yellow vegetable*
She always puts a red *pepper* and a green *pepper* in her salads.

per
preposition
1. *(to) each*
The principal gave ten minutes of his time *per* student.
2. *(for) each*
We could buy the books at one dollar *per* book.

perceive
verb: perceiving, perceived, perceived
see (and understand)
I *perceived* that she was not pleased with the meeting.

perfect
adjective
the very best
His explanation was *perfect*; it was easy, and everyone understood it.

perfectly
adverb
1. *in the very best way*
He did his work *perfectly*; there was no mistake in it.
2. *completely*
She understood her lesson *perfectly*. The meeting was *perfectly* successful.

perform
verb
do
He *performs* his work very well; he does it successfully.

performance
noun
1. *an act, a play*
We saw a school *performance* last week; the play was good, and the actors were wonderful.
2. *the way one does (work)*
His *performance* as a driver was not good; he went too fast, and his attention was not on driving.

perhaps
adverb
maybe
I don't know if she is in her office now; *perhaps* she is; *perhaps* she isn't.

period
noun
1. *full stop (.)*
Use a *period* at the end of a sentence.
2. *a length of time*
They lived in Africa for a *period* of three years.

perish
verb
die
The truck was carrying a cow and ten chickens; all of them *perished* in the accident.

permanent
adjective
lasting for ever
Some important laws are *permanent*; they are practiced for a very long time.

permission
noun
something said or written that will allow someone to do something
The teacher gave us *permission* to go out and see our parents.

permit
noun
something written that allows someone to do something
The police gave the man a *permit* to park his car in the street for three hours.

permit
verb: permitting, permitted, permitted
allow
The teacher *permitted* us to leave the classroom to see our parents.

person
noun
an individual, a man, a woman, a boy, or a girl
Six *persons* came to dinner last night: three men and three women.

personal
adjective
relating to a private individual
I had something *personal* to tell her; I didn't want anyone else to know it. What you do with your money is a *personal* matter.

personality
noun: personalities
the qualities and nature of an individual
I met an important *personality* yesterday; he is the head of a big company.

persuade
verb: persuading, persuaded, persuaded
make someone think in a certain way to want what you want him or her to want
She wanted to study in a big college, but I *persuaded* her to go to a small college.

pet

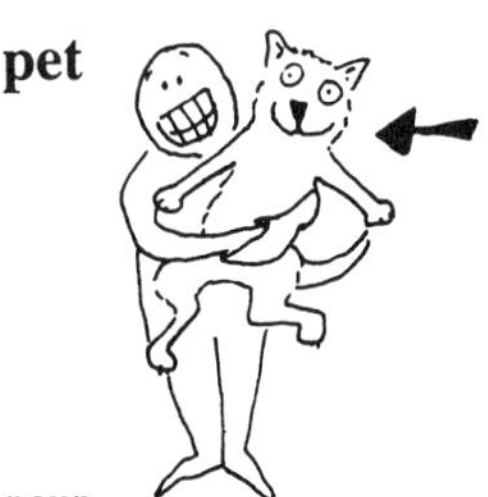

noun
an animal that is kept at home
She has four *pets*: a cat, a dog, and two birds.

phone
noun
a telephone
I spoke with my friend on the *phone* for a few minutes.
verb: phoning, phoned, phoned
use the telephone to speak to someone
I *phoned* my friend to tell him that I was waiting for him.

photograph
noun
a picture taken with a camera
I have a *photograph* of my parents in the living room.
verb
take a picture with a camera
We *photographed* the animals when we went to the zoo.

photographer
noun
a person who takes pictures with a camera
My friend is a good *photographer*; all his pictures are very clear.

phrase
noun
a group of words that go together
In the morning is a *phrase*.
verb: phrasing, phrased, phrased
put in words
I did not understand what you said; can you *phrase* it in another way?

physical
adjective
1. *related to material things*
The seas and mountains are parts of our *physical* world.
2. *related to the body*
He went to the hospital because of a *physical* problem; his stomach was hurting him.
3. *related to physics*
We learned some *physical* laws in our physics class.

physician
noun
a doctor
They took their sick child to a *physician*.

physics
noun
the study of the physical world and its laws
We learned about electricity in *physics*.

piano

noun
a musical instrument at which people sit to play the keys
My sister plays the *piano* and I sing.

pick
noun
a choice
The coat she bought was a good *pick*; it fits her very well.
verb
1. *choose*
She *picked* a good coat to buy; she *picked* the blue coat out of ten coats.
2. *take something off a tree*
They *picked* their own grapes in the garden.

pick up
verb
lift something from the floor or ground
I dropped my keys on the floor; my brother *picked* them *up* for me.

picnic
noun
a short trip to a place where people eat and have fun
We went on a *picnic* to a small forest with our friends; we took the food; they brought lemonade and tea.

picture
noun
a photograph or a drawing
We have two *pictures* on the wall in our living room.
verb: picturing, pictured, pictured
imagine
Can you *picture* a horse flying in the air?

piece
noun
a part (of something)
I had a small *piece* of cake after lunch.

pig

noun
an animal
A *pig* has a very funny nose.

pigeon

noun
a bird
Many *pigeons* come to our garden to eat.

pile

noun
a heap, a number of things on each other
She had a *pile* of books on the table; I think she has about twelve books on top of each other.

verb: piling, piled, piled
heap, put things on each other
She *piled* the books on the table before she put them in a box to take them to school.

pill

noun
a small round piece of medicine to take through the mouth
The doctor told me to take two *pills* of that medicine three times a day.

pillow
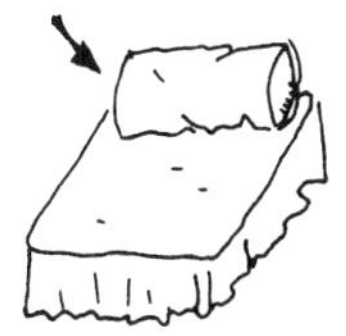
noun
the soft thing we put our heads on in bed
She sleeps without a *pillow*; I like a big *pillow* under my head at night.

pilot
noun
a person who flies an airplane
The *pilot* told the passengers on the plane to put their seat belts on.

pin

noun
a small metal piece with one sharp end and a head
He held the three pieces of paper together with a *pin*.

pine

noun
a tree with very thin leaves
I like the smell of *pine* in my friend's garden.

pineapple

noun
a fruit
She eats some *pineapple* with her breakfast every day.

ping-pong
noun
a table game with bats, a ball, and a net
I won the *ping-pong* game by 21 to 17.

pink
noun
a color
You can get *pink* if you mix red and white.
adjective
a color
My sister has a pretty *pink* dress.

pipe

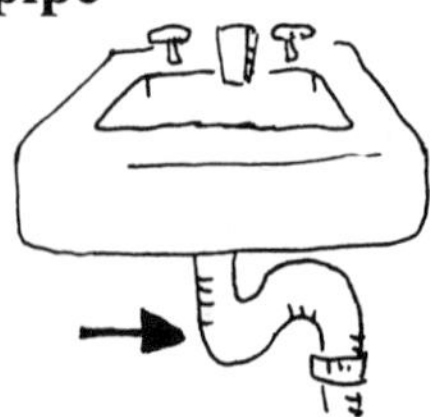

noun
a long hollow metal piece that allows gas or a liquid to go through
The water in our bathroom comes through *pipes*.

pitch
noun
a degree that shows how high or low a voice or musical note is
I can't listen to her for a long time, because she speaks with a very high *pitch*.

pitied
See **pity**.

pity
noun
a feeling for someone who has a problem or is sad
We had *pity* on the poor man who couldn't find work; my uncle tried to help him.
verb: pitying, pitied, pitied
feel for someone
We *pitied* the poor man who couldn't find work, and we asked our uncle to help him.

place
noun
1. *a position somewhere*
She always finds her things, because she always puts them in the right *places*.
2. *somewhere to live*
They have moved to a new *place* in the city.
verb: placing, placed, placed
put (something) somewhere
She *placed* her books in her room before she went to dinner.

plain
noun
a large piece of flat land
Iowa has many *plains* that have corn fields.
adjective
simple and clear
We didn't understand the lesson when we read it, but the teacher gave us a *plain* explanation of it.

plan
noun
1. *a scheme*
We had a *plan* to go to the beach; we had to change our *plan* when it rained.
2. *a drawing to show places*
The engineer showed us the *plan* for his new house.
verb: planning, planned, planned
make a scheme
We *planned* to go to the beach, but we changed our plan when it rained.

plane

noun
airplane
We didn't drive from Washington to New York; we took the *plane*.

planet

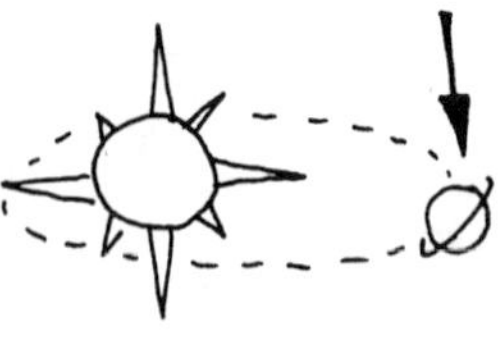

noun
a body or world in space
The earth and the moon are two of the very

many *planets* in space.

plant

noun
a living thing that grows in the ground
Trees and flowers are *plants*. She has many green *plants* at home.
verb
put in earth to grow
She *planted* many kinds of flowers in her garden.

plastic
noun
a material that is not natural from which we can make many things
Some bags, cups, forks, and spoons are made of *plastic*.

plate

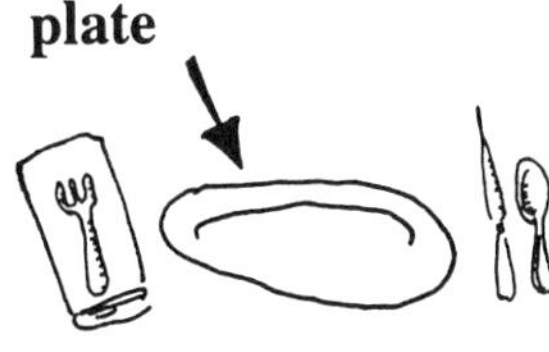

noun
a dish to put food on
I put my steak, potato, and peas on my *plate* and ate them.

platform
noun
1. *a stage*
The actors performed the play on the school *platform*.
2. *a raised level in a room*
The speaker stood on the *platform* to give his talk.

play
noun
a performance that tells a story
We saw a nice *play* in the city; the actors were very good and the story was interesting.
verb
do things for pleasure
The children are *playing* in the garden.

player
noun
a person who plays
Our basketball team is very strong; my cousin is one of the *players*.

playground
noun
a place where children play
The school has a big *playground* for the children; there are swings and many other things in it.

plead
verb: pleading, pleaded or pled, pleaded or pled
ask for something strongly
The thief *pleaded* to the policeman to let him go, but the policeman didn't listen to him.

pleasant
adjective
nice, enjoyable, pleasing
We had a very *pleasant* afternoon with our friends.

please
verb: pleasing, pleased, pleased
make (someone) happy
The music we heard *pleased* us very much; it was the kind of music we like.
interjection
be kind enough to
Please help me with this bag.

pleasure
noun
happiness
The music we heard gave us great *pleasure*. It is a *pleasure* to know you.

plenty
pronoun
a big amount
He doesn't need any more money; he has *plenty* of it now.

plot
noun
1. *a piece (of land)*
They built a new house on the *plot* of land they bought last year.
2. *a scheme*
The thieves had a *plot*

to rob a bank.
verb: plotting, plotted, plotted
plan
The thieves *plotted* to rob a bank, but the police caught them before they could do it.

plow

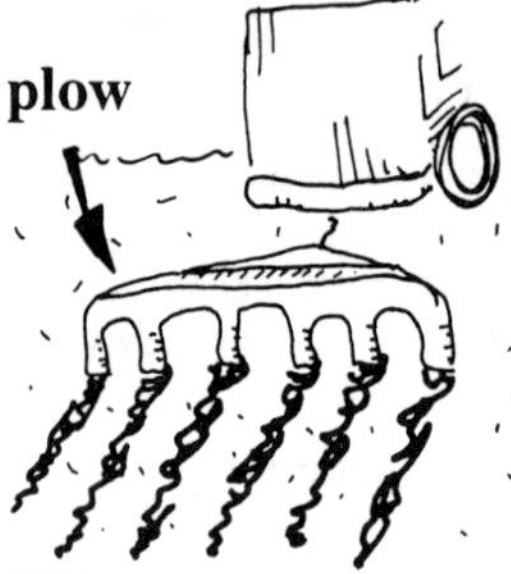

noun
a big tool to cut the earth and prepare it for planting
The farmer used two horses to pull his *plow* on the farm.
verb
cut the earth and prepare it for planting
The farmer *plowed* his land and had it ready for his seeds.

plunge
verb: plunging, plunged, plunged
fall down or forward
The car *plunged* into a hole when the driver went off the road.

plural
noun
more than one
Cats is the *plural* of *cat*.
Men is the *plural* of *man*.

plus
preposition
with, and
Five *plus* two make seven.

p.m.
adverb
after 12:00 o'clock noon
They arrived in the morning and left at 2:00 *p.m.*

pocket

noun
a small bag or container in one's clothes
His jacket has five *pockets*; he puts his money in one of them.

poem
noun
a form of language that expresses ideas in a special way
She likes the *poems* of Edgar Allan Poe.

poet
noun
a person who writes poems
Edgar Allan Poe is a famous American poet; he wrote many wonderful *poems*.

poetry
noun
poems
Writing *poetry* is not easy; it takes skill and practice.

point
noun
1. *a sign that shows part of a number or fraction*
He has 3.5 (three *point* five) acres of land.
2. *a sharp end*
He broke the *point* of his pencil.
3. *a place*
Meet me at this *point* tomorrow.
4. *a sharp end of a piece of land going into the sea*
The *Point* of Good Hope is in Africa.
verb: pointing, pointed, pointed
show a direction
The arrow *pointed* to the north.

pointed
See **point** also.
adjective
having a sharp end
She wrote with a *pointed* pencil.

poison
noun
a substance that may kill a living thing, a substance that some snakes give out
Poison is very dangerous for living creatures.
verb
give this substance (to some living thing)

Very bad food can *poison* the body.

pole
noun
1. *a tall thick stick that holds wires or ropes*
The electric wires in our city are tied to *poles* on the sides of streets.
2. *the North or South Pole*
The North *Pole* is always cold; there is a lot of snow there.

police
noun
a group of men and women who keep the law in a city or town
The *police* caught the thief who tried to rob a bank.

policeman
noun
a man who keeps the law in a city and protects people
My uncle is a *policeman*; he stops drivers who drive too fast.

policewoman
noun
a woman who keeps the law in a city and protects people
The *policewoman* helped catch the thief in the store.

polish
noun
a substance to make things shine
I used a new black *polish* on my black shoes.
verb
shine
I *polished* my black shoes to make them shine.

polite
adjective
kind and gentle
We must always be *polite* with other people; we must be kind and gentle in the way we deal with them.

political
adjective
related to politics
There are two main *political* parties in the U.S.: the Democratic Party and the Republican Party.

politics
noun
the study of government and relations among nations
His father went into *politics*; he wanted to become a governor.

pond
noun
a small body of water
People give food to the ducks near the *pond* in the park.

pony

noun: ponies
a young horse
The little girl likes to ride on a *pony* in the park.

pool

noun
a place with water where people can swim
They have a small *pool* in the back of their house; they swim in it in summer.

poor
adjective
1. *not rich, with little money or material things*
They helped the *poor* man find a place to live.
2. *not good, weak, bad*
He did *poor* work in school and got *poor* grades.

popular
adjective
liked by many
She is a *popular* singer; everybody wants to

hear her sing.

population
noun
people in a city or country
The *population* in our city grew from one million to two million in the last ten years.

porch

noun
a covered outside part of a building
In the summer, my neighbors like to sit on their *porch* and eat their dinner.

pork
noun
the meat of pigs
Some of my neighbors like their *pork* roasted; other neighbors don't eat pork.

port
noun
a harbor
The ship sailed from the *port* after it took the passengers.

portion
noun
a part
The children divided the money among themselves; they all had equal *portions*.

position
noun
1. *the way a person or animal sits or stands or sleeps*
My brother puts his head back on his chair; he likes to sit in that *position*.
2. *a place (in relation to other places)*
From our *position* on the top of the hill, we could see the shore very well.
3. *a job*
She has a good *position* in that company; she helps the manager.

positive
adjective
1. *yes*
He gave a *positive* answer to my question; he said yes.
2. *sure*
He is *positive* that it will rain today.

possess
verb
have, own
They *possess* a large piece of land on the hill, but they are planning to sell it soon.

possession
noun
the act of having or owning
The land is in their *possession*; nobody can have it unless they sell it.

possibility
noun: possibilities
the state when something may or may not happen
There is a *possibility* that it will rain today; we can see some clouds, but we are not sure about the rain.

possible
adjective
1. *may or may not happen*
Rain is *possible* today; we'll wait and see.
2. *able, can*
Is it *possible* for you to help me with this bag?

possibly
adverb
perhaps
Do you think your uncle will be coming today? *Possibly*.

post
noun
mail
We received a parcel by *post* yesterday.
verb
mail
I *posted* a letter to my friend yesterday.

postcard
noun

a card with a picture on one side sent by mail
When I went to Europe last summer, I sent *postcards* to my friends in the U.S.

post office
noun
a place where one can buy stamps and mail letters and parcels
I went to the *post office* yesterday to buy some stamps and to mail a few letters.

pot

noun
a container that one can use to put hot liquids in or to cook in
She served us tea from a colored tea *pot*. They boiled the vegetables in a *pot*.

potato

noun: potatoes
a vegetable that grows in the ground
I like a baked *potato* with my meat; my brother prefers fried *potatoes*.

pound
noun
1. *a measure of weight: lb., 16 ounces*
It takes 2.2 *pounds* to make 1 kilogram.
2. *an amount of money*
In England, they use *pounds*, not dollars, for money.

pour
verb
1. *send or throw a liquid out of a container*
I asked the waiter to *pour* me another cup of coffee.
2. *rain*
You can't go out now without an umbrella; it's *pouring*.

powder
noun
very small dry particles of a substance
She puts *powder* on her face before she goes out. Their milk comes in the form of *powder*; they add water to it to drink it.

power
noun
strength
His new car has great *power*; he can take four passengers in it and go quite fast.

powerful
adjective
strong
He has a *powerful* light in his office; he can see everything very easily.

practical
adjective
related to practice and how one applies things
It is more *practical* to have one suitcase when you travel than to have two; it makes moving about much easier.

practically
adverb
almost, nearly
He is *practically* done with his work; he will be ready to go with us in a few minutes.

practice
noun
exercise
He needs more *practice* playing tennis to become a good player.
verb: practicing practiced, practiced
exercise
She *practiced* using a typewriter until she could type fifty words a minute.

praise
verb: praising, praised, praised

say nice things about
My teacher *praised* me for my good work in class; she was very pleased with me.

pray
verb
speak to God to thank Him or to ask Him for things
She *prayed* to have her son get well.

prayer
noun
the words spoken to God
In her *prayer*, she thanked God and asked Him to make her son well again.

preach
verb
speak about one's religion or about good behavior
He *preached* to his people to be good and honest.

precious
adjective
having value
She has a very *precious* ring; it has a big jewel in it. I have a very *precious* friend; she is a very good person.

prefer
verb: preferring, preferred, preferred
like or want (something) more
I don't like cold weather; I *prefer* warm weather. I *prefer* warm weather to cold weather.

preparation
noun
1. *the act of making something*
In the *preparation* of a salad, use the oil and lemon last.
2. *the act of getting ready*
He is putting his clothes in the suitcase in *preparation* for leaving.

prepare
verb: preparing, prepared, prepared
1. *make*
She is *preparing* a salad for lunch.
2. *get or make ready*
She is *preparing* herself for the test; she is studying very hard.

preposition
noun
a part of speech
We use many *prepositions* in our sentences. In the last sentence, the word *in* is a *preposition*.

presence
noun
the act of being present
The students were very quiet in the *presence* of the teacher.

present
noun
1. *gift*
She received many *presents* on her last birthday.
2. *now, at this time*
In the past, people didn't have cars; at *present*, they have cars, trains, and airplanes.
adjective
1. *here, attending*
He was *present* in class when the teacher talked about the rules; he should know them.
2. *now, (at) this time*
At the *present* time, I don't need the car; I may need it later.

present
verb
1. *offer*
They *presented* me with a letter from the chief.
2. *introduce*
The manager *presented* the new secretary to the company.

presently
adverb
soon
We sat at a table in the restaurant for a few minutes; *presently*, the waiter came and took our order.

preserve
verb: preserving, preserved, preserved
keep

Salt can help *preserve* some foods for a longer time.

president
noun
the elected head (of a government or organization)
The *president* gave a talk on television to the people of his country.

press
noun
1. *a printing machine or office*
He took his book to the *press* to have it printed.
2. *newspapers, radio, and television*
We knew about the president's talk from the *press*; all the papers and televisions mentioned it.
verb
put pressure (on)
She couldn't close her suitcase, because it was full; her husband *pressed* on the cover and closed it.

pressure
noun
force put on something or someone
He put too many books on the glass table; the *pressure* broke the glass.

pretend
verb
act to show what one is not
The thief *pretended* to be a policeman; he wore a policeman's clothes and talked like a policeman, but he was a thief.

pretty
adjective: prettier, prettiest
beautiful
The little girl had a very *pretty* dress on; it was lovely.

prevent
verb
stop (from happening)
The mother *prevented* her child from going out into the street alone; it was too dangerous with all the cars there.

previous
adjective
coming before
Last week the manager wanted his company to sell cars and trucks; the *previous* week, he wanted to sell cars only.

price
noun
the amount of money asked for to sell something
We couldn't buy the coat; the *price* was too high.

pride
noun
a feeling of value or worth
She paints beautiful pictures, and she takes great *pride* in her work.

prince
noun
a son of a king, queen, or prince
They prepared the *prince* to become the king after his father.

princess
noun
a daughter of a king, queen, or prince
The *princess* became queen when the king, her father, died.

principal
noun
a head of a school
Our school *principal* talked to the new teachers and students.
adjective
main
In this plain, the *principal* food grown is wheat.

principle
noun
a rule, an ideal
He has many good *principles*; one of them is that he is very honest.

print
noun
1. *letters or words printed on paper or some other material*

I couldn't read the story, because the *print* was too small.
2. *a mark left when something presses on something else*
They left their *prints* on the sand when they walked near the shore.
verb
put letters or words on paper by using a tool or a machine
The manager *printed* the name of his company on all his envelopes.

prison
noun
a building where people who do something wrong are locked up
The thief spent five years in the city *prison*; his family could visit him there once a week.

prisoner
noun
a person who is in prison
The *prisoner* escaped from the prison, but he was caught by the police before he got too far.

private
adjective
personal, not public
I didn't want anyone to hear what we were saying; it was a *private* matter between us.

prize
noun
something one receives for doing something very well
Ten students ran in the race; the first three received *prizes*; the first *prize* went to a friend of mine.

probable
adjective
likely
Rain is very *probable* today; there are many dark clouds in the sky.

probably
adverb
likely, perhaps
It will *probably* rain today; there are many dark clouds in the sky.

problem
noun
a difficult situation
They have a *problem* with their son; he doesn't study and he doesn't do much; they don't know what to do.

proceed
verb
go on, continue
The speaker stopped talking for a moment to drink some water; then he *proceeded* with his talk.

process
noun
the steps followed in doing things
He wanted to wash the dishes in the kitchen; in the *process* of doing that, he broke one dish.

produce
verb: producing, produced, produced
make something
Michigan *produces* different kinds of cars.

product
noun
a thing made or produced
Good companies have good *products*, but their prices are high.

production
noun
the act of producing or making
Detroit is known for its *production* of cars.

professional
adjective
done by an expert
Our clock stopped running; we asked a very clever man to fix it; he did a *professional* job; he is an expert, and he fixed it well.

professor
noun
a rank of a college or university teacher
The book we used in class was written by

one of my university *professors.*

profit
noun
gain
He bought the car for $2,000 and sold it for $2,150; he made a *profit* of $150.
verb
gain
You don't *profit* much if you don't work hard.

program
noun
1. *a plan*
The guide has a full *program* for us today; he is taking us to the zoo and to two museums.
2. *a list of things that will be happening*
We bought a *program* as we walked into the hall to see the play; the *program* had the names of the actors and something about each act.

progress
noun
improvement
She is making *progress* in her English lessons; now she can speak and write.

progress
verb
improve
She is *progressing* in her English lessons; now she can speak and write well.

promise
noun
something said that should be followed
He made a *promise* to come early, and he did. He kept his *promise.*
verb: promising, promised, promised
say something that should be kept and followed
He *promised* to come early, but he didn't; he broke his promise.

prompt
adjective
on time
He is very *prompt* in his appointments; he is never late.

promptly
adverb
on time
They opened the meeting very *promptly* at 8:00 a.m.

proof
noun
evidence that something is true
We have *proof* that John was at the meeting; five people saw him there.

proper
adjective
correct, right
What he wore to dinner was not *proper*; he didn't have a jacket on.

property
noun: properties
1. *land and buildings*
He owns some *property* in the city.
2. *what one owns*
He feels that the bicycle is his *property*, not his brother's.

prophet
noun
a messenger of God
Abraham was a *prophet.*

propose
verb: proposing, proposed, proposed
1. *suggest*
She *proposed* to go with us to see the principal; we let her.
2. *ask (someone) to marry*
The young man *proposed* to the girl; she accepted; they are getting married next summer.

protect
verb
keep (someone or something) safe
My coat *protected* me from the cold. The guard *protected* the palace.

protection
noun
the act of keeping someone or something safe
A coat is good *protection* from the wind and cold.

protest
noun
an expression showing what someone does not like
Some people marched in *protest* against higher prices.

protest
verb
express dislike of something
The people *protested* when prices went up; they didn't like that.

proud
adjective
feeling good about oneself or someone else
The children received high grades and reports in school; their father was *proud* of them.

prove
verb: proving, proved, proved
show that something is right
They didn't believe that the boy was in school yesterday, but he *proved* it; two teachers saw him.

provide
verb: providing, provided, provided
give (something) as needed
They *provided* the guests with food and a place to sleep.

province
noun
a part of a country
Canada has many *provinces*; one of them is Ontario.

provision
noun
the act of supplying
The camp had tents and beds; we were only worried about the *provision* of covers for the beds.

public
noun
the people
If our newspaper has the story, the *public* will know it tomorrow.
adjective
common, not private
The city has a *public* garden; everybody can go there.

publish
verb
put in print and spread
The newspaper *published* the news about the king's visit here.

pudding
verb
a soft dessert
She offered us rice *pudding* for dessert.

pull
noun
a draw towards oneself
If you can't open the door easily, give it a *pull.*
verb
draw towards oneself, opposite of push
The carriage was *pulled* by two horses.

pump

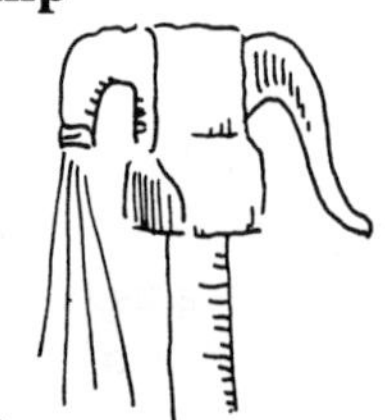

noun
an instrument that draws or pushes a liquid
They used a *pump* to open the closed water pipe.
verb
draw a liquid towards or away from something
They *pumped* water out of the well to drink.

punish
verb
do something to somebody for something wrong done
The boy was *punished* for stealing some money; he paid a fine and was told to stay at home for three days.

punishment
noun
something one is to do for doing something wrong
The boy was punished for stealing some money; his *punishment* was to stay at home for three days.

pupil
noun
student, young student
She has twenty-four *pupils* in the fourth grade: twelve boys and twelve girls.

purchase
noun
a buy
The car he has was a very good *purchase*; the car is in good condition, and the price was low.
verb: purchasing, purchased, purchased.
buy
We *purchased* a few books from the new bookstore; the prices were good.

pure
adjective
clean, not mixed with anything else
They wanted to drink *pure* water; so they boiled it.

purely
adverb
only, completely
She gave everything she had to the poor; she did that *purely* because she loved them.

purple
noun
a color
You can get *purple* if you mix red and blue.
adjective
a color
She has a *purple* dress.

purpose
noun
reason
She went to the library for one *purpose* only: to read.

purse

noun
a small container for money
She puts her money in a black *purse.*

pursue
verb: pursuing, pursued, pursued
follow, go after
She *pursued* her studies until she became a nurse.

push
verb
put force away from oneself, opposite of pull
She *pushed* her baby's carriage up the street.

put
verb:putting, put, put
place
She *put* her books in her school bag before she left the house.

put on
verb: putting on, put on, put on
wear
She *put on* a beautiful dress for the party.

puzzle
noun
a difficult matter to explain
I gave him a *puzzle* to solve; he couldn't do it; it was difficult for him.
verb: puzzling, puzzled, puzzled
make difficult to understand
The situation in their home *puzzles* me; I don't know what to do about it.

pyramid

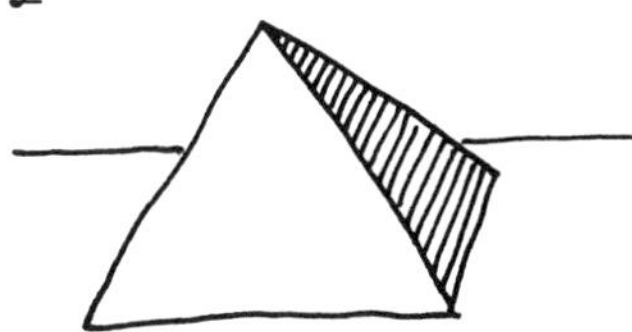

noun
a structure that has a square bottom and a pointed top
The children built a *pyramid* in the sand on the beach.

Qq

qualification
noun
ability (for something)
They took him for the job, because he had the right *qualifications* for it; they knew he would do well in it.

qualify
verb: qualifying, qualified, qualified
make (someone) able to do something
She took a special course in nursing to *qualify* her to work in that hospital. The course she took *qualified* her for the job.

quality
noun: qualities
the degree of how good or bad a thing is
The blue car is more expensive than the red car; it is of a better *quality*.

quantity
noun: quantities
amount
We have a big *quantity* of sugar at home; it will take us a long time to use it all.

quarrel
noun
a fight
The two brothers had a little *quarrel* over the cake; in the end, they divided it between them.
verb
fight
They *quarreled* over the piece of cake; then they divided it between them.

quarter
noun
1. *one fourth*
The four children divided the apple among them; each one of them had a *quarter*.
2. *an area in a city or town*
They live in a rich *quarter* of the city.

queen
noun
a female head of a country, feminine of king
The *queen* sat on her throne and spoke to her government.

queer
adjective
strange
He acts in a *queer* way; I don't know if he is normal.

question
noun
a language form that asks for an answer
The teacher asked me three *questions*, and I knew the correct answers to them.
verb
raise doubt about
He told us his story, but we *questioned* some of the details; we did not think they were correct.

queue
noun
line
They stood in a *queue* to get into the music hall.
verb: queuing, queued, queued
stand in line
The people *queued* up to buy tickets for the play.

quick
adjective
fast
Joe is very *quick* in his answers; he gives you his answers as soon as he hears the questions.

quickly
adverb
fast, in a quick way
When they saw the fire in the house, they *quickly* ran out to the street.

quiet
adjective
without noise

I like a *quiet* library; I can read and write in it easily; I don't like noise when I'm working.

quietly
adverb
in a quiet way, without making noise
The students sat *quietly* in the library; I heard no noise when I was in it.

quit
verb: quitting, quit, quit
leave
He *quit* his job in Virginia; he is going to live in Michigan.

quite
adverb
to a certain degree
It is *quite* cold today; wear your coat. I know him *quite* well; he used to live near us.

quiz
noun: quizzes
a small test
The teacher gave us a short *quiz* in mathematics in class; I finished it in fifteen minutes.
verb: quizzing, quizzed, quizzed
give a small test
The teacher *quizzed* us on the lesson we had last week; I answered the questions well.

quorum
noun
the number of people needed to hold a meeting
The president could not open the meeting before we had a *quorum.*

quotation
noun
the words taken from somebody's speech or writing
I read an interesting book and found some interesting *quotations* in it that I can use in my next report in class.

quote
verb: quoting, quoted, quoted
use someone's words
I read an interesting book last week; some of the ideas and words were excellent; I am *quoting* a short paragraph from the book in my report to the class next week.

Rr

rabbit

noun
a small animal with long ears
Some people keep *rabbits* in their gardens. Some people like *rabbit* meat.

race
noun
1. *a running contest*
My friend is running now; he is practicing for the *race*. He won the *race* last year.
2. *people belonging to the same country or color or origin*
In my city, all the people of different *races* live nicely together.
verb: racing, raced, raced
1. *run in a running contest*
My friend is *racing* with seven other runners; I think he will win the race.
2. *hurry, rush*
He is always in a hurry; he is *racing* to work and *racing* back home all the time.

racket

noun
an instrument for hitting balls

Tennis players and badminton players use *rackets* when they play.

radar
noun
an electric device that sees objects
The police use *radar* equipment to catch drivers who drive too fast.

radiator

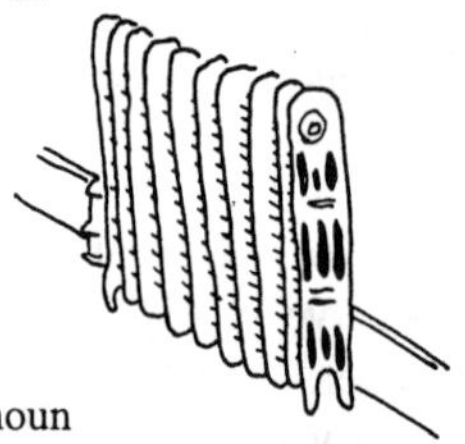

noun
an electric heater that uses oil
They have a *radiator* in every room to keep them warm in winter.

radio

noun
a device that receives sounds from a station
We listened to the news on our *radio* at home.
verb: radioing, radioed, radioed
send a message by radio
The policeman *radioed* his station and told them that he had caught a thief.

rage
noun
a strong anger
The mother went into a *rage* when her child walked out into the street alone.

raid
noun
a sudden attack
There was a *raid* on the camp outside the city; some thieves stole all they could carry from the camp.
verb
attack suddenly
The thieves *raided* the camp and stole many things.

rail
noun

1. *a long bar to hold or hang things on*
The old woman held the *rail* as she walked down the steps.

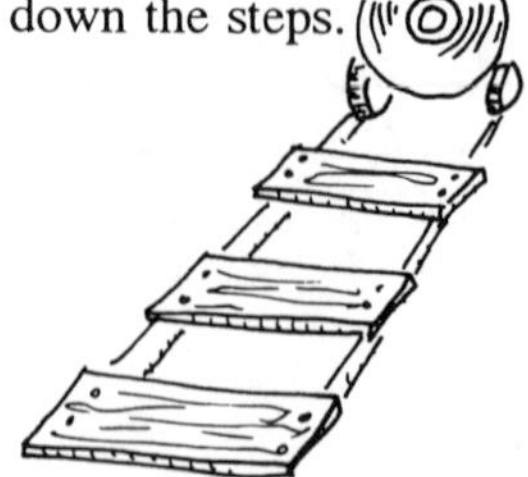

2. *a long bar for trains to move on*
Trains run on *rails*.

railway
noun
a line for trains to move on
There is a *railway* from New York to Boston.
You go to a *railway* station to catch a train.

rain
noun
the drops of water that come from the clouds
The *rain* we had made all the roads very wet.
verb
let drops of water fall from the clouds
It is not *raining* now; there are no clouds in the sky.

rain check
noun
a ticket for an activity that one can use at a later date
Because of bad weather, there was no football game last Sunday. People with tickets got *rain checks*.
They invited me to dinner, but because I was busy, I joked and said I would take a *rain check*!

raincoat
noun
a coat to protect a person from the rain

He didn't get wet, because he was wearing a *raincoat.*

rainy
adjective: rainier, rainiest
with rain
Today is sunny, but yesterday it rained very hard; it was *rainy.*

raise
noun
an increase
In her second year of work, she received a *raise* in pay; she was happy.
verb: raising, raised, raised
1. *bring up*
They *raised* their children to love people.
2. *gather*
He *raised* a lot of money in his job.
3. *build*
The company *raised* a new office building.
4. *lift*
Raise your hand before you speak in class.

raisin
noun
a dried grape
She put *raisins* in the cake she baked.

ran
See **run**.

ranch
noun
a field to raise cattle
The man from Texas has horses on his *ranch.*

rang
See **ring.**

range
noun
1. *a number of things in a row*
There are many mountain *ranges* in the world.
2. *a stove*
She cooked the food in a *range*.

rank
noun
a level or grade
The army captain moved up in time to the *rank* of general.

rapid
adjective
fast
He is very *rapid* in his work; he finishes it in a very short time.

rare
adjective
1. *seldom found, not common*
Diamonds are *rare*; that is why they are expensive.
2. *not cooked long*
Some people like their steaks well done, and some like them *rare*. When the steak is *rare*, it is red in color.

rarely
adverb
seldom, not often
I *rarely* see him in the library; he reads and studies at home.

rat

noun
a small animal with a long tail
Rats are afraid of cats, because cats can catch them and kill them.

rate
noun
an amount paid for a length of time
These workers work at the *rate* of twelve dollars an hour.

rather
adverb
1. *preferably*
I would *rather* play a game than watch that film.
2. *quite*
He arrived *rather* early to the meeting.
3. *instead*
She didn't go to the doctor; *rather*, she went back to school.

raw
adjective
not cooked
She likes to eat *raw* fruits and vegetables.

ray
noun
a line or beam of light
Look at the *rays* of the sun shining on the water.

reach
verb
get to
He is very tall; he can *reach* the top shelf of the cupboard.

read
verb: reading, read, read
1. *understand something written or printed*
She *read* a story and enjoyed it.
2. *say aloud what is written or printed*
She *read* us a story from her favorite story book.

readily
adverb
without hesitation
I asked them to go with us; they *readily* accepted.

ready
adjective: readier, readiest
prepared
They are *ready* to leave now; they have their coats on.

real
adjective
actual
In a zoo, you can see *real* animals.

realize
verb: realizing, realized, realized
1. *understand*
I *realize* that you are busy, but may I ask you a question?
2. *reach, fulfill, obtain*
He always wanted to become a doctor. After studying and working hard, he *realized* his dream.

really
adverb
actually
I saw a movie last night; I liked it very much; it was *really* very good.

rear
noun
the back
I sat in the front of the class; my friend sat in the *rear*.
verb
bring up
They *reared* their children to like music and help others.

reason
noun
cause
She had a *reason* for not going to school; she was sick.
verb
think logically
They *reasoned* that if they spent their money on travel, they wouldn't have enough for a car.

recall
verb
remember
The old men talked about their school days; they *recalled* many stories.

receive
verb: receiving, received, received
get
I *received* a letter from my cousin; it arrived yesterday.

recent
adjective
of a time past that is near the present
Their wedding was very *recent*; it happened last week.

recently
adverb
at a time past that is near the present
They were with us for a long time, and they left

recently; they left two days ago.

reception
noun
a social party or meeting
We invited our friends to an afternoon *reception* to meet my cousin who arrived here recently.

recess
noun
a break, a time for rest
The workers have a thirty-minute *recess* for coffee.

reckless
adjective
in a hurry and without thinking
He is a *reckless* person; he is not careful, and he doesn't look where he is going.

recognize
verb: recognizing, recognized, recognized
know
I had not seen her for many years, but I *recognized* her as soon as I met her.

record

noun
a disc
I listened to a music *record* at home.

record
verb
put on disc or tape
She *recorded* her voice on tape and listened to it later.

recover
verb
get back what was lost
He lost a lot in his business last year, but this year he *recovered* his loss and made a profit.

rectangle

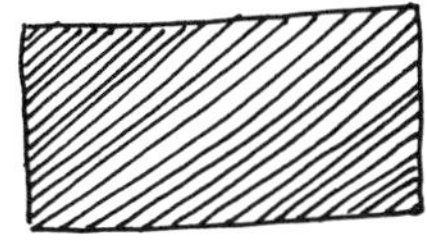

noun
a shape that has 90° angles, four sides, and whose length is longer than its width
A football field, a basketball court, and a tennis court are *rectangles.*

recur
verb: recurring, recurred, recurred
happen again
If you don't correct your mistakes, they may *recur*.

recycle
verb: recycling, recycled, recycled
separate paper, glass, metal, and plastic so that they can be used again
We are *recycling* our waste products now; it is a good thing to do.

red
noun
a color
She likes *red*; she always wears *red.*
adjective: redder, reddest
a color
She has *red* roses in a vase and a *red* dress in her closet.

reduce
verb: reducing, reduced, reduced
make less
She wants to *reduce* her weight from 150 pounds to 135 pounds.

refer
verb: referring, referred, referred
send or go to someone or something
I didn't know the answer to her question; so I *referred* her to the teacher. When I don't know a word, I *refer* to a dictionary.

reflect
verb
1. *think*

They asked me about the film. I *reflected* on it for a moment and then I gave them my opinion.
2. *send back*
A mirror *reflects* any light that shines on it.

reform
noun
improvement
The government is bringing about some *reform* in health practices.
verb
improve
The government is trying to *reform* health practices.

refrigerator

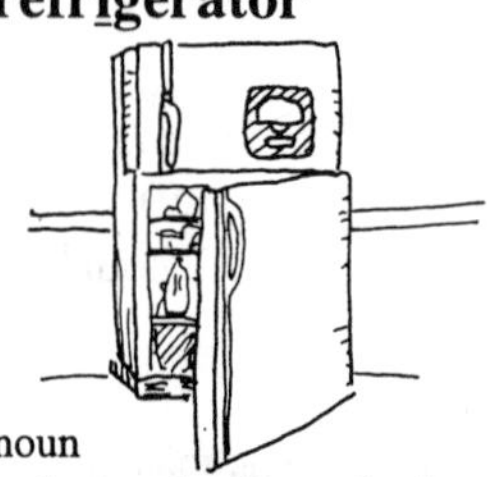

noun
a device that keeps food and drink cold and makes ice
Milk, meat, fresh fruits and vegetables should be kept in the *refrigerator*.

refuse
verb: refusing, refused, refused
not to accept
She *refused* to pay for the radio, because it was broken.

regard
verb
consider
We *regard* our good friends as family.

regarding
preposition
in connection with
Regarding the weather, I think it is too cold to go out without a coat.

register
verb
put one's name down for something
The college is *registering* new students next week.

regret
verb: regretting, regretted, regretted
be sorry for something
Thank you very much for the dinner invitation, but I *regret* I shall not be in town. I'm sorry to miss your dinner.

regular
adjective
1. *normal*
The taxi driver charged you the *regular* price; that's what we always pay.
2. *not changing*
He is very *regular* in his work; he always comes on time and works well.

relate
verb: relating, related, related
see or make a connection
She asked about the weather; he asked about the clothes to wear; I *related* the questions together.

related
See **relate** also.
adjective
belonging to the same family
She is *related* to him; he is her uncle.

relation
noun
1. *connection*
There is a *relation* between quality and price.
2. *a member of the same family*
All the people here are *relations* of mine: they are uncles, aunts, and cousins of mine.

relative
noun
a member of the same family
This is a *relative* of mine; he is my cousin.
adjective
seen in relation to (something)
Rich and poor are *relative* words; they mean different things to different people at different times.

release
verb: releasing, released, released
let go, let free
The judge *released* the prisoner after he had served two years in prison.

relief
noun
help when there is a problem
She had a bad headache, but the medicine she took gave her some *relief.*

relieve
verb: relieving, relieved, relieved
help when there is a problem
The medicine she took *relieved* her pain when she had a headache.

religion
noun
a system of faith
Judaism, Christianity, and Islam are three of the *religions* of the world.

religious
adjective
related to religion
The Bible and the Koran are *religious* books. My aunt is a *religious* person; she prays regularly.

remain
verb
stay
The students *remained* in their seats after the bell rang.

remainder
noun
that which is left
If you subtract 5 from 8, the *remainder* is 3.

remark
noun
a comment or statement
I made a *remark* about the cold room, and they closed the window.
verb
make a comment or statement
I *remarked* about the cold room we were in, and they closed the window.

remarkable
adjective
deserving notice
This boy is *remarkable*; he is only six years old and he is playing tennis like a champion.

remedy
noun: remedies
cure
The medicine she took was a good *remedy* for her illness; she got well.

remember
verb
bring back to mind
I forgot his name; I couldn't *remember* it; I couldn't call him by name.

remind
verb
make (someone) remember
She had forgotten my name; so I *reminded* her of it; now I hope she remembers it.

remove
verb: removing, removed, removed
take away
I had books on a shelf; I wanted to put a picture there; so I *removed* the books and put the picture in their place.

renew
verb
1. *stretch the time for (something)*
I *renewed* my membership in the club for another year.
2. *replace*
We *renewed* our beds at home; we bought new ones.

rent
noun
money paid for the use of something for a time
We paid our house *rent*

for the month yesterday.
verb
pay for the use of something for a time
We *rented* a house for a year before we bought our own.

repair
noun
fixing
Their television is not working; it needs *repair.*
verb
fix
They *repaired* their television when it stopped working.

repeat
verb
do something again
I didn't hear his name when he gave it, but when he *repeated* it, I heard it well.

repetition
noun
doing something again
She sang so nicely that the people asked for a *repetition* of her last song.

reply
noun: replies
an answer
I tried to phone my friend twice, but there was no *reply.*
verb: replying, replied, replied
answer
The teacher asked the student to *reply* to his question.

report
noun
an oral or written statement on a subject
The students gave a *report* on their visit to the museum.
verb
give an oral or written statement on a subject
The students *reported* in class on their visit to the museum.

reporter
noun
a person who reports
The newspaper received the news about the war from a *reporter* who was with the soldiers.

represent
verb
1. *act for someone else*
The principal *represented* the school at a meeting of educators.
2. *be an example of*
That picture *represents* the wonderful things you can see in the country.

representative
noun
a person who acts for someone or a group
Every country has a *representative* at the United Nations.
adjective
be an example
This picture is *representative* of what the artist can do.

reputation
noun
the public view of a person's character
She has a good *reputation* because she is good and behaves very well.

request
noun
demand
The *request* she made was granted; she wanted to sit in the front row.
verb
make a demand
She *requested* a seat in the front row; she was given what she wanted.

require
verb: requiring, required, required
need
Passing courses *requires* hard work.

requirement
noun
a need

The *requirement* for passing is hard work.

rescue
noun
an act of saving from danger
The *rescue* of the animals from the fire was a wonderful action.
verb: rescuing, rescued, rescued
save from danger
The animals were *rescued* from the fire.

reserve
verb: reserving, reserved, reserved
ask to have (something) held
We *reserved* a table for six persons at our favorite restaurant.

resolve
verb: resolving, resolved, resolved
decide
She has *resolved* to continue her studies; she wants to become a teacher.

respect
noun
high regard
People have *respect* for honesty.
verb
give high regard to
We *respect* honest people.

responsibility
noun: responsibilities
a duty
We wash the dishes in turn at home. Today it is my brother's *responsibility* to wash them.

responsible
adjective
able to carry out one's duties
My uncle is *responsible* for all the activities in his company.

rest
noun
1. *remainder*
He had $10; he spent 6 dollars on a book; the *rest* he used to buy a sandwich.
2. *comfort by not working*
He worked for three hours; then he took a little *rest*.
verb
get comfort by not working
He *rested* for half an hour after working for five hours.

restaurant
noun
a place where one can sit and buy food to eat
My favorite *restaurant* has very good fish and chicken dishes.

restore
verb: restoring, restored, restored
bring back to a good condition
After resting and taking the right medicines, his health was *restored*; he was quite ill, but now he is healthy again.

result
noun
something that happens as an effect
He studied and worked very hard; the *result* was good; he passed.
verb
cause an effect
His hard work *resulted* in success.

retain
verb
keep
The judge allowed him to *retain* his driver's license even though he had two speeding tickets.

retire
verb: retiring, retired, retired
1. *leave one's work*
She worked for 25 years for one company, and she *retired* this year. Now she wants to travel and read.
2. *go to bed*
He *retired* at 9:00 p.m. because he worked hard all day.

retreat
verb
move back
The enemy *retreated* in the face of a strong attack.

return
noun
the act of coming back
She was away for a year; upon her *return*, we had a party for her.
verb
come or go back
He went to work early in the morning and *returned* late in the evening.

reveal
verb
show, let (something) show
She baked a surprise for us and covered it up; when she removed the cover, she *revealed* a chocolate cake.

review
noun
the act of going over (something)
The teacher gave us a good *review* of our lessons to prepare us for the test.
verb
go over (something)
We *reviewed* the lesson in class before our test.

revolution
noun
1. *a very big change*
We learned about the French *Revolution* in our history class.
2. *going around*
The *revolution* of the earth around the sun takes one year.

revolve
verb: revolving, revolved, revolved
go around
The earth *revolves* around the sun.

reward
noun
something given for something done
The student with the highest grades received a prize as a *reward.* The thief got his *reward*: he was put in prison.
verb
give something for something done
The clever student was *rewarded* for his fine work.

rib

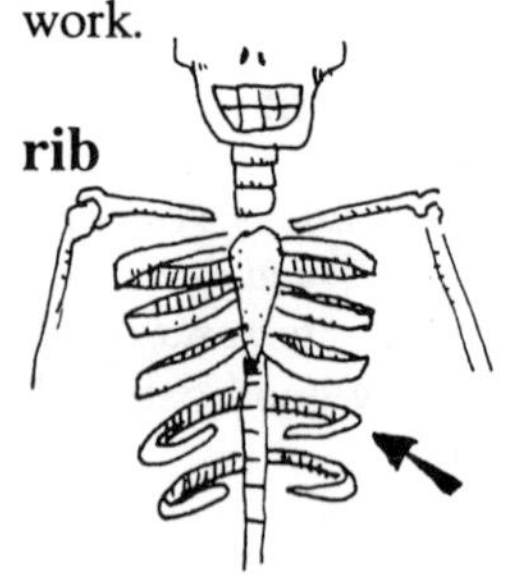

noun
one of the bones of the chest
Our *ribs* protect our hearts and other parts of our bodies.

ribbon

noun
a long and narrow piece of cloth used to tie around hair or presents
She has a blue *ribbon* in her hair. All the presents were wrapped with colored paper and *ribbons.*

rice
noun
a grain that people cook and eat
Some people like potatoes with their meat; I like *rice.*

rich
adjective
not poor
Rich people can buy very expensive things.

rid
verb: ridding, rid, ridden
relieve
The doctors in the city were working very hard to *rid* the people of a bad disease.

ridden
See **rid** and **ride**.

ride
noun
the act of going in a car or bus or on a bicycle
My brother was planning to drive to work; I asked him to give me a *ride* to school on his way.
verb: riding, rode, ridden
She *rides* her bicycle to school every day.

ridge

noun
a number of hills in a row
The view from the top of the *ridge* was beautiful; we could see the valley and the sea below.

rifle
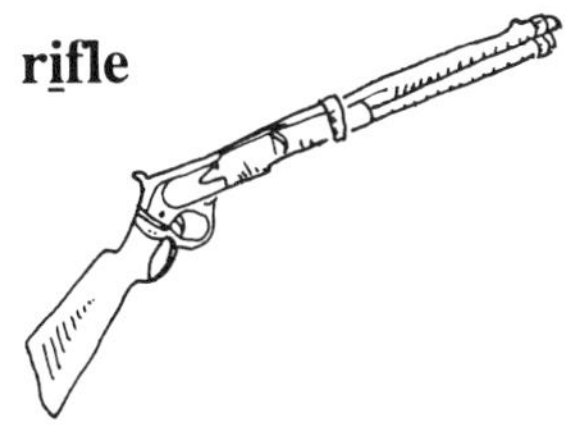
noun
a gun that one puts on a shoulder before firing
The hunter used a *rifle* when he went hunting.

right
noun
one of two sides: left and right
I stood in the middle for a picture; my sister was on my left, and my brother was on my *right*.
adjective
correct
I answered all five questions on the test; four of my answers were *right* and one was wrong.

ring
noun
1. *the sound of a bell*
Our door bell has a musical *ring*; it sounds like a tune.
2. *something one wears on a finger*
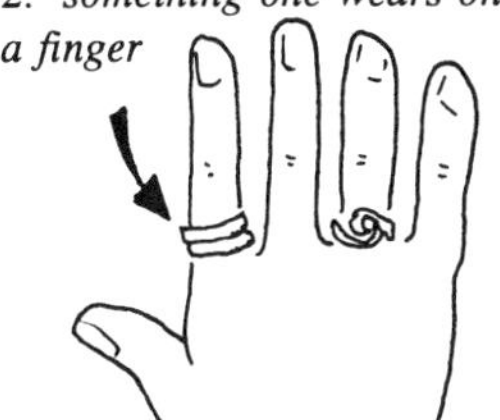
She has a lovely gold *ring* on her finger.
3. *something round*
We danced in a *ring* around the fire.
verb: ringing, rang, rung
make a sound like a bell
The students went to class when the bell *rang*.

ripe
adjective
ready to eat
We picked the *ripe* oranges from the tree; we did not touch the green ones.

ripen
verb
become or get ready to eat
I like fruits to *ripen* on the trees before we pick them.

rise
noun
going up, becoming higher
The doctor was not happy with the *rise* in the patient's temperature.
verb: rising, rose, risen
1. *go up*
The price of cars *rose* this year.
2. *get up*
He sat in his chair for an hour; then he *rose* to open the door.

risk
noun
danger
There is a greater *risk* of losing your money if you are not careful.
verb
face a danger
He *risked* losing money by buying a bad business.

risky
adjective: riskier, riskiest

capable of being in danger
Doing business with people who are not honest is very *risky*.

rival
noun
a person or thing trying to get ahead
The best runner in our school has a new *rival*; he is a new student who runs very fast.

river
noun
a body of water that flows down
It is dangerous to swim in *rivers*.

road
noun
a way, a street, a highway
The *roads* in our city are very wide.

roar
noun
a loud sound
We heard the *roar* of lions in the zoo.
verb
make a loud sound
Lions *roar* when they are hungry.

roast
noun
a piece of meat that is cooked in an oven
We had a lamb *roast* for dinner last night.
verb
cook meat in an oven
We *roasted* a leg of lamb in the oven for dinner.

rob
verb: robbing, robbed, robbed
steal from (someone or some place)
Thieves went into a store last week and *robbed* it; they stole some food and some money.

robber
noun
a person who steals
The three *robbers* who stole money from a bank last month were caught and put in prison.

robbery
noun: robberies
an act of stealing
A store had a *robbery* last week; robbers went in and stole some food and some money.

robe
noun

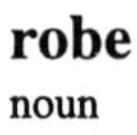

1. *a loose outer garment worn at home*
She wore her morning *robe* when she came to the breakfast table.

2. *an official garment*
The judges wore their *robes* in court.

robot

noun
a machine that acts like a person
The *robot* in the store walked around without hitting anything; it also said some things.

rock

noun
a hard stone
Driving up the mountain, we saw very big *rocks*.
verb
move (something) in one direction and then in the other

She *rocked* her baby's cradle to make her sleep.

rocket

noun

a bomb or a device that is shot up over a long distance

The fighter plane shot *rockets* that hit a tank. Some *rockets* with cameras are going around the earth.

rocky

adjective: rockier, rockiest

full of rocks

The mountain we climbed was very *rocky*; we saw rocks everywhere.

rod

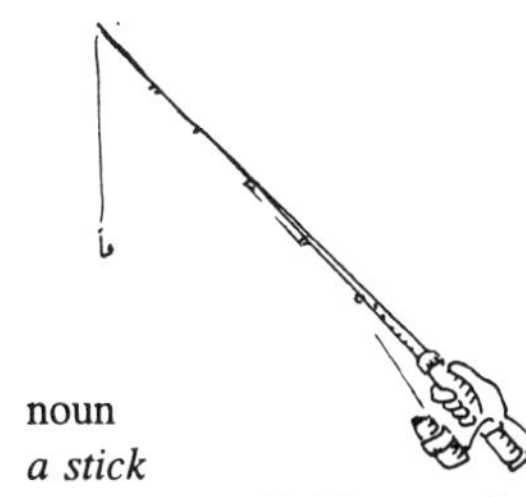

noun

a stick

He uses a fishing *rod* when he goes fishing.

rode

See **ride.**

roll

noun

a round bundle (of something)

I bought a *roll* of paper towels.

verb

turn around on the ground

Some rocks *rolled* down the hill to the road below; it was dangerous for drivers.

roof

noun

the top outer part of a building

Some large buildings have a swimming pool on the *roof.*

room

noun

1. *a part of a house or an apartment*

We have five *rooms* in our house. The dining *room* is one of them.

2. *space*

I couldn't enter the car; there was no *room* for me; it was full.

root

noun

1. *the bottom part of a plant that is not seen*

The old tree in our garden spread its *roots* very far.

2. *source*

Money is the *root* of his problems; when he has money, he gets in trouble.

rope

noun

a thick and strong string

They used heavy *ropes* when they climbed the high mountains.

rose

See **rise** also.

noun

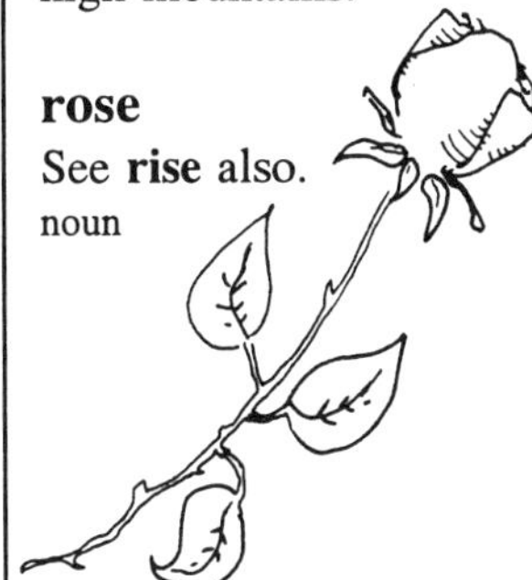

a flower

She has red and white *roses* in her garden.

rough

adjective

1. *not smooth*

His hands became very *rough* after he worked in the garden for a long time.

2. *not calm*

The wind was blowing, and the sea became very *rough.*

round
adjective
1. *like a ball*

Tennis balls are *round.*
2. *like a circle*

Their dining room table is *round.*

route
noun
way, road
One of the *routes* we took to the farm had heavy traffic.

row
noun
a line
We stood in three *rows* in front of the school.
verb
use oars to move a boat on the water
When I go to the beach, I like to rent a boat and *row* it.

royal
adjective
1. *related to a king or queen*
The queen lived in a *royal* palace.
2. *good for a king or queen*
We had a *royal* dinner last night; it was truly grand.

rub
verb: rubbing, rubbed, rubbed
push one surface on another
She *rubbed* her leg where it hurt her. We *rub* the soap on our hands when we wash them.

rubber
noun

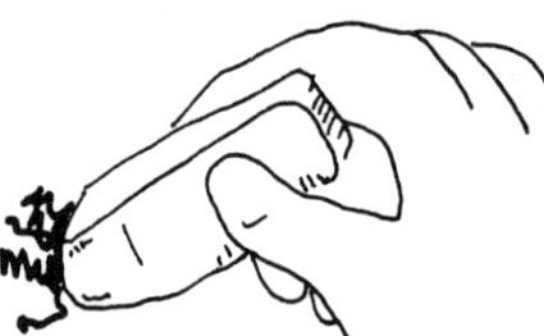

1. *an eraser*
My pencil has a *rubber* on top.
2. *a kind of material used for shoes and tires*
His shoes are made of *rubber*; they are good for walking in the snow.

rude
adjective
not polite
We don't like him, because he is *rude*; he uses bad words and a loud voice when he speaks to others.

rug

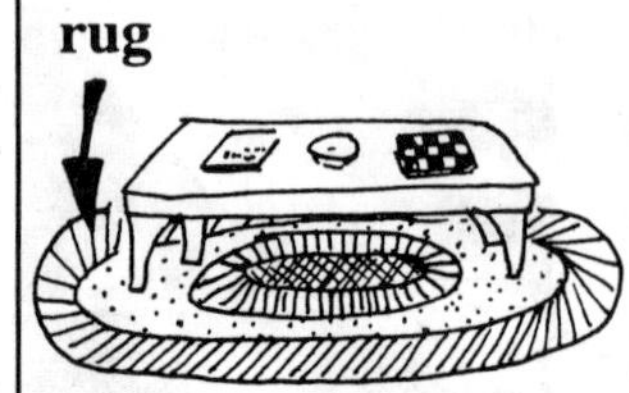

noun
a piece of fabric to put on the floor
They have a wool *rug* in their living room.

rugged
adjective
rough
The land was *rugged*; it was not easy to drive on it.

ruin
noun
part of an old building or structure
There are many Roman *ruins* in different parts of the world.
verb
destroy
The bombs *ruined* five buildings; now people can't live in them.

rule
noun
a law
Drivers must obey all the traffic *rules* of the country.
verb: ruling, ruled, ruled

govern
The chief *ruled* the camp where he and his men lived; he gave all the orders.

ruler

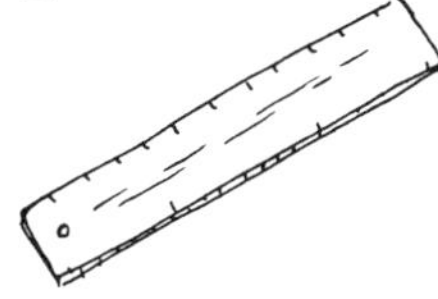

noun
1. *a flat stick that has measurements on it*
I used a *ruler* to draw straight lines.
2. *a person who governs*
The chief was the *ruler* of his tribe.

run
noun
the act of running
The students wanted to get the ball in the field; they made a *run* for it.
verb: running, ran, run
move fast on the legs
We *ran* to class, because we thought we were late.

rung
See **ring**.

runner
noun
a person who runs
My friend is the fastest *runner* in school; he always wins the races.

running
See **run**.

rush
noun
hurry
He is in a *rush* to get to work; he is late.
verb
hurry, move fast
He *rushed* to work; he was late.

rye
noun
a grain
Some bread is made of *rye*; some bread is made of wheat.

Ss

sack

noun
a big bag
I put all the fruits I bought in a *sack* and brought them home.
verb
fire, make (someone) leave work
The manager didn't like one of his workers; so he *sacked* him; the worker had to get another job.

sacred
adjective
holy
The Bible and the Koran are *sacred* books.

sacrifice
noun
a loss
The time I spent trying to help them was a *sacrifice*; I could do nothing, and my time was wasted.
verb: sacrificing, sacrificed, sacrificed
spend something and lose it for a purpose
I *sacrificed* three hours of my time trying to help them.

sad
adjective: sadder, saddest
not happy
He was *sad* to learn that his friend had been killed in the war.

saddle

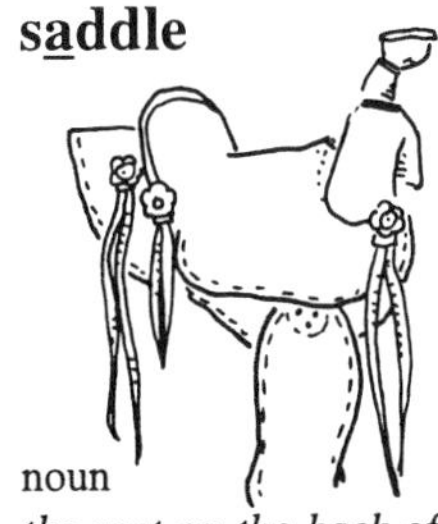

noun
the seat on the back of an animal for a person to ride on
Saddles make riding on animals much more comfortable.

safe

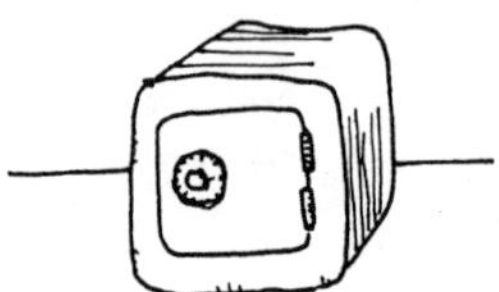

noun
a strong container to keep valuable things
She put her rings and necklaces in a *safe* in the bank.
adjective
not in danger
There was a car accident on the road, but my friend was *safe* in a car ten yards away.

safety
noun
being away from danger
There was a strong storm outside, but the parents were happy about the *safety* of their children at home.

said
See **say**.

sail

noun
a piece of cloth used on a boat to help it move on the water
The *sails* they had didn't help them, because there was no wind blowing.
verb
move on the water
Their ship *sailed* from one port to another.

sailor

noun
a person who works on a ship
The *sailors* went on land when their ship arrived in the harbor.

salad
noun
a side dish of vegetables (and fruits)
She put lettuce, tomatoes, and cucumbers in her *salads.*

salary
noun: salaries
pay for work
His *salary* as a teacher is enough for him and his family.

sale
noun
1. *the act of selling*
They could not move to a new house before the *sale* of their old one.
2. *an occasion when prices are brought down*
The store I go to had a *sale* on shoes; the prices were low, and I bought two pairs for the price of one.

salt
noun
a seasoning for food that comes from sea water
I put *salt* and pepper on my food.
verb
use salt as a seasoning
I usually *salt* my food after I taste it.

same
adjective
not different
My friend and I went to different libraries, but we borrowed the *same* book to read.

sand
noun
very small particles found on beaches and in deserts
The children played in the *sand* and swam in the sea when we went to the beach.

sandwich

noun
two slices of bread with some food between them
She asked for a cheese *sandwich* for lunch.
verb
put in the middle
The three of us sat in the back of the car; I was *sandwiched* between my friends.

sang
See **sing**.

sank
See **sink**.

sat
See **sit**.

satisfaction
noun
a feeling of pleasure
She wanted her name to appear on the teacher's special list. When it did, you could see the *satisfaction* on her face; she was happy.

Saturday
noun
a day of the week
Saturday comes after Friday and before Sunday.

saucer
noun

1. *a small plate for a cup*
She put the tea cups on *saucers* before she served her guests.
2. *a vehicle that looks like a plate and flies in the air*

Do you think there are flying *saucers* coming from outer space?

savage
noun
a rough and wild person
He acted like a *savage* when he hit his dog and horse.

save
verb: saving, saved, saved
put away for use in the future
Every month she *saves* some money; she is planning to buy a car next year.

savings
noun
the amounts saved for future use
She used a part of her *savings* to buy a car.

saw
See **see** also.
noun
an instrument used to cut wood and iron
A carpenter uses a *saw* to cut his wood into smaller pieces.

say
verb: saying, said, said
speak, pronounce
She *said* something in Spanish; I didn't understand it.

scale
noun

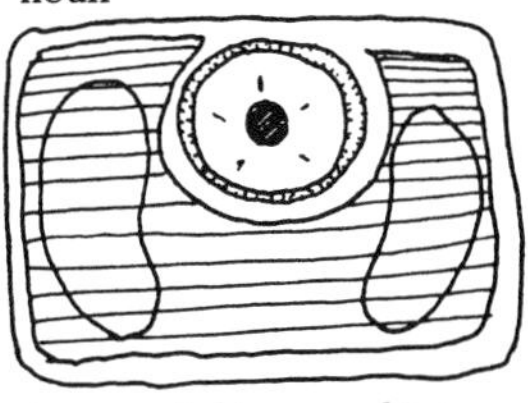

1. *a weighing machine*
She stood on her *scale* in the bathroom; she was happy that her weight was down.
2. *a measure of something*
The weather today is not very good; on a *scale* of one to ten, I would give it a four.

scar

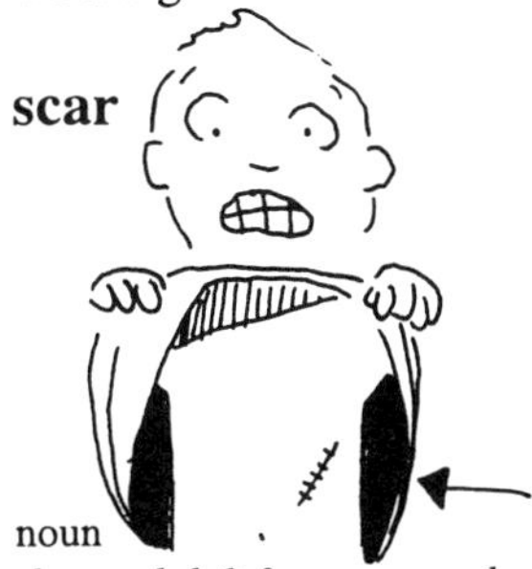

noun
the mark left from a wound

He still has a *scar* on his hand; he wounded it last month.

scarce
adjective
rare
It didn't rain for three months, and water was very *scarce*.

scarcely
adverb
near not, barely
We had *scarcely* enough water when it didn't rain

scare
noun
a feeling of fear
She had a *scare* last night when the lights went out.
verb: scaring, scared, scared
frighten
The loud noise in the middle of the night *scared* her.

scared
adjective
afraid
She is *scared* of the dark.

scarf
noun: scarves
a piece of cloth to put around the neck or head
I keep my neck warm with a wool *scarf* in cold weather.

scatter
verb
distribute and separate over a wide area
The war *scattered* the people of the country all over the world.

scheme
noun
a plan
The school had a good *scheme* to build a new gym.

school
noun
a place where students go to classes
Our *school* has 40 teachers and 500 students.

science
noun
the study of areas like biology, physics, etc.
We learn about our bodies and natural laws in our *science* classes.

scientific
adjective
related to science
We arrive at many facts and truths by using the *scientific* method.

scientist
noun
a person whose work is related to some science
Many *scientists* do experiments in laboratories.

scissors
noun
an instrument that cuts with two edges
She cut the piece of cloth in half with a pair of *scissors*.

score
noun
the points made in a game
The final *score* in basketball last night was 80-70; our team had the higher *score*.
verb: scoring, scored, scored
make points in a game
My brother *scored* 18 points in the basketball game.

scout
noun
1. *a person who goes out to find out something*
The army sent a *scout* out to locate the enemy soldiers.
2. *a Girl Scout or a Boy Scout*

His sons and daughters are *scouts*.

scratch
noun
a small shallow wound made by a rough rub
He got a *scratch* on his hand when he fell down.
verb
rub roughly
He *scratched* his face with his nails and cut himself.

scream
noun
a shout or cry
I heard the child's *screams* when she fell.
verb
shout or cry
She *screamed* when she fell; I heard her and went to help her.

sea
noun
a big body of water
Three continents are around the Mediterranean *Sea*. I prefer swimming in the *sea* to swimming in a pool.

search
verb
examine (something) to find (something)
The police *searched* the house and found ten radios; thieves had stolen them.

season
noun
one of the four parts of a year
The four *seasons* we have are spring, summer, autumn, and winter.
verb
add spices or flavors to food
The food she prepares is delicious; she *seasons* it with spices.

seat

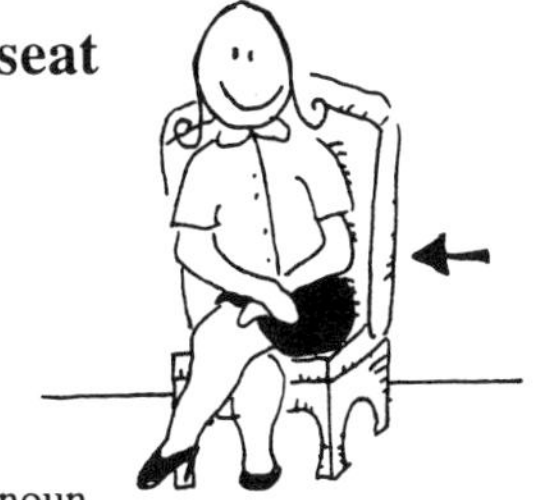

noun
a place to sit
We had very good *seats* when we went to see the play; we could see the whole stage.

second
noun
1. *a measure of time*
One minute has sixty *seconds*.
2. *a number showing order: 2nd*
I was the first to arrive in class; my friend was the *second*.
adjective
a number showing order: 2nd
My friend was the *second* student to arrive in class.

secondary
adjective
in a second place or position
Secondary education comes after eighth grade and before college education.

secret
noun
something kept from others
She can't keep a *secret*; she tells her sister everything she hears.

secretary
noun: secretaries
a person who types and files and answers telephones in an office
It is a very busy office; the manager has three *secretaries*.

secure
verb: securing, secured, secured
get
We needed some help, and we *secured* it from the neighbors.
adjective
safe
She gave him very important papers to keep; he told her they were *secure* in his office.

see
verb: seeing, saw, seen
observe with the eyes
I *saw* an interesting movie last week.

seed

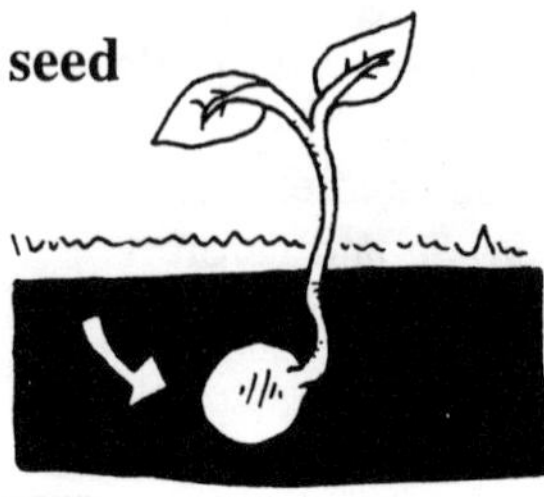

noun
the inner part of a plant or fruit that one can plant
We planted new *seeds* to have more flowers in our garden next summer.

seek
verb: seeking, sought, sought
look for, try to get
They *sought* some help for their sick child; they got it in the hospital.

seem
verb
appear
Although they had a small problem, they *seemed* to be happy.

seen
See **see.**

seize
verb: seizing, seized, seized
take and hold
She *seized* her child's hand as they crossed the street. The army attacked the city and *seized* it.

seldom
adverb
rarely
We don't see her in the library very often; she *seldom* goes there.

select
verb
choose
I wanted to buy a necktie; I went to a store and saw ten lovely ones; I *selected* a red one to buy.

sell
verb: selling, sold, sold
give (something) and get paid (for it)
I wanted to buy a used car; my neighbor *sold* me his.

senate
noun
a branch of government
A *senate* makes laws for a country.

senator
noun
a member of a senate
The U.S. Senate has two *senators* from every state.

send
verb: sending, sent, sent
make (something) go (somewhere)
I *sent* a letter to my cousin last week; he received it yesterday.

sense
noun
1. *one of people's five abilities and powers*
Seeing and hearing are two of our *senses.*
2. *meaning*
What he said made no *sense*; it meant nothing.
verb: sensing, sensed, sensed
feel, know
From what he said, I *sensed* that he was not very happy.

sent
See **send**.

sentence
noun
an independent language structure that is a statement or a question
We start a *sentence* with a capital letter and end it with a period or a question mark.

separate
verb: separating, separated, separated
put things apart
The merchant *separated* the large eggs from the small eggs; he wanted to sell the small eggs for a lower price.
adjective

single
Each of the children has a *separate* bedroom at home.

September
noun
the ninth month of the year
September comes after August and before October.

series
noun
a number of things put in some order
The doctor had a *series* of books on medicine in his office.

serious
adjective
1. *needing much thinking*
The father asked his son a *serious* question; the boy had to think hard to answer it.
2. *dangerous*
The patient had a *serious* illness; he needed to stay in the hospital for a long time.
2. *not joking, not light*
She has a *serious* look on her face; she is not smiling.

servant
noun
a person who works for pay at home
They had two *servants* at home to do the house work.

serve
verb: serving, served, served
1. *work in a house for pay*
The two servants they had *served* them for fifteen years.
2. *offer*
The hostess was ready to *serve* dinner at 7:00 p.m.
3. *be good for*
The food we bought *served* eight persons.

service
noun
1. *benefit*
I just need one car; a second car is of no *service* to me.
2. *the act of serving or helping*
The food in that restaurant is very good, but the *service* is slow; they take a long time to bring you your food.

set
noun
a number of things that belong together
I have a new ping pong *set*; I have a net, bats, and balls.
verb: setting, set, set
1. *put, place*
I asked my sister to *set* the vase of flowers on the table.
2. *go down*
The sun rises in the east and *sets* in the west.

settle
verb: settling, settled, settled
1. *live in a place for a long time*
They moved from New York and *settled* in Florida.
2. *be calm*
Stop moving and talking; just *settle* down.
3. *come to some agreement*
We argued about a matter, but we *settled* it between us later.

seven
noun
a number: 7
Four and three make *seven.*

seventeen
noun
a number: 17
Ten and seven make *seventeen.*

seventeenth
noun
a number showing order: 17th
Seventeen students ran across the field. My friend came last; he was the *seventeenth.*
adjective
a number showing order: 17th
There are 16 days before the *seventeenth* day of a month.

seventy

noun
a number: 70
Seventy is ten more than sixty.

several
adjective
a few
Several students decided not to play basketball in the rain; there were about four or five or six of them.

severe
adjective
1. *hard to handle*
We couldn't leave the house because of the *severe* weather; it was too cold.
2. *hard in ways of doing things*
The father was *severe* with his children; he wanted them to do what pleased him only.

sew

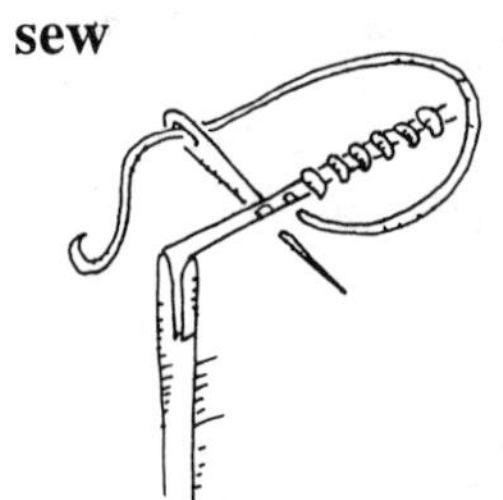

verb: sewing, sewed, sewn
use a thread and needle to work on pieces of cloth
She *sewed* herself a silk dress.

shade
noun
a place on the ground where there is no sun
After working in the field, the man stood in the *shade* for a short time to feel cool.

shadow

noun
an area that the light does not shine on
If you stand in the sun, you will be able to see your *shadow* on the ground.

shake
noun
a drink with milk and ice-cream
I like chocolate *shakes* to drink.
verb: shaking, shook, shaken
move (something) fast
Don't *shake* your glass; it is full; you might spill some water.

shall
auxiliary verb
1. *(to show future action)*
I *shall* be at the station at nine in the morning.
2. *(to ask if an action is wanted)*
Shall I prepare your dinner now?

shallow
adjective
not deep
It is safe for the children to play in the pool; it is *shallow*; it is only one foot deep.

shame
noun
a bad feeling for doing something wrong
It is a *shame* to tell lies.

shape
noun
a form
She made a cake in the *shape* of a book; it was her husband's birthday, and he had just written a book. The cake looked like an open book.

share
noun
1. *a part that belongs to one person*
We divided the apple between us; my *share* was half the apple.
2. *one of many portions of a company*
She bought 100 *shares* in a company.
verb: sharing, shared, shared
1. *divide among people*
We *shared* the money we made equally.

2. *give a part (of something) as a kind act*
I would like you to *share* some of the food I have; please have a sandwich.

sharp
adjective
1. *with a cutting edge*
He shaves his beard with a *sharp* razor.
2. *with a thin point*
I can make thin lines with my pencil; it is very *sharp*.
3. *intelligent, clever*
She is a *sharp* student; she understands things very fast.

sharpen
verb
make sharp or pointed
I *sharpened* the knives in the kitchen to make them cut well. The student *sharpened* his pencil in school.

shave
noun
the act of cutting the hair with a razor
He has a smooth beard; he has just had a good *shave*.
verb: shaving, shaved, shaved or shaven
cut hair with a razor
He *shaved* his beard twice yesterday; he had a party in the evening.

shaven
See **shave**.

she
pronoun: her, hers
third person feminine singular
She is a very fine person; I know her and her brother.

shed
noun

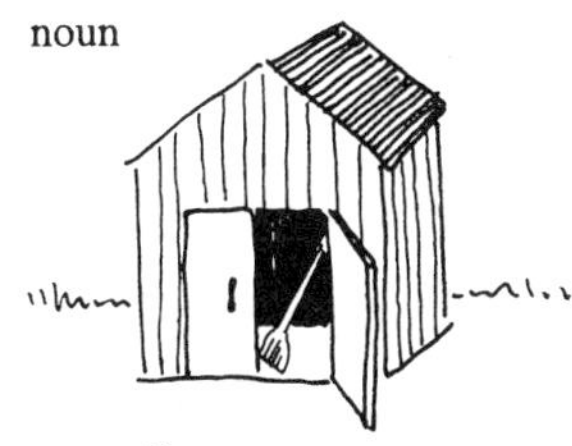

a small room or structure to put things in
He keeps his garden tools in a *shed* behind his house.
verb: shedding, shed, shed
1. *get (something) off*
When the sun came out, we *shed* our coats.
2. *give*
We didn't understand the situation, but my brother *shed* some light on it.
3. *let (something) flow*
She *shed* some tears when she heard the sad news.

she'd
pronoun and auxiliary verb
1. she had
She'd finished her work when I saw her.
2. *she would*
She'd like to go to the zoo with us tomorrow.

sheep

noun: sheep
an animal
Sheep like to eat grass. We get wool from *sheep*.

sheet
noun
1. *a piece of cloth for a bed*

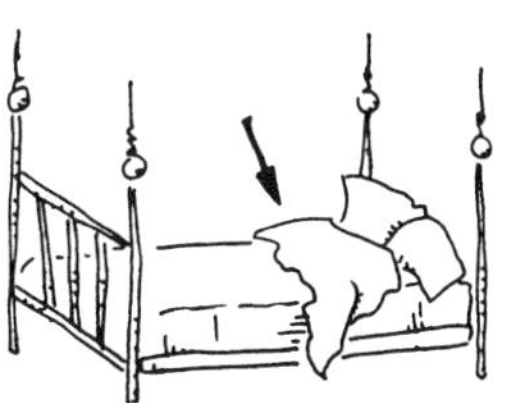

We usually use two *sheets* on a bed.
2. *a flat piece (of paper)*

My notebook has 60 *sheets* of paper.

shelf
noun: shelves
a flat piece of wood or metal on which one puts things in

a room

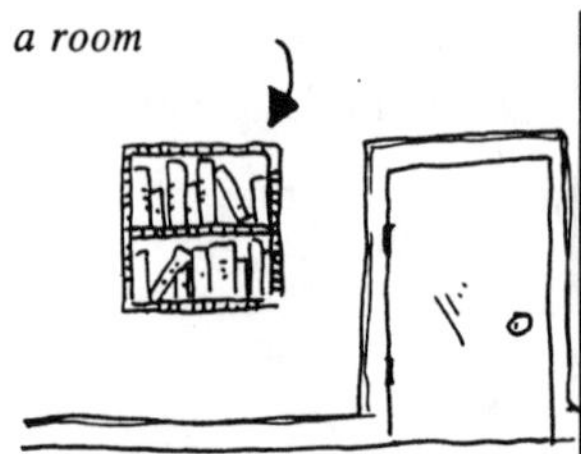

She has her books on four *shelves*; each *shelf* has about twenty books.

shell

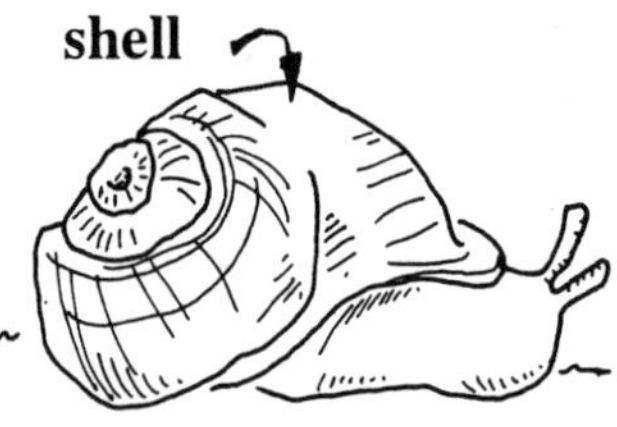

noun

the hard outer cover of an animal or a fish

Crabs and shrimp have *shells* to protect them.

she'll

pronoun and auxiliary verb

she will

She'll be going with us to the zoo tomorrow.

shelter

noun

a place to go to be away from a problem

During the war, many people felt safer in *shelters*. When it rained, we looked for a *shelter* from the rain.

verb

give a safe place (to someone)

The city *sheltered* the poor people in special homes during the cold months.

shelve

verb

put on a shelf

She *shelves* her books after she reads them; she has a shelf full of books.

shelves

See **shelf**.

shepherd

noun

a person who takes care of sheep and goats

The *shepherd* took his sheep to the field to feed them.

sheriff

noun

a person who keeps order in a county

Every county in the U.S. elects a *sheriff*; the *sheriff* makes sure that the laws are obeyed.

she's

pronoun and verb

she is

She's a tall girl.

pronoun and auxiliary verb

she has

She's been waiting here for an hour.

shield

noun

a device that protects

An umbrella is a good *shield* from the sun in summer.

verb

protect

The umbrella *shielded* us from the sun on the beach.

shine

verb: shining, shone or shined, shone or shined

1. *give light*

The sun is *shining* brightly in the sky. It *shone* brightly yesterday too.

2. *polish*

He *shined* his black shoes before he went to work.

ship

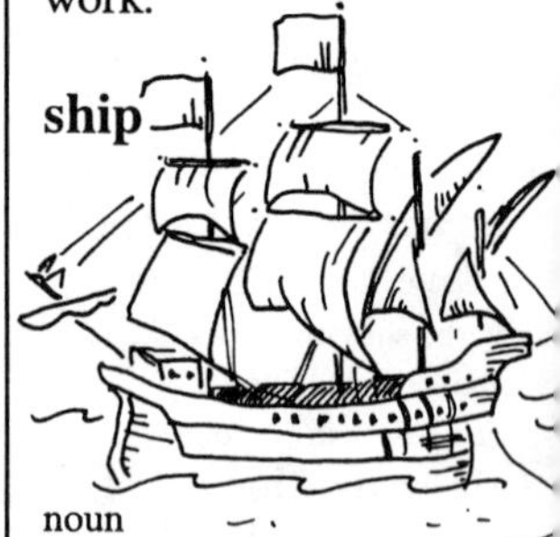

noun

a sea or river vessel

We crossed the Atlantic on a big *ship*.

verb: shipping, shipped, shipped
send (something) by land, sea, or air
The company *shipped* the television I ordered to my address at home; I received it yesterday.

shirt

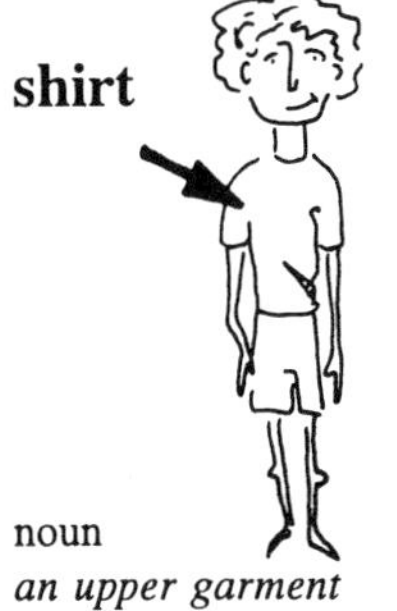

noun
an upper garment
He bought a *shirt* and tie to go with his new suit; his *shirt* has long sleeves.

shock
noun
a sharp surprise
I got a *shock* when he said he was leaving town; I didn't expect it.
verb
give a sharp surprise
The news about his leaving *shocked* me.

shoe

noun
the outer wear on a foot
She bought a new pair of brown leather *shoes*.

shone
See **shine**.

shook
See **shake**.

shoot
verb: shooting, shot, shot
1. *fire*
The soldiers *shot* their guns towards the enemy.
2. *hit (with a bullet or sharp object)*
The hunter *shot* the lion and killed it.

shop
noun
a place where you can buy things
There is a new flower *shop* near our house; now we can buy flowers without going very far.
verb: shopping, shopped, shopped
look for (things) to buy in shops
I *shopped* for a new shirt yesterday, but I didn't find what I was looking for.

shopping
See **shop** also.
noun
buying things
We did our *shopping* for the party last week; we bought everything we needed.

shore
noun
land by a lake or sea
We drove along the *shore*; we saw the waves coming in.

short
adjective
1. *not tall*
My brother is six feet tall; I am not as tall; I am *shorter* than my brother.
2. *not long*
Our school is a *short* distance away from our home; we can walk there in six minutes; it takes a *short* time to get there.

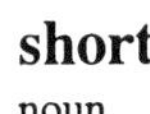

shorts
noun

1. *trousers that don't reach below the knee*
The boys wore *shorts* on the trip.
2. *underpants*
He was alone at home and it was warm; he walked around the house in his *shorts*.

sh<u>o</u>rtly
adverb
soon
They will be here *shortly*; I expect them within an hour.

shot
See **shoot**.

should
auxiliary verb
1. *(showing what one has to do)*
If you want to pass your courses, you *should* study hard.
2. *(showing condition)*
Should they come, we would be able to talk with them.

sh<u>ou</u>lder

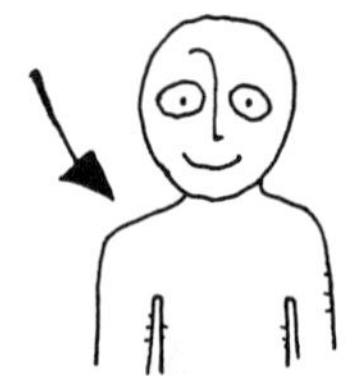

noun
a part of the body that is at the top of an arm
He carried the bag easily when he put it on his *shoulder*. She wore her scarf over her *shoulders*.

shout
noun
a loud cry
I heard a *shout* in the dark; it was a boy's cry; he was lost.

verb
speak with a loud voice
He *shouted* to make the old man hear him.

show
noun
a performance
We saw a lovely *show* last night; people danced and sang.
verb: showing showed, shown
let (someone) see
I *showed* my friend my new bicycle; he liked it.

sh<u>o</u>wer
noun

1. *a bath taken with the water coming down like rain*
I take a *shower* every morning; it makes me feel clean and fresh.
2. *a short fall of rain*
We had a *shower* a little while ago; now the roads are wet.

shown
See **show**.

shut
verb: shutting, shut, shut
close
We *shut* the windows when we felt cold.
adjective
closed
All the doors and windows are *shut*; now nobody can leave.

sick
adjective
ill, not well
The boy is *sick*; we are calling our doctor.

side
noun
1. *a surface of a thing*
Write the address on this *side* of the envelope.
2. *either the left or right part of a thing*
One *side* of the boat hit a wall in the harbor.
verb: siding, sided, sided
support one person or group against another
My brother and I had an argument. My friend *sided* with me; my brother wasn't happy about that.

sigh
verb
giving out a sound with a breath of air through the mouth
He *sighed* when he heard the same story again.

sight
noun

1. *view*
The sea and the valley make a beautiful *sight* from our windows.
2. *ability to see*
His *sight* is not as good as it was; he needs eye-glasses.
verb
see
We *sighted* a boat far out at sea.

sign
noun
1. *a mark*
He put a little *sign* on his paper to show that it was his.
2. *a notice*
The school put up a *sign* about test times.
verb
write one's name in a special way
She *signed* the letter after she wrote it.

signature
noun
the writing of one's name in a special way
She put her *signature* at the end of the letter she sent.

silence
noun
no sound
We like to have *silence* in the library; people need to work in a quiet place.

silent
adjective
quiet
The students were *silent* in the library; nobody spoke or made any noise.

silk
noun
a kind of cloth
Silk, cotton, and wool are different kinds of cloth.

silver
noun
a metal
She has two rings: one made of gold and one made of *silver*. *Silver* is not as expensive as gold.

similar
adjective
alike
His bicycle and mine are very *similar*; they have the same shape and weight, but they have different colors.

simple
adjective
1. *plain*
We had a *simple* dinner last night: a piece of meat, a potato, and a small salad.
2. *easy*
He gave us a *simple* job to do; we did it very quickly.

simply
adverb
1. *in a plain way*
They arranged the furniture in their house very *simply*: the chairs were around a big table.
2. *only*
He works very hard *simply* to make more money.

since
adverb
from that time
She graduated from college in 1991. She has been working ever *since*.
conjunction
after that time in the past
We have been living in this house *since* we moved here from Canada.
preposition
from a time in the past until the present
She has been working *since* 1991.

sincere
adjective
loyal, honest
He is very *sincere* in his work; he comes on time, he leaves on time, and he serves the company well.

sing
verb: singing, sang, sung

use the voice to make music
She has a beautiful voice; she *sang* two lovely songs last night.

singer
noun
a person who sings
This little girl has a lovely voice; one day she will be a good *singer*.

single
adjective
1. *one (and no other)*
We are a large family, but we have a *single* car.
2. *not married*
She would like to get married; she is *single* now.

singular
adjective
1. *(showing) one*
Cat is a *singular* word; the plural form is *cats*.

sink

verb: sinking, sank, sunk
go down in water
The boat *sank* in the river when it was hit.

sir
noun
a title
Sir Winston was an important man in history. "Yes, *sir*," the student said to his teacher.

sister
noun
a female who has the same parents as another person
Mr. and Mrs. Brown have two sons and two daughters; the boys and the girls are bothers and *sisters*.

sit
verb: sitting, sat, sat
rest with the head and body up and the legs bent
I have a comfortable chair at home to *sit* on. We *sat* at the table to have our dinner. She *sat* up in bed to read the newspaper. Don't stand; please *sit* down.

situation
noun
condition
The *situation* in the company is very good; everybody is happy and business is good.

six
noun
a number: 6
Six is what you get when you multiply three by two.
adjective
a number: 6
I have *six* uncles and aunts.

sixteen
noun
a number: 16
Four times four gives you *sixteen*.
adjective
a number: 16
This room has four rows of chairs; each row has four chairs; *sixteen* people can sit in the room.

sixty
noun
a number: 60
Sixty is ten more than fifty.
adjective
a number: 60
Sixty people came to the party; ten had to stand, because we had fifty chairs.

size
noun
a measure of how big or how small a thing or person is
His shoes are a large *size*, because he is very tall.

skate

noun
the shoes with wheels or blades worn to move smoothly on the ground or ice
She bought a pair of *skates* to roll on the street.
verb: skating, skated, skated
move in shoes with wheels or blades on the ground or ice
She *skates* very fast on the ice.

skill
noun
ability
That carpenter has great *skill* doing things with wood.

skillful
adjective
clever, showing skill
She is very *skillful* as a tennis player; she runs and hits the ball very well.

skin
noun
the outer cover of a person, animal, fruit, or vegetable
She loves to eat potato *skins.* Her *skin* is soft, because she uses a lot of cream on it.

skinny
adjective: skinnier, skinniest
thin
She used to be fat; now she is *skinny,* because she hasn't eaten much lately; she has been sick.

skirt

noun
a dress that goes from the waist down
She bought a white blouse to wear with her black *skirt.*

sky
noun: skies
the space outside the earth
The sun is high up in the *sky.* Planes fly in the *sky.* The *sky* is blue.

slave
noun
a person who is owned by another and who works for him or her
In the past there was a big trade in *slaves*; people bought them and sold them in many countries.

sleep
noun
the condition of not being awake
He was so tired he had a good and long *sleep.*
verb: sleeping, slept, slept
be in a condition not awake
He went to bed at 10:00 p.m. and woke up at 6:00 a.m.; he *slept* for eight hours.

sleepy
adjective: sleepier, sleepiest
feeling like going to sleep
She was so *sleepy* that she fell asleep on her chair.

slender
adjective
thin
He is tall and *slender*; he is not fat.

slept
See **sleep**

slice
noun
a thin piece cut from a bigger piece
I couldn't eat much; so I just had a small *slice* of the cake.
verb: slicing, sliced, sliced
cut a thin piece
We *sliced* the loaf of bread into 24 slices.

slid
See **slide**.

slide
noun
a surface on which one goes down sitting or lying on it
The children enjoyed going down the *slide* into a small pool.
verb: sliding, slid,

slid
move easily on or down something
The children *slid* down the snow slope.

slight
adjective
small, little
He is fine, but he has a *slight* headache.

slightly
adverb
a little
He is *slightly* tired; he needs a little rest.

slip
noun
1. *a small mistake*
He didn't mean what he said; it was just a *slip*.
2. *a woman's garment that is worn under a dress*
Her *slip* was too long; it showed below her dress.
verb: slipping, slipped, slipped
1. *make a mistake*
He *slipped* when he said *bet*; he meant to say *pet*.
2. *slide*
There was some snow on the ground; he *slipped* on the snow and fell.

slipped
See **slip**.

slipping
See **slip**.

slipper
noun
a shoe worn at home
He has warm *slippers* to wear at home in winter.

slippery
adjective
easy to slip on
The snow and ice made the road very *slippery*.

slope
noun
a bit of land that goes down or up
The children enjoyed sliding down the snow *slope*.

slow
adjective
not fast
He is *slow* in his work; it takes him a long time to finish it.

slowly
adverb
in a slow way, not fast
Her foot hurts her; she is walking *slowly*.

small
adjective
little
I am not very hungry; I can only have a *small* sandwich.

smart
adjective
clever
She is quite *smart*; she knows what to say and how.

smell
noun
a sense with the nose
There is a bad *smell* in the room; let us open the window.
verb: smelling, smelled or smelt, smelled or smelt
sense with the nose
My mother was cooking in the kitchen; I could *smell* the food in the living room.

smelt
See **smell**.

smile
noun
an expression one gives with the mouth to show that one is happy
When he heard the good news, we saw a *smile* on his face.
verb
show an expression of happiness with the mouth
He *smiled* when he heard the good news.

smoke
noun
white or black gas that comes out of something burning

We see a lot of *smoke* coming out of chimneys in winter.
verb: smoking, smoked, smoked
take in smoke from a cigarette, cigar, or pipe
We do not *smoke* in public places.

smooth
adjective
not rough
There were no waves; the sea was very *smooth*. Silk is a *smooth* material.

snack
noun
a small meal
They didn't want to eat much before the movie; so they had a *snack* on the way.
verb
eat a small amount of food
He couldn't wait for dinner; so he *snacked* on some bread and cheese.

snake

noun
an animal that creeps without legs
A *snake* bite can be very dangerous.

snow
noun
the white stuff that falls from the clouds on very cold days
When there is a lot of *snow*, everything is white.

so
adverb
1. *in order to*
He studied hard *so* he could pass.
2. *to the degree mentioned*
He is *so* tall, he can reach the ceiling when he jumps.
3. *as mentioned*
I told her to repeat the story, and she did *so*.
conjunction
as a result
He had no money; *so* he couldn't buy a new car.

soap
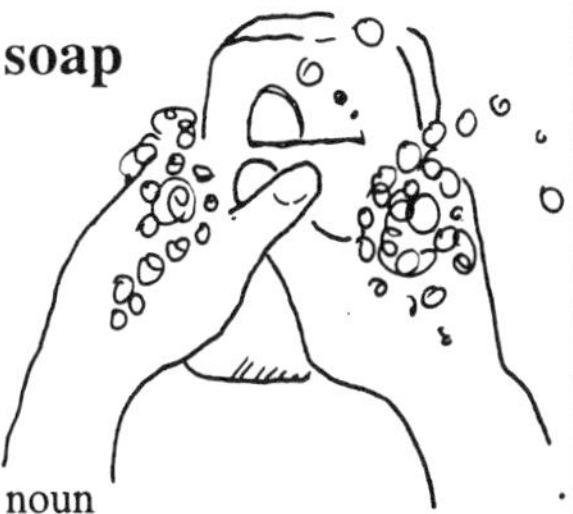
noun
the material we use with water for washing
She uses a new kind of *soap* for her dishes.

social
noun
a social gathering
A *social* is a good place and time to meet new people.
adjective
related to society
We had a *social* party last night; people ate and played games.

society
noun: societies
1. *an organization*
The teachers formed a *society* to discuss teaching and learning methods.
2. *a community*
In our *society*, people dress well.

sock
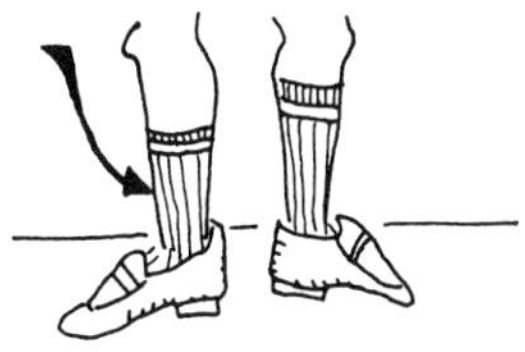
noun
a short foot garment
She never wears tennis shoes without *socks*. They walked around at home in *socks*.

soft
adjective
1. *not hard*
She puts cream on her hands to keep them *soft*.
2. *not loud*
He always speaks in a *soft* voice; he never shouts.

soil
noun
earth
Plants grow better when the *soil* is good and rich.
verb
make dirty
The children *soiled* their clothes playing in the garden.

sold
See **sell**.

soldier
noun
a person in the army
The *soldiers* fought very bravely in the war.

solid
noun
something hard, not a gas or a liquid
Air is a gas; water is a liquid; iron is a *solid.*
adjective
hard, strong
This is a *solid* building; it is very strong.

solution
noun
the way a problem is solved
He is poor; the *solution* to his problem is work.

solve
verb: solving, solved, solved
find a solution
Our mathematics teacher gave us five problems to *solve*.

some
adjective
1. *an indefinite number*
Some students play football.
2. *a little*
I need *some* money; I have no money now.
pronoun
an indefinite number
Some of the secretaries left the office early.

somebody
pronoun
some person, a person
Somebody is at the door; I hear the door bell.

somehow
adverb
in some way
He doesn't speak Italian, but he will manage in Italy *somehow.*

someone
pronoun
some person, a person
Someone is at the door; I hear the door bell.

something
pronoun
some thing, a thing
Something is in my glass; I don't know what it is, but it is black.

sometime
adverb
at some time
I don't know what day he's coming, but it will be *sometime* next week.

sometimes
adverb
at times, occasionally
The weather changes here; *sometimes* it's warm and *sometimes* it's cold.

somewhat
adverb
to a certain extent
He is *somewhat* angry with me, because I didn't lend him my pen.

somewhere
adverb
in some place
I don't know where he is now, but I'll find him *somewhere* in school.

son
noun
a male child of a parent
Mr. and Mrs. Lee have five children: two *sons* and three daughters.

song
noun
words and music that one sings
She sang two lovely *songs* for us. She has a beautiful voice.

soon
adverb
in a short time
She has already left the office; she should be home very *soon.*

sore

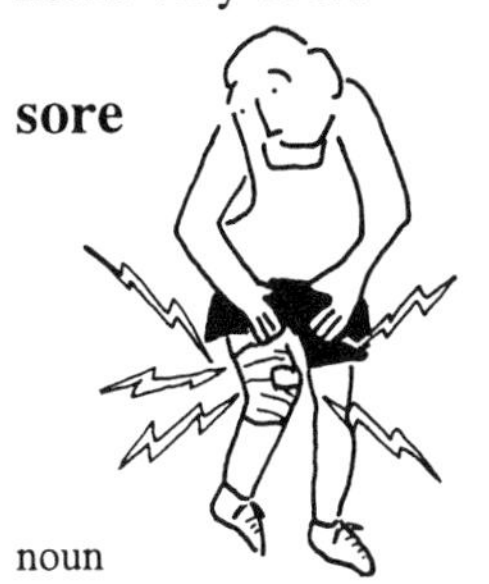

noun
a spot on the body that is not healthy or well
He has a *sore* on his foot where he cut it last week.
adjective
causing pain
He drank hot lemonade for his *sore* throat.

sorrow
noun
sadness
I noticed his *sorrow* over the death of his uncle.

sorry
adjective: sorrier, sorriest
showing regret
I was *sorry* to hear that she was in the hospital.

sort
noun
a kind
A jet is a *sort* of plane that goes very fast.

sought
See **seek.**

sound
noun
1. *a noise*
I heard the *sound* of thunder.
2. *something heard*
I like the *sound* of soft music.
verb
1. *be heard*
His voice *sounded* very clear.
2. *seem*
Your plan *sounds* good.

soup
noun
a liquid food with some chicken or meat or rice or vegetables
I had a cup of tomato *soup*; it was hot and delicious.

source
noun
a place from which things come
Money can be the *source* of trouble or happiness. The river is our *source* of water.

south
noun
a direction opposite north
The *south* is warmer than the north in the U.S.
adjective
from the south
There is a *south* wind blowing today.
adverb
to the *south*
We drive *south* to go from New York to Florida.

southern
adjective
related to the south
Wisconsin is a northern state; Alabama is a *southern* state in the U.S.

souvenir
noun
an object that reminds a person of something or someone
When I visited Washington, D.C. for the first time, I bought a *souvenir;* it was a small model of the Washington Monument.

sow
verb: sowing, sowed, sown
plant seeds
She *sowed* some seeds in her garden to have flowers.

sown
See **sow.**

space
noun
1. *the sky*
Rockets fly through *space.*
2. *an empty place*

The teacher asked us to fill the *spaces* on the paper with new words. When we write, we leave *spaces* between words.
verb: spacing, spaced, spaced
put an empty place between
Space your words when you write.

spare
verb: sparing, spared, spared
do without
I cannot *spare* my pen now; I need it.
adjective
extra, additional
We must always have a *spare* tire when we drive a car.

speak
verb: speaking, spoke, spoken
say things
She *spoke* to me on the telephone; she told me that she would meet me soon.

speaker
noun
one who speaks
They had a good *speaker* after dinner; she gave a good speech.

special
adjective
not common
Every day the dinner in that restaurant is steak and salad; last night they gave us a *special* dinner: steak, salad, and dessert.

speech
noun
1. *the way a person talks*
His *speech* is not very clear, because he has something in his mouth.
2. *a talk*
He gave a good *speech* to the students. They liked what he said.

speed
noun
fastness
He couldn't stop his car very easily, because he was going at a high *speed*.

spell
verb: spelling, spelled or spelt, spelled or spelt
name or put the letters of a word
She *spells* words correctly; she writes words without mistakes.

spelling
noun
naming or putting letters of a word
Her *spelling* is excellent; she makes no mistakes in writing words.

spend
verb: spending, spent, spent
1. *pay (for something)*
She *spent* a lot of money on her clothes; she didn't have much left for other things.
2. *let (something) pass*
They *spent* a lot of time playing; they didn't have enough time to study.

spent
See **spend**.

spice
noun
a plant used to flavor food
The food she cooks tastes good, because she uses pepper and other *spices* in it.
verb: spicing, spiced, spiced
use plants to flavor food
She *spices* her food, and it always has a good flavor.

spied
See **spy**.

splash
verb
distribute liquid on (someone or something)
I was standing near the pool, and when my friend jumped into the pool, he *splashed* me.

spoil
verb: spoiling, spoiled or spoilt, spoiled or spoilt
ruin

He kept playing with his watch until he *spoiled* it; now it is not working at all.

spoilt
See **spoil**.

spoke
See **speak**.

spoken
See **speak**.

spoon

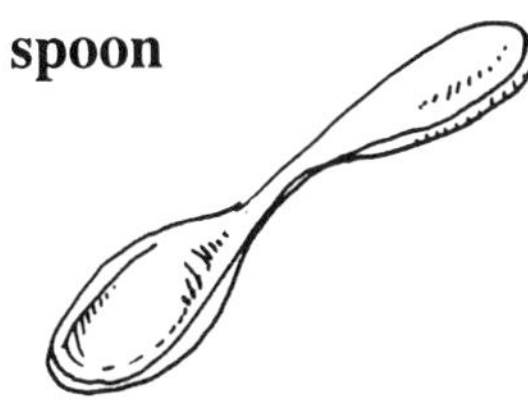

noun
a tool used to eat with
We use a fork and knife to eat our meat; we use a *spoon* to have our soup.

sport
noun
1. *a physical activity or game*
Football and basketball are *sports*.
2. *a person who accepts any result with a good spirit*
He lost the game, but he continued to smile; he is a good *sport*.

spot
noun
a dot

One drop of soup came on her dress; now she has a *spot* on her dress; she needs to clean it.
verb: spotting, spotted, spotted
locate
I lost my friend at the party for a time; then I *spotted* him talking with our neighbor.

sprang
See **spring**.

spread
noun
1. *a cover for a bed*
She bought a new bed *spread* to match her curtains.
2. *a soft food that one can put on a piece of bread or a biscuit*
She offered us toast and a cheese *spread*.
verb: spreading, spread, spread
distribute over an area
We *spread* the butter on our toast. The news about the football player *spread* all over the city.

spring
noun
1. *a season*
Tree leaves come out in the *spring*.
2. *a source of water*
They got their water from a *spring* in the village.
3. *a round metal device that moves up and down when weight is put on it*

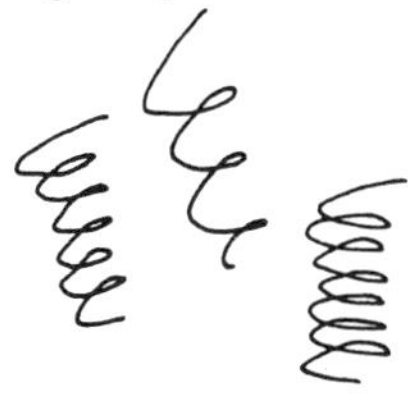

My bed is very comfortable; it has many *springs* in it.
4. *a jump*
He could reach the light with a *spring*.
verb: springing, sprang, sprung
1. *jump*
The rabbit *sprang* up and down in the garden.
2. *arise*
The subject of money *sprang* up during our conversation.

sprung
See **spring**.

spy
noun: spies
a person who tries to get information about another country secretly
The police caught an enemy *spy* and put him in prison.

verb: spying, spied, spied
1. *get information secretly*
The agent *spied* on the movements of the enemy.
2. *get a fast look*
He *spied* his friend at the party and then lost him.

square

noun
1. *a shape that has four equal sides*

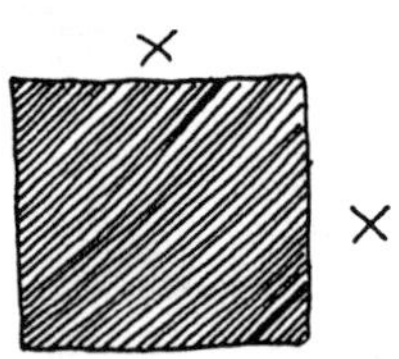

A *square* has four equal sides and four equal angles.
2. *a place in a city or town that has four streets around it*
Our favorite store is in the middle of the city *square*.

staff

noun
the people working for someone
The manager has a *staff* of four persons in the office; all of them work well together.

stage

noun
1. *a platform for acting*
They performed the play on the school *stage*.

2. *a level in a process*
Children go through *stages* as they are growing up.

stairs

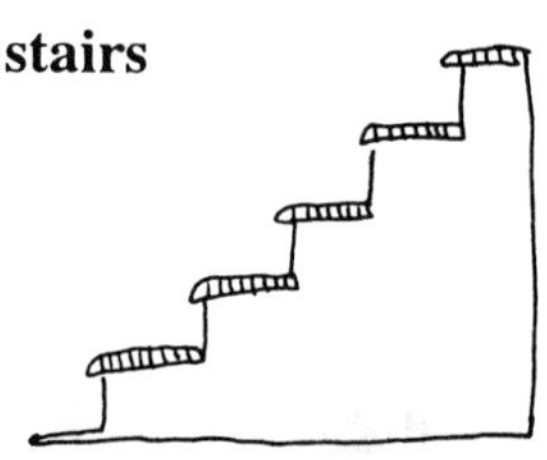

noun
the steps going up and down a place
We walk up the *stairs* to our apartment on the third floor.

stamp

noun
1. *a small paper with a design and a value put on an envelope to send it by mail*

We bought some *stamps* from the post office.
2. *a device for putting a mark on something*
I have a *stamp* with my name on it; I can print my name with it.

stand

verb: standing, stood, stood
be straight up on one's feet
She *stood* at the station waiting for the train.

stand up

verb: standing up, stood up, stood up
go from sitting to being straight up on one's feet
The people in the room *stood up* when the president entered.

standard

noun
a model or a rule
The way my father did things was a *standard* for me to follow.

star

noun
a body far up in space
We can see the moon and some *stars* on a clear night.

stare

verb: staring, stared, stared
give a hard look

We *stared* at the actor; we wanted to see every movement he made.

start
noun
a beginning
They finished their work early, because they had an early *start*.
verb
begin
She *started* cooking at 4:00 p.m. and she was ready to serve dinner at 6:00 p.m.

state
noun
1. *a country*
The *State* of Bahrain is an island.
2. *a part of a country that has its own government*
The U.S. has 50 *states*.
verb: stating, stated, stated
say, utter, express
Every person in the room *stated* his name and address.

statement
noun
an expression in words
The principal made a very important *statement* to the students; he told them about a new rule.

station
noun
a place where a bus or train stops

We caught the train at the city *station*.

statue
noun
a solid structure in the form of a person
There is a *statue* of the president in the museum.

stay
verb
remain
They came here and *stayed* one week before they left.

steady
adjective: steadier, steadiest
not changing
The temperature remained *steady* for a week; it didn't change.

steal
verb: stealing, stole, stolen
take (something) belonging to someone else
The police caught the thief who *stole* money from a store.

steam
noun
the vapor that comes from hot water
There was a lot of *steam* in the bathroom when she took her bath.

steel
noun
a metal
Steel is used in cars and buildings because it is hard and strong.

steep
adjective
with a sharp slope
We were very careful driving down the *steep* mountain.

stem
noun
the lower part of a plant or tree above the ground
A vase holds the *stems* of flowers.

step

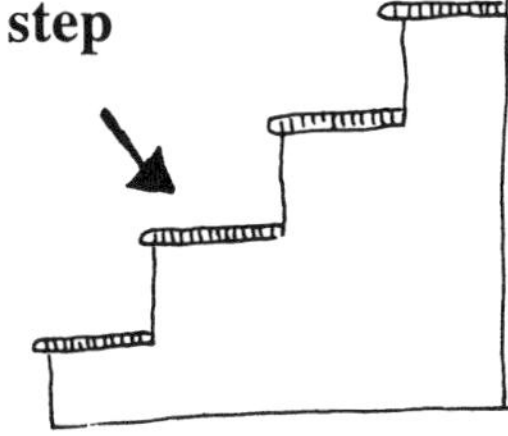

noun
1. *one of several parts of stairs*
There are forty *steps* from the ground floor to our apartment.
2. *one movement of a foot in walking*
The captain asked the soldiers to take two *steps* forward and stop.

verb: stepping, stepped, stepped
put a foot down
His shoes are dirty, because he *stepped* in the mud.

stern
adjective
severe
The manager is rather *stern* in the office; he is very strict.

stick

noun
a long and thin piece of wood or metal
The old man used a *stick* to help him walk.
verb: sticking, stuck, stuck
attach
I wanted the papers to be together; I *stuck* them to each other.

stiff
adjective
not bending
He hurt his arm; now he can't bend it; it is *stiff*.

still
adjective
not moving
The wind is very *still*; it is not blowing.
adverb
1. *not moving*
They sat *still* in their seats.
2. *till now*
They are *still* here; I don't know when they are leaving.
3. *with all that*
It is raining hard; *still* we need to leave.

stir
verb: stirring, stirred, stirred
1. *turn and move something to mix it*
I *stirred* the sugar in my tea cup.
2. *move*
Children can't sit still for a long time; they need to *stir*.

stocking

noun
a long sock that covers the leg
She always wears shoes and *stockings* that match her dresses in color.

stole
See **steal**.

stolen
See **steal**.

stomach

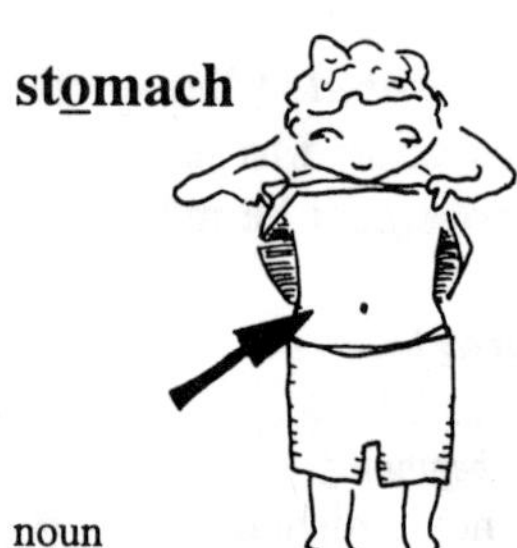

noun
a part of the body that receives the food we swallow
His *stomach* hurts him; he ate too much.

stone

noun
a piece of rock
There were many *stones* in the field; it wasn't easy to walk.

stood
See **stand**.

stoop
verb
bend down
She dropped her bag, and she *stooped* to pick it up.

stop
noun
an end, no action
The cars came to a *stop* at the red right.
verb: stopping, stopped, stopped

come to an end, bring something to an end
The driver *stopped* the car at the red light.

stopped
See **stop**.

stopping
See **stop**.

store
noun
a shop
The *store* we buy things from has good products and good prices.
verb: storing, stored, stored
put in a place for future use
We bought a lot of rice and *stored* it in the kitchen cupboard.

stories
See **story**.

storm
noun
heavy rain or snow with a strong wind
Everybody stayed at home during the snow *storm*.

story
noun: stories
1. *an account of something that has happened*
She told us a very interesting *story* about herself.
2. *a level of a building*
We live on the third *story* of the building.

stove

noun
a place that gives heat for cooking
We use an electric *stove* to heat liquids and cook food.

straight
adjective
1. *without curves or bends*
The road is very *straight*; we could see it for miles.
2. *direct*
I gave her a *straight* answer to her question; it was short and to the point.

strange
adjective
not known, different
They took me to a *strange* place; I had never seen it before.

stranger
noun
a person who is not known
A *stranger* came to our door; he had lost his way.

straw
noun
1. *dry stems of a grain*
Animals on a farm like to sleep on *straw*.
2. *a soft pipe used for sucking up a liquid*

I used a *straw* to drink my iced tea.

stream
noun
a body of water flowing down
The *stream* became deeper when it rained. They found some fish in the *stream*.

street
noun
a road in a town or city
Their house is on a main *street* in the city. The driver drove up and down the *street* looking for their house.

strength
noun
the degree of how strong a thing is
This man has great *strength*; he can carry very heavy loads.

stretch
verb
make longer or bigger
He *stretched* my sweater when he pulled it; now it looks too big for me.

strict
adjective
hard and stern in dealing with others
They are very *strict* with their children; they don't give them much freedom.

strike
verb: striking, struck, struck
1. *hit*
The thief *struck* the manager on the head and took his money.
2. *make a sound*
I like to hear our clock when it *strikes* each hour.

striking
See **strike** also.
adjective
very nice, remarkable
We saw a *striking* view from the mountain; the trees, the valley, and the sea looked very beautiful.

string

noun
a thick thread to tie things with
I tied the box with a *string* before I took it to the office. He had a very long *string* for his kite.

strip
noun
a long piece
She owns a *strip* of land near the sea; it is too narrow to build a house on.

stripe
noun
a line that has a different color
She wore a white dress with red *stripes.*

striped
adjective
something with lines of a different color
She wore a *striped* dress; I liked the red stripes on her white dress.

stroke
verb: stroking, stroked, stroked
rub softly
My sister puts her cat near her and *strokes* its head and back; the cat likes that.

strong
adjective
1. *healthy*
He was ill last week, but now he is *strong* and going to school.
2. *not weak, powerful*
This is a very *strong* box; it won't break easily.

struck
See **strike**.

structure
noun
1. *a construction, something built*
They have a little *structure* in the garden; it looks like a round wall.
2. *the way things are put together*
The *structures* of the following sentences are a bit different: He is a captain. Is he a captain?

struggle
verb: struggling, struggled, struggled
1. *try with difficulty*
The old man *struggled* up the hill; it was steep, and he was weak.
2. *fight*
The two armies *struggled* together before the rulers ordered peace.

stuck
See **stick**.

student
noun
a person who is learning
There are 15 teachers and 220 *students* in that school.

study
verb: studying, studied, studied
learn
They are *studying* the history of their country in school.

stuff
noun
the things one owns
When he moved to his new room, he took all his *stuff* with him.
verb
fill
They *stuffed* his suitcase with warm clothes; he was going to a cold place.

stupid
adjective
not clever
He is a clever boy, but sometimes he acts in *stupid* ways; he does things without thinking.

style
noun
1. *a fashion*
That store has the latest *styles* of clothes.
2. *a way of doing things*
She has a good *style* in writing; you can read what she writes and enjoy it.

subject
noun
1. *topic, head of a sentence*
In the following sentence, the word *children* is the *subject*: Children like to play.
2. *an area studied in school*
Science is his favorite *subject* in school.

submit
verb: submitting, submitted, submitted
present
She wrote her homework in the evening and *submitted* it to the teacher the next morning.

substance
noun
1. *the most important thing*
A policeman spoke to the students; the *substance* of his talk was that they should drive carefully.
2. *material*
To build that wall, they mixed a number of *substances* together.

subtract
verb
take (from)
If you *subtract* eight from twenty, you get twelve.

succeed
verb
come to a good result
He worked hard and *succeeded* in his business.

success
noun
arriving at a good result
His *success* in business is based on hard work.

successful
adjective
having a good result
He is *successful* in his work, because he is honest in his dealings with people.

such
pronoun
one like
He has a car with three wheels. I don't care to have *such* a car myself.
adjective
like
I have many pencils *such* as the one I am holding.
adverb
so
She is *such* a good singer that we asked her to sing many times.

sudden
adjective
coming very quickly
The weather was good all day; then we had a *sudden* shower.

suddenly
adverb
very quickly
The birds were eating in the garden; *suddenly*, they all flew away at the same time.

suffer
verb
1. *feel pain*
They *suffered* during the war; they had very little to eat.
2. *bear (something)*
He *suffered* a broken leg in the war.

sufficient
adjective
enough
They didn't have very much money, but what they had was *sufficient* for them; they didn't need any more.

sugar
noun
a sweet substance
He puts a lot of *sugar* in his tea; he likes it sweet.

suggest
verb
give an idea
My friends wanted to do something interesting; I *suggested* going to a museum; they liked that.

suggestion
noun
an idea given
My friends wanted to do something interesting; I suggested going to a museum; they liked my *suggestion*.

suit

noun
a number of things to wear together
He and his wife wore *suits*. She wore a skirt and jacket; he wore a jacket and a pair of trousers.
verb
fit
He and his wife *suit* each other; both of them like music. This kind of food *suits* me; it is good for me.

sum
noun
1. *a total, an amount reached by adding*
The *sum* of 3, 4, and 5 is twelve.
2. *an amount of money*
She bought the car for a *sum* of 5,000 dollars.

summer
noun
a season
Summer comes after spring and before autumn.

summon
verb
ask (someone) to come
All the secretaries were *summoned* to a meeting with the manager.

sun
noun
the body in the sky that gives us light and heat
The earth and the moon go around the *sun* once a year.

Sunday
noun
a day of the week
Sunday comes after Saturday and before Monday.

sung
See **sing**.

sunk
See **sink**.

sunny
adjective: sunnier, sunniest
with the sun shining
Yesterday was a cloudy day; we didn't see the sun. Today is *sunny* and warmer.

superior
adjective
of higher rank or importance
Their performance was *superior* to anything I've seen. It was truly excellent.

supper
noun
a light evening meal
I had soup and a salad for *supper* last night.

supply
noun: supplies
a quantity of some product
We still have a good *supply* of rice at home; we don't need to buy any more now.
verb: supplying, supplied, supplied
furnish (someone) with (something)
The school *supplied* each teacher with enough paper and chalk for a week.

support
noun
something which holds something else up
A pillow is a good *support* for my head when I sleep.
verb
1. *hold something up*
My pillow *supports* my head when I sleep.
2. *give enough to live*
His father *supported* him when he was a college student.

suppose
verb: supposing, supposed, supposed
assume, think something to be true
I don't see their suitcases; I *suppose* they have left.

sure
adjective
certain
I am *sure* they have left; my uncle told me so.

surely
adverb
certainly, of course
Surely they have left; otherwise, they would have been here.

surface
noun
1. *the outer side of something*
That piece of land has a flat *surface*.
2. *the upper side of something*
When I opened the box, I found some apples on the *surface*; there were oranges below.
verb: surfacing, surfaced, surfaced
come to the top
A dead fish *surfaced* on the river; we took it and threw it away.

surname
noun
family name
His name is Jack Brown; his first name is Jack; his *surname* is Brown.

survey
verb
examine
She *surveyed* the living room before her guests arrived; she wanted to be sure it was ready.

suspect
noun
a person who is thought to have done wrong
They don't know for sure if the thief is the killer also, but he is a *suspect*.

suspect
verb
think that (someone) has done wrong
The police *suspected* the thief to be the killer also.

swallow
verb
take (something) down from the mouth to the stomach
When we *swallow* our food, it goes to the stomach.

swam
See **swim**.

sweater

noun
a knitted jacket made of wool or some other material
She wore a *sweater* when she felt cold. His mother made him a wool *sweater*.

sweep

verb: sweeping, swept, swept
clean by using a broom
She *swept* the house to make it look clean before her guests arrived.

sweet

adjective
1. *tasting like sugar*
He likes his coffee *sweet*; he adds a lot of sugar to it.
2. *not with salt*
I bought some *sweet* butter for my aunt, because she can't have salt.
3. *kind and nice*
I received a very *sweet* letter from a friend; the letter had very kind words in it.

swell

verb: swelling, swelled, swollen
become bigger
He fell on his hand and hurt it; now it has *swollen*; it looks bigger than his other hand; the doctor told him to put ice on it.
adjective
very fine, excellent
We saw a *swell* play last night; the actors were very good.

swept

See **sweep**.

swift

adjective
fast
He is very *swift* in his work; he does it in a very short time.

swiftly

adverb
quickly
He does his work *swiftly*; it doesn't take him a long time.

swim

noun
moving in the water
He feels a little hot; he wants to go for a *swim* in the lake.
verb: swimming, swam, swum
move in the water
After she *swam* for half an hour, she sat in the sun.

swimmer

noun
a person who swims
Five *swimmers* swam across the pool; my friend was the second.

swimming

See **swim** also.
noun
the act of moving in water
Swimming is a very good exercise.

swing

noun

something at the end of a rope that one can hold or sit on to move backwards and forwards
The children like to sit on the *swing* for a long time.
verb: swinging, swung, swung
move backwards and forwards
Monkeys like to *swing* from trees.

switch

noun
a device to turn electric things on or off

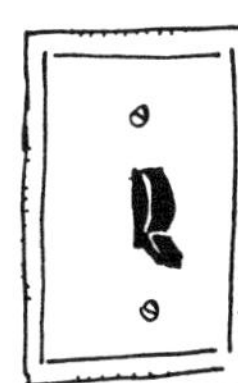

She turned on the *switch* for some light.
verb
exchange
My friend and I *switched* places in class; she took my place, and I took hers.

sword

noun
a weapon that looks like a very long knife
In the old days, soldiers fought with *swords*.

swum
See **swim**.

swung
See **swing**.

sympathy
noun: sympathies
a feeling for others
She had *sympathy* for her brother when he needed help, and she gave him some.

system
noun
a group of things working together
Language is a *system*; the sounds, words, and grammar of a language work together as one unit. The company is using a new *system* to keep their accounts.

Tt

table

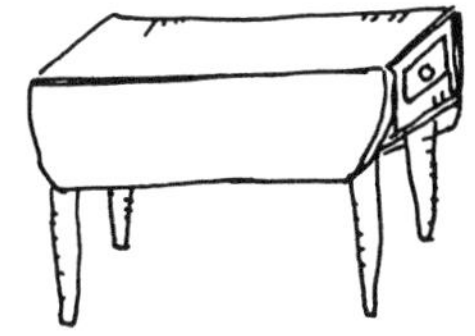

noun
1. *a flat surface with four (or three) legs*
We sat at the *table* to eat.
2. *a body of figures*
I could tell the prices of different cars from the *table*.

tail

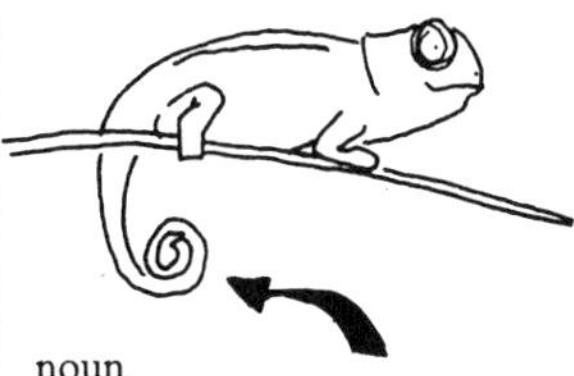

noun
the end part of an animal
Don't hold a dog by its *tail*; dogs don't like that.

tailor
noun
a person who makes or fixes clothes
I took a piece of cloth to my *tailor*, and he made me a new suit.

take
verb: taking, took, taken
1. *hold*
I *took* the child's hand before we crossed the street.
2. *capture*
The army *took* the city.
3. *remove, subtract*
If you *take* three from seven, you are left with four.

taken
See **take**.

talk
noun
a speech
The manager gave the workers a *talk* at the beginning of the year; he told them to work hard.
verb
speak
I *talked* with my friend on the telephone for a long time.

tall
adjective

opposite of short
He is a *tall* boy; he is six feet *tall*. There are many *tall* buildings in New York.

tank
noun

1. *a big container*
The water for the city is stored in big *tanks*.

2. *a strong vehicle used in fighting*
The army used big *tanks* to advance against the city.

tanker

noun
a ship that takes oil across seas
Tankers can carry thousands of tons of oil.

tap

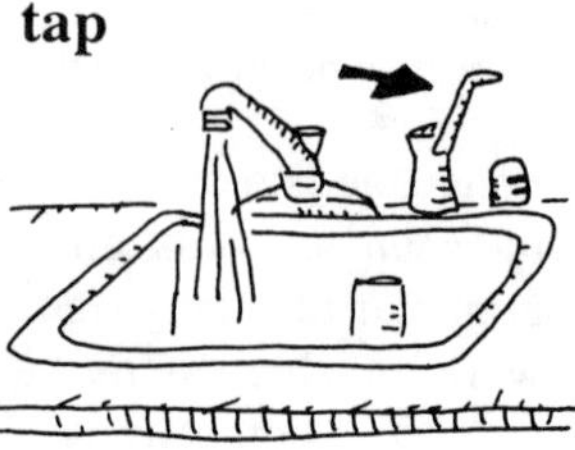

noun
the device that one opens at home to get water
We get cold and hot water from the same *tap* in our bathroom.

task
noun
job
One of my *tasks* in school as a student was to bring enough chalk to class.

taste
noun
1. *trying the flavor of some food*
I had a *taste* of the dessert to see if I liked it; it was good.
2. *knowing and liking things of quality*
She has very good *taste* when it comes to clothes; she wears the nicest dresses.
verb: tasting, tasted, tasted
try the flavor of some food
I *tasted* the food on the plate; I didn't like it.

taught
See **teach**.

tax
noun
an amount that is paid to the government by people
When we buy things from a store, we pay for them, and we pay a *tax* on them too. Everybody who works must pay *taxes* to the government.
verb: taxing, taxed, taxed
ask (someone) to pay a tax
The government *taxes* people on their income.

taxi
noun
a car that people ride in for pay
We took a *taxi* from our house to the airport.

tea
noun
a drink that comes from leaves
My brother puts milk and sugar in his *tea*. I like iced *tea*.

teach
verb: teaching, taught, taught
give knowledge and skills (to someone)
Mr. Smith *taught* us to write well.

teacher
noun
a person who teaches
Mr. Smith was a good *teacher*; he taught us English and he cared for us.

team
noun
a group of persons who do something together
Our basketball *team* won the game last night. He and his wife ran their business as a *team*.

tear

noun
a drop that falls from the eye
The sad news brought *tears* to her eyes.

tear

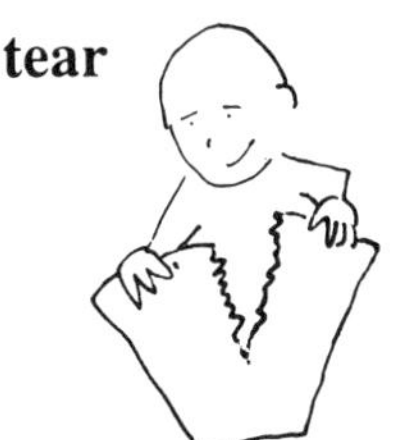

verb: tearing, tore, torn
take a piece of paper or cloth apart
She *tore* her dress as she was going down the steps. Now she has to fix it before she can wear it again.

teeth
See **tooth**.

telephone

noun
the device we use to talk with others who are not with us
I spoke with my friend for ten minutes on the *telephone*.
verb: telephoning, telephoned, telephoned
use a telephone, call (someone)
I *telephoned* my friend and invited him to come to dinner.

television

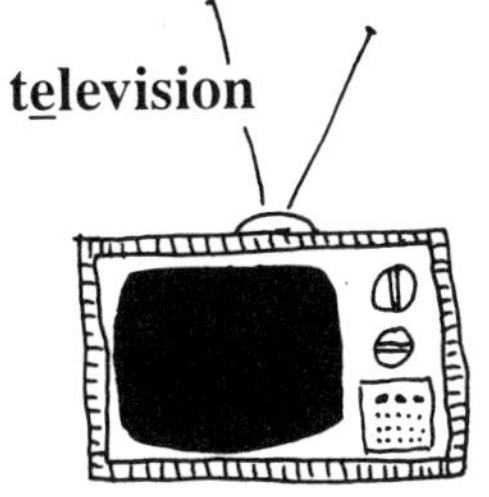

noun
a device that gives us pictures on a screen
We saw an old movie on *television* last night.

tell
verb: telling, told, told
1. *say to*
She *told* me about the new film. I listened as she spoke.
2. *relate*
She *told* us a very interesting story.

temperature
noun
a degree showing how hot or cold something or someone is
His *temperature* went up today; he is not well. Water turns to ice at a *temperature* of 32°F or lower.

ten
noun
a number: 10
Ten is the lowest number with two digits.
adjective
a number: 10
What can you buy with *ten* dollars?

tend
verb
1. *look after*
He *tended* to his business every day; that is why he did so well.
2. *show how one is inclined*
He *tends* to like western movies.

tender
adjective
soft
It was easy to eat my steak; it was very *tender*.

tent

noun
a room or shelter made of strong cloth
The camp had ten *tents*; each *tent* held six people.

tenth
noun
1. *a number showing order: 10th*
I was the *tenth* to walk into the room; nine persons went in before me.
2. *one of ten equal parts*
We divided the cake among the ten of us; each of us had one *tenth* of it.
adjective
a number showing order: 10th
October is the *tenth* month of the year.

term
noun
a fixed period of time
The president of the U.S. is elected for a *term* of four years.

terrible
adjective
very bad
The food they gave us was *terrible*; it was cold, and it wasn't cooked well.

terribly
adverb
1. *in a very bad way*
He spoke *terribly*; he didn't have much to say, and he didn't say it well.
2. *very much*
She is *terribly* clever; she understands things very quickly.

territory
noun: territories
an area of land
The *territory* between the two hills became a small city.

test
noun
an examination
The teacher gave us a *test* in English; we did very well in it.
verb
examine
The teacher *tested* us yesterday; he found out that our English is quite good.

than
conjunction
(showing comparison)
He is taller *than* his brother.

thank
verb
show that one is grateful
We *thanked* our teacher for teaching us English so well.

thankful
adjective
grateful
We are very *thankful* to our teacher for teaching us English in such a short time.

that
pronoun (plural: those)
1. *the (thing) there*
That is our house; it is at the end of the street.
2. *the thing already mentioned*
We went to the library to borrow some books; after *that*, we went to class.
adjective
the (thing) there or just mentioned
That book is very interesting.
conjunction
the thing that will be mentioned
He knew *that* we were coming.

that's
pronoun and verb
that is
That's a book.
pronoun and auxiliary verb
1. *that is*
That's going too far.
2. *that has*
That's been here for a week.

the
article
(showing something definite)
The boy I am talking

about is *the* same boy you mentioned.
adverb
(to that degree)
The taller you are, *the* easier it will be for you to play basketball.

theater
noun
1. *a place where plays are acted*
I went to the *theater* to buy tickets for the play.
2. *plays or performances*
I like the *theater*; I see one play or two a month.

their
adjective
(showing possession)
This is not *their* book; it's ours.

theirs
pronoun
(showing possession)
This is not their book; *theirs* is a blue one; this is green.

them
pronoun: they, them, their, theirs
(third person plural)
They are good teachers; I like *them*.

themselves
emphatic pronoun
they alone
They did the work *themselves*.
reflexive pronoun
their own selves
They hurt *themselves* playing with knives.

then
adverb
1. *at that time*
He didn't eat the apple at 3:00 p.m.; he wasn't hungry. He felt hungry at 5:00 p.m.; he ate the apple *then*.
2. *after that*
First we went to the library; *then* we went to class.

theory
noun: theories
a thought, a principle
The merchant bought a lot of sugar on the *theory* that the price of sugar will be going up; he was right; he gained a lot of money.

there
adverb
in that place
I live here; my friend lives somewhere else; here I have three rooms; *there* he has four. Go to the library; you will find my friend *there*.
pronoun
(to begin a sentence)
There is a story I would like to tell you.

thereby
adverb
by that way
He drove through the field, *thereby* saving a lot of time.

therefore
adverb
as a result
She saved her money for two years; *therefore*, she had enough money when she wanted to buy a car.

there's
pronoun and verb
there is
There's a book on the table.
pronoun and auxiliary verb
there has
There's been an accident in the street.

these
pronoun (singular: this)
the ones here
These are the books I told you about.
adjective
the ones here
These books are very interesting.

they
pronoun: they, them, their, theirs
third person plural
I know Jack and Mary; *they* are good friends of mine.

they'd
pronoun and auxiliary verb
1. *they had*
They'd done their work before they went home.
2. *they would*
They'd like to see a new film.

they'll
pronoun and auxiliary verb
they will
They'll be here in five minutes.

they're
pronoun and verb
they are
They're good people.
pronoun and auxiliary verb
they are
They're doing their work well.

they've
pronoun and auxiliary verb
they have
They've been studying for a long time.

thick
adjective
not thin (for things)
I have a *thick* blanket to keep me warm in winter.

thief
noun: thieves
a person who steals
A *thief* went into a house and stole some money; he was caught by the police.

thieves
See **thief**.

thin
adjective
1. *not thick (for things)*
I cut a *thin* slice of cake to eat; I wasn't very hungry.
2. *not fat (for persons)*
She's very *thin*; she doesn't eat much.

thing

noun
1. *an object*
There are two *things* in this box: a pen and a pencil.
2. *a matter*
I have a *thing* or two to tell you about.

think
verb: thinking, thought, thought
use the mind
We must *think* before we act. I *thought* of something last night.

third
noun
1. *a number showing order: 3rd*
I was the *third* on the list of runners in school.
2. *one of three equal parts*
We divided the money among the three of us; each got one *third.*
adjective
a number showing order: 3rd
I was the *third* person in line; two people were ahead of me.

thirsty
adjective: thirstier, thirstiest
needing water
When we are hungry, we eat; when we are *thirsty*, we drink.

thirteen
noun
a number: 13
Six and seven make *thirteen.*
adjective
a number: 13
I have *thirteen* friends in class: six boys and seven girls.

thirty
noun
a number: 30
Thirty is three times ten.
adjective
a number: 30
Thirty students were in class today: fifteen boys and fifteen girls.

this
pronoun (plural: these)
the one here
This is the book I told

you about.
adjective
the one here
This book is very interesting.

thorough
adjective
very careful
He is very *thorough* in his work; he does everything very well.

thoroughly
adverb
1. *very carefully*
He does his work *thoroughly*; he makes no mistakes.
2. *completely*
She is *thoroughly* satisfied with her results; they are exactly what she wanted.

those
pronoun (singular: that)
the ones there
Those are the new cars they have.
adjective
the ones there
Those cars are the ones they bought last week.

though
adverb
however
They wanted to travel yesterday; the weather stopped them from doing that, *though*.
conjunction
with that
Though it is raining, they are planning to play outside.

thought
See **think** also.
noun
idea
He has a good *thought*; he would like us to cook a meal for hungry people.

thousand
noun
a number: 1,000
She can count to one *thousand*.
adjective
a number: 1,000
More than a *thousand* people were at the airport to meet the football players.

thread

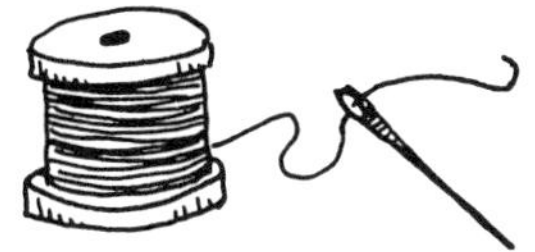

noun
a very thin string used in sewing
She used a needle and *thread* to fix the button on my shirt.

threat
noun
words that show that something bad will happen
The thief made a *threat* that he would shoot the manager of the store if he tried to telephone the police.

threaten
verb
say that something bad will happen
The thief *threatened* to kill the manager if he tried to call the police.

three
noun
a number: 3
Two and one make *three*.
adjective
a number: 3
They have *three* children: two girls and a boy.

threw
See **throw**.

thrill
noun
joy and excitement
Flying in an airplane for the first time gave the children a *thrill*; it made them very happy.
verb
give joy and excitement
Flying in an airplane for the first time *thrilled* the children; it made them very happy.

throat
noun

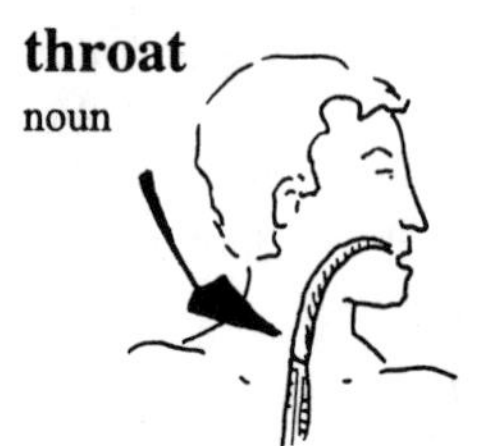

the front part of the neck on the inside
He hurt his *throat* when he swallowed a big piece of bread.

throne

noun
a king's or queen's chair
The king sat on his *throne* with a crown on his head.

through
adjective
open to let (things) pass
We drove down a *through* street to the museum.
adverb
from begining to end
I read the book *through*.
proposition
from one side to the other
I walked *through* the garden and saw the beautiful flowers.

throughout
adverb
everywhere
You don't have to go to the main branch of the bank in the city; you will find branches *throughout*.

throw
verb: throwing, threw, thrown
use the hand to send (something) through the air
I *threw* the ball to my friend; he caught it.

thrown
See **throw**.

thumb

noun
the thick "finger" on the hand
People have eight fingers and two *thumbs*.

thunder
noun
the noise made by clouds
The child was afraid when she saw the lightning and heard the *thunder* during the storm.

Thursday
noun
a day of the week
Thursday comes after Wednesday and before Friday.

thus
adverb
1. *in that way*
I told him to drive slowly down the hill; he drove *thus*.
2. *therefore*
He was ill; *thus* he couldn't play basketball.

tick
noun
a check mark
I put a *tick* on the words I knew; then I studied the others.
verb
put a check mark on
I *ticked* the words I knew; then I studied the others.

ticket
noun

1. *a paper showing that one has paid for something*
We bought six *tickets* for the play.
2. *a paper given by a police officer to someone who does something wrong*
When he parked his car in the wrong place in

the city, he found a *ticket* on his car.

tide
noun
the rising and falling of sea water
When the *tide* is high, we can't see the rocks on the shore.

tidy
adjective: tidier, tidiest
having things in place and in order
He is a very *tidy* person; his room always looks neat and clean.

tie

noun
1. *a long piece of cloth worn around the neck*
He has a *tie* to go with every suit.
2. *a connection*
They have good *ties* with the president's office; they know many people there.
verb: tying, tied, tied
connect

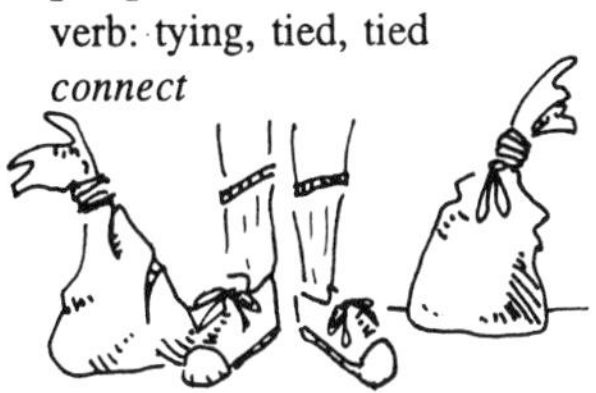

We *tied* the two bags together with a string.

tiger

noun
a big and strong male animal
Tigers can catch deer and eat them.

tight
adjective
firm, not loose
Her shoes hurt her feet; they are *tight*.

tigress
noun
a female tiger
Tigresses sometimes help tigers catch deer.

till
verb
plow and plant the land
The farmer *tilled* his land.
preposition
until
He stayed in the office *till* eight o'clock in the evening.

time
noun
1. *a period of minutes, hours, days, weeks, months, years, or so*
It takes a shorter *time* to fly to a place than to drive there.
2. *exact minute of the day that a watch or clock gives*
The *time* now is 4:40 p.m.
verb: timing, timed, timed
see how long a thing takes
They *timed* the runner; he ran the distance in ten seconds.

tin
noun
a metal
Many containers that have soft drinks are made of *tin*.

tiny
adjective: tinier, tiniest
small
The baby was *tiny*; it was only four pounds in weight.

tip
noun

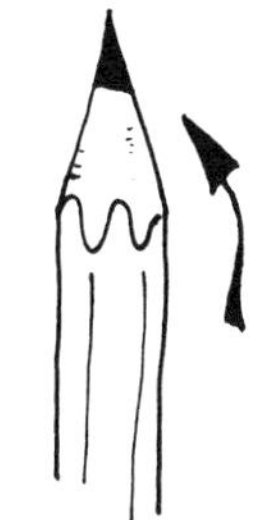

1. *an end*
To write well, your pencil must have a sharp *tip*.

2. *money given to someone who does some work for you*
When I eat in a restaurant, I leave a *tip* for the waiter.
verb: tipping, tipped, tipped
give money to someone who does some work for you
We *tipped* the waitress in the restaurant; she was very kind to us.

tire
noun

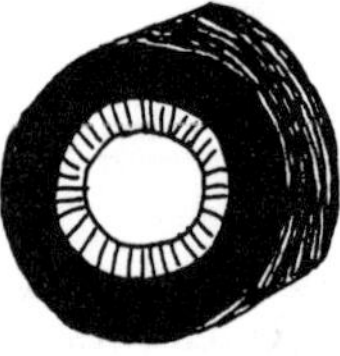

a wheel
She bought four new *tires* for her car.

tired
adjective
feeling the effect of work, needing rest
He worked for hours on his car; he got very *tired*; he sat down to rest.

title
noun
subject
He bought a new book; the *title* of the book is *The English Language.*

to
preposition
1. *(showing direction)*
We walked from the library *to* class.
2. *as far as*
I can stay here up *to* one hour; after that, I must leave.
3. *until*
They were with us from six *to* eight o'clock in the evening.

today
noun
this day
Today is Wednesday; tomorrow is Thursday.
adverb
on this day
They are arriving *today*.

toe

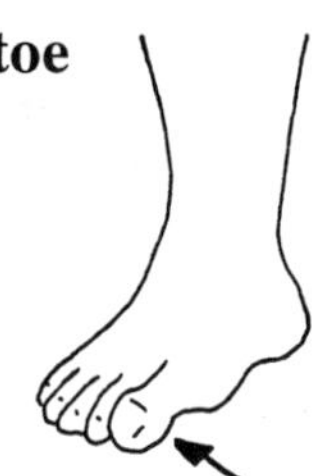

noun
a foot finger
When she took off her shoes and hit her foot, she hurt her *toes*.

together
adverb
1. *with each other*
We worked *together* in the office.
2. *at the same time*
Can you read and watch television *together*?

toilet
noun
a bathroom
He went to the *toilet* to wash his hands.

told
See **tell**.

tomato

noun: tomatoes
a red fruit used on sandwiches or in salads as a vegetable
She likes to put red *tomatoes* in the salads she prepares.

tomorrow
noun
the day after today
If *tomorrow* is Monday, today must be Sunday.
adverb
on the day after today
They arrived today, and they are leaving *tomorrow*.

ton
noun
a weight: 1,000 kilograms
Tankers can hold thousands of *tons* of oil.

tongue
noun

the part of the month that we use to taste and to talk with
Cats and dogs use their *tongues* to drink water or milk.

tonight
noun
this night or the coming night
Tonight is the time to see the film.
adverb
on this night or the coming night
We can see them tomorrow; they are arriving *tonight*.

too
adverb
1. *also*
She goes to school, and I go to school *too*.
2. *more (than necessary or than one can take)*
It is *too* hot to walk outside.
3. *very*
Thank you for your help; you are *too* kind.

took
See **take**.

tool
noun

an instrument that we use to do things
He keeps all his garden *tools* in a shed in the garden.

tooth

noun: teeth
one of the white bones in the mouth that we use when we eat
Her *teeth* showed when she smiled.

top
noun

1. *the highest point*
The boys climbed to the *top* of the mountain.

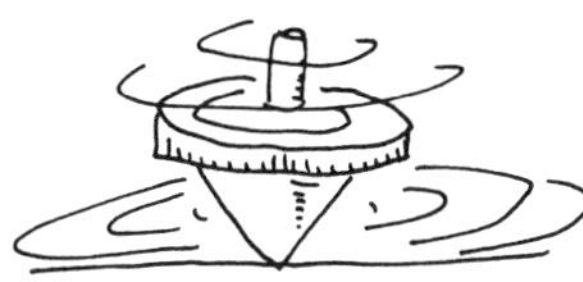

2. *a toy that turns around*
The boy played with his *top*.

tore
See **tear**.

toss
verb
throw up or down
He *tossed* a coin up in the air to see which side would be up when it fell to the floor.

total
noun
sum
We added the numbers 15, 20, and 32; the *total* was 67.
verb
We *totaled* what we paid for the clothes; it was a bit more than we expected.

touch
noun
1. *a light stroke*
He felt my *touch* on his hand.
2. *a small bit*
All she needs is a *touch* of kindness. He has a *touch* of a cold.
verb
contact with the hand
The store manager did not want people to *touch* the things on the shelves.

tour
noun
a journey
They took a *tour* to some of the small islands and then returned home.
verb
make a journey
They *toured* the islands and returned home in three days.

tourist
noun
a visitor to a place
Many *tourists* from all over the world visit Washington, D.C. to see the important buildings and places.

toward
See **towards**.

towards or toward
preposition
1. *in the direction of*
We walked *towards* the beach, but we turned back before we got there.
2. *as part of a payment for*
She paid $1,000 *towards* her car.

towel

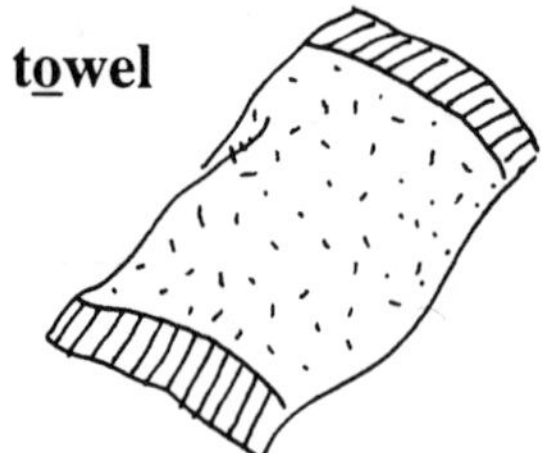

noun
a piece of material to dry oneself with
He dried his hands with a face *towel.* She has a big *towel* for the beach.

town
noun
1. *a small city*
The *town* they live in has a hospital and post office.
2. *an area with stores and shops*
They went to *town* to buy what they needed for the party.

toy

noun
a play thing
Children like to play with *toys.*
He has small cars and planes and other *toys.*

trace

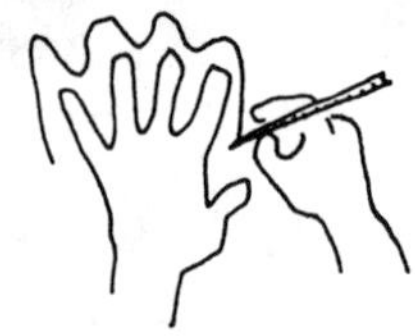

noun
a mark left by something
He left some *traces* behind him when he walked on the wet floor.
verb: tracing, traced, traced
copy by following marks or lines
She drew a picture of the face when she *traced* it on a piece of paper.

track

noun
a mark left by someone walking or driving
They followed the *tracks* of the wheels until they got to the house.

tractor

noun
a big machine that moves on wheels and cuts the earth for farming
The farmer has his *tractor* in the field; he plows the earth with it before he plants his seeds.

trade
noun
buying and selling

There was a lot of *trade* between travelers and natives in the old world.
verb: trading, traded, traded
1. *buy and sell*
The merchants are *trading* their jewels in the city.
2. *exchange*
The boys are *trading* their toy cars; John wants the blue one instead of the red one.

trader
noun
a person who buys and sells
Traders can make a lot of money if they move from city to city.

tradition
noun
an old way of doing things
The people of that tribe still follow old *traditions*. Eating turkey on Thanksgiving day is an American *tradition*.

traffic
noun
the movement of cars and other vehicles
Traffic is heavy early in the morning and late in the afternoon. We drove very slowly because of the heavy *traffic*.

trail
noun
a trace, a mark left by someone or something that has gone before
The thieves left a *trail* that the police could follow.

train

noun
a vehicle that runs on rails and takes passengers
I like to travel by *train*; I see the country that way.
verb
give practice
The teacher *trained* us to write English correctly.

translate
verb: translating, translated, translated
say or write something in another language
The new student didn't understand English; so I *translated* what the teacher said into Spanish for him.

trap

noun
a way to catch someone or something
They put a little *trap* in the kitchen to catch mice; it worked.
verb: trapping, trapped, trapped
use a way to catch someone or something
They *trapped* the mouse in the kitchen.

travel
noun
journey
She met many new people and saw many new places in her *travels*.
verb: traveling, traveled, traveled
journey
They *traveled* to many countries in Europe.

traveler
noun
a person who travels
The planes were full; there were many *travelers* going to Europe.

tray

noun
a flat piece of wood, glass, or metal to serve things on
The waiter brought the food and drinks on a *tray*.

treasure
noun
things of value put somewhere
In the past, people put their *treasures* in boxes in the ground.
verb: treasuring, treasured, treasured
give value to
He is a very wise person; I *treasure* his words.

treat
noun
something liked very much
She made a delicious cake; it was a *treat.*
verb
1. *deal with (someone or something)*
He *treats* his friends well; he is always kind to them.
2. *offer someone something and pay for it*
My uncle *treated* my friends and me to ice-cream.

treatment
noun
the way a person deals with someone or something
I like his *treatment* of the dog; he takes care of his dog kindly.

treaty
noun: treaties
agreement between nations
After the war, the two countries signed a peace *treaty.*

tree

noun
a big plant with a stem and branches
They picked some oranges from the orange *tree.*

tremble
verb: trembling, trembled, trembled
shake
The child *trembled* when he saw a big dog near him; he was afraid of the dog.

triangle

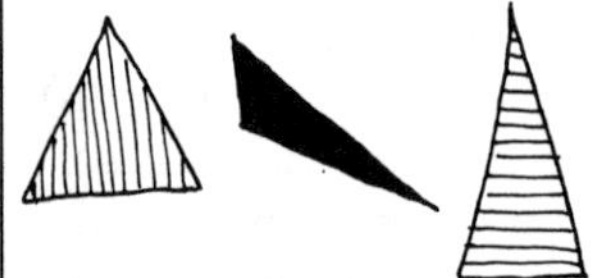

noun
a shape with three sides
A *triangle* has three sides and three angles.

tribe
noun
a number of families that belong to one group
In the past, tribes *fought* against each other.

trick
noun
1. *a clever way to make things look like something that they are not*
He is very fast with his hands; he does some card *tricks.*
2. *a way to deceive*
They played a *trick* on us; they made us stand, and they took our seats.
verb
deceive
They *tricked* us into leaving our seats, so that they could sit.

tried
See **try**.

trim
verb: trimming, trimmed, trimmed
cut and let (something) look neat
When the branches of the tree grew too long, I *trimmed* them. He *trims* his moustache once a week.

trip
noun
a journey
We took a *trip* to Europe last summer.
verb: tripping, tripped, tripped
fall
She *tripped* over a stone in the street.

triumph
noun
victory
We were very happy with our team's *triumph* in basketball.

trouble
noun
a problem, something that makes one not very comfortable
They have some *trouble* with their mail; it is getting to them late.
verb: troubling, troubled, troubled
cause a problem
Their son is *troubling* them; he is not doing very well in school.

trousers

noun
long pants
He wanted to buy a new suit; he tried one on; the jacket fit well, but the *trousers* were a bit small on him.

truck

noun
a vehicle for carrying heavy things
The army used *trucks* to move soldiers and guns to the field.

true
adjective: truer, truest
correct
This is a *true* statement: The sun rises in the east and sets in the west.

truly
adverb
honestly
We were *truly* very tired after our trip; we needed to rest.

trunk
noun

1. *the thick part of a tree above the ground*
The cat climbed up the *trunk* of our tree in the garden.

2. *the container in the back of a car*
We put our suitcases in the *trunk* and drove to the airport.

trust
verb
1. hope
I *trust* you will visit the zoo in our city; it is a very interesting place to see.
2. *depend on*
She *trusts* her husband to do the hard things around the house.

truth
noun
a correct statement
He told the *truth*; he broke the cup and told his mother about it.

try
verb: trying, tried, tried
test
We *tried* the food in that restaurant and didn't like it very much.

tube
noun

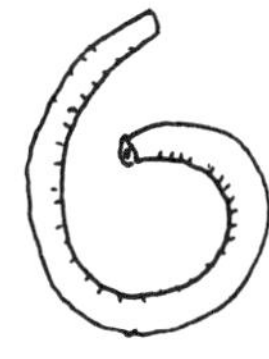

1. *a round and hollow thing for liquids to go through*
The nurse passed the blood *through* a tube in the hospital room.

2. *a container for soft material*
She put some cream on her hands from a *tube*.

Tuesday
noun
a day of the week
Tuesday comes after Monday and before Wednesday. They arrived on *Tuesday*.

tumble
verb: tumbling, tumbled, tumbled
fall
He *tumbled* down the steps; he went down too fast.

tune
noun
a number of musical notes
We listened to some music, and we felt like dancing to the *tune*.

turn
noun
1. *the place and time for something to happen*
My friends and I took *turns* to throw the ball into the basket; when my *turn* came, I threw it in.
2. *a bend*

He drove slowly at the *turn* in the road.
verb
change direction
He drove down the street; then he *turned* to a side street to get to the restaurant.

turn on
verb
put on
He *turned on* the lights when he entered the house.

twelfth
noun
a number showing order: 12th
They were married on the *twelfth* of June.
adjective
a number showing order: 12th
The *twelfth* month of the year is the last month of the year.

twelve
noun
a number: 12
Ten plus two make *twelve*.
adjective
a number: 12
There are *twelve* students in my class: six boys and six girls.

twenty
noun
a number: 20
Fifteen and five make *twenty*.
adjective
a number: 20
There are *twenty* classrooms in our school: ten in one building and ten in another.

twice
adverb
two times
He tried to jump over the wall *twice*; the first time, he couldn't do it; the second time, he did it.

twist
verb
1. *turn from the right way*
I told him a story, but he *twisted* it when he told it to his brother; he changed many things in it.
2. *turn to hurt*
She *twisted* her finger; the doctor said it would take three days to get well again.

two
noun
a number: 2
Two and *two* make four.
adjective

a number: 2
They have *two* uncles: Sam and Ray.

tying
See **tie.**

type
noun
a kind
There is a new *type* of jacket in the store; I don't like it very much.
verb: typing, typed, typed
print on a typewriter
She wrote a letter to her friend, but she *typed* a letter to the manager of her company.

typing
See **type.**

typewriter
noun
a machine that types letters, numbers, and other signs
She bought a new electric *typewriter* for herself; now she can type her own letters and reports.

Uu

ugly
adjective: uglier, ugliest
not nice, not pretty
With all the paper and other things thrown in the garden, the place looked *ugly*.

umbrella

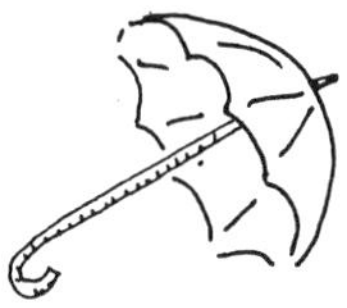

noun
a protection to carry from the rain or sun
When it rains, I open my *umbrella* and use it.

un-
prefix
not
He is *un*wanted here. He is *un*desirable. He is *un*fit to be here.

unable
adjective
not able, cannot
After he broke his leg, he was *unable* to walk without a stick.

uncle
noun
the brother of a father or mother
My *uncle* has two children; they are my cousins.

under
preposition
beneath, opposite of over
The cat is *under* the table.

underground
noun
a train system that goes partly under street level
We went to the market by *underground*; it was fast and comfortable.

underneath
preposition
below, just under
My book is *underneath* my school bag.

understand
verb: understanding, understood, understood
1. *know (in the mind)*
She can read a bit of French, but she doesn't *understand* it very well.
2. *see the point*
A. I'm sorry I have a meeting; I can't come to your party.
B. I *understand.*

understanding
See **understand** also.
noun
agreement
He and his wife have an *understanding*: she cooks the main dish, and he makes the salad.

understood
See **understand**.

undress
verb
take off clothes
She *undressed* her child before she gave him a bath.

undressed
adjective
without clothes
He wouldn't open the door because he was *undressed.*

unfortunate
adjective
unlucky
They were a bit *unfortunate*: they decided to go on a picnic on a very rainy day.

unfortunately
adverb
unhappily
They could have paid for their dinner by cash or credit card. *Unfortunately*, they had neither.

unhappy
adjective
sad
They were very *unhappy* when they listened to the news and learned that the airport was closed; they wanted to fly that day.

uniform

noun
a dress or costume worn by a group of people
All students in that school wear the same blue *uniform.*
adjective
regular, unchanging
The weather here is very *uniform*; it doesn't change very often.

union
noun
1. *unity, oneness*
The two governments decided on a *union* between the two countries.
2. *a group of people in an organization that helps them with their rights*
All the workers in the factory are members of their local *union.*

universal
adjective
belonging to the whole world
The physics laws we learned are really *universal.* They apply everywhere.

university
noun: universities
an institution of higher learning that gives high degrees
My cousin is studying medicine in the *university*; he wants to become a doctor.

unknown
adjective
not known
When he first came to this city, he was an *unknown* person; later he became quite famous.

unless
conjunction
except if
I don't think we can leave now *unless* it has stopped raining.

until
conjunction
1. *except at the time when*
We can't leave *until* it stops raining.
2. *till the time when*
Wait *until* he comes to start the meeting.

unusual
adjective
not ordinary
He is always on time. Today he was late. This is very *unusual* for him.

up
adverb
opposite of down
He is moving *up* in the company; he was a salesman and now he is director.
preposition
opposite of down
This man is climbing *up* the ladder.

upon
preposition
1. *across*
I came *upon* an interesting book in the library.
2. *over, on top of*

He put his hat *upon* his head.

upper
adjective

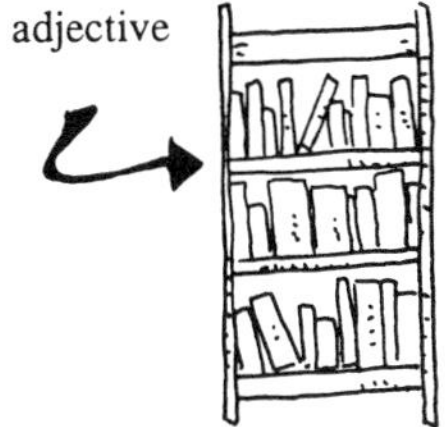

the one on top
There are two shelves in this bookcase. My books are on the *upper* shelf.

upside down

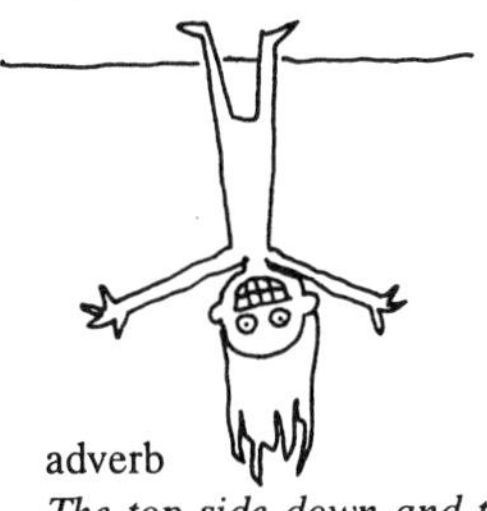

adverb
The top side down and the bottom side up
This boy is holding his book *upside down.* He doesn't know that; he can't read.

upstairs
adverb
on a higher level in a building
We live on the middle floor of our building. The neighbors who live *upstairs* walk up and down more steps than we do.

upward
adverb
in a direction towards the top
He is moving *upward* in the company. He was a salesman and now he is a manager.

urge
noun
a strong desire to do something
He had the *urge* to do some exercise, so he went for a long walk.
verb: urging, urged, urged
press, encourage, push (someone to do something)
You are facing an important examination. I *urge* you to study hard for it.

us
pronoun: we, us, our, ours
first person plural
We like them, and they like *us*. All of *us* like each other.

use
noun (pronunciation: s)
the way we make things work for us
I made good *use* of the telephone: I spoke with five of my friends.
verb (pronunciation: z): using, used, used
make things work for us
I *used* the telephone to speak with my friends.

useful
adjective
good to use
The telephone is very *useful* when you want to contact people who are far away.

usual
adjective
ordinary
Arriving late is not very *usual* for him; he is always on time.

usually
adverb
ordinarily
He is *usually* on time; I don't know why he is late today.

utter
verb
say, speak
The baby *uttered* his first word; he said, "Ba-ba."

Vv

vacation
noun
holiday
Students like their summer *vacation* when they can play and swim.

valley

noun
a low place between mountains
We drove over a mountain and down to a *valley* where we saw a farm.

valuable
adjective
having value or worth
My books are very *valuable*; they have good information in them, and I paid a lot of money for them.

value
noun
worth
There is a high *value* on his land; it is on a corner.
verb: valuing, valued, valued
put a worth (on something or someone)
I *value* my friends very highly. Do you *value* your free time?

vanish
verb
disappear
He was playing with us; then he *vanished*; we didn't know where he was. An hour later he appeared again.

various
adjective
different
There are *various* ways of cooking meat: you can boil it, bake it, or fry it.

vary
verb: varying, varied, varied
differ
Vary your colors; sometimes use red, sometimes blue, and sometimes green.

vase

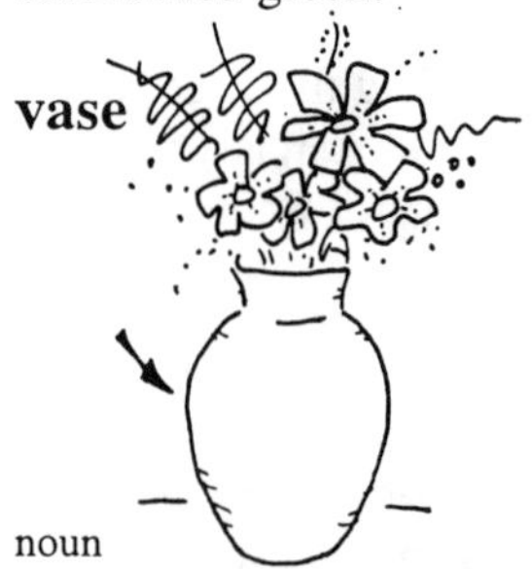

noun
a container for flowers
She put three red roses in a tall glass *vase*.

vast
adjective
huge and wide
We drove over *vast* areas of farm land; the trip took hours.

vegetable

noun
a white, green, or red plant that is not a flower or a fruit
She made a salad with four different *vegetables*: lettuce, carrots, cucumbers, and beans.

veil

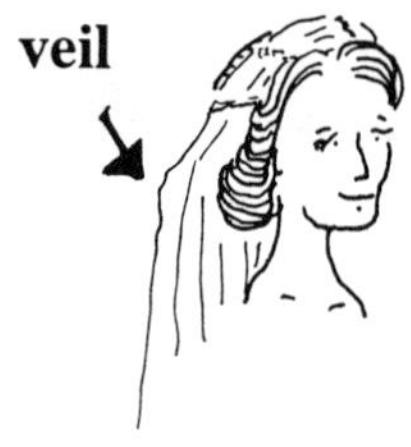

noun
a cover for the face
The bride wore a white *veil* over her face.

vein

noun
a tube that blood goes through in the body

Our *veins* take the blood to different parts of our bodies.

venture
noun
a daring experience
He tried climbing to the top of the mountain on his last *venture*.
verb: venturing, ventured, ventured
dare to try something
They *ventured* into the dark without knowing the area.

verb
noun
a part of speech like a noun or an adjective
In the sentence, "He came here yesterday," *came* is the *verb*.

verbal
adjective
oral
His *verbal* language is good; he speaks well, but his written language is poor.

very
adverb
extremely, much
He is a *very* clever student; he gets high grades in all his courses.

vessel
noun
1. *a container*
All the washed fruits were in a plastic *vessel* in the refrigerator.

2. *a ship*
Three *vessels* sailed into the harbor this morning.

vice
noun
a bad habit or behavior
Smoking and eating too much are among his *vices*. He knows he shouldn't do them.

victim
noun
a person who has been hurt
The thief was put in prison; his *victim* got back the money that had been stolen.

victory
noun: victories
winning a game or battle
Our basketball *victory* last night was wonderful; we won by a score of 88 to 53.

view

noun
the things one sees by looking out
We have a commanding *view* of the river from our house.

village
noun
a small town in the country
They have a small cottage in a *village* half way up the mountain.

vine

noun
a plant that gives grapes
We have a *vine* tree in our garden; it gives us red grapes in summer.

violet
noun
a color which one can get by mixing blue and red
She doesn't like *violet*; she prefers blue.
adjective
has that color
She doesn't like her *violet* dress as much as her blue dress.

virtue
noun
a very good personal quality
My father was a man of *virtue*; he was honest and kind.

visa

noun
a stamp on a passport that allows a person to enter a country
They applied for *visas* to Italy; they wanted to visit Rome and Florence.

vision
noun
sight, seeing
Before you become a driver, you must have your *vision* tested. One must see well in order to drive.

visit
noun
going to and seeing people or places
Our neighbors paid us a *visit* last night. They come and see us once a week.
verb
go and see people or places
Our class *visited* the zoo last week. We were studying about animals.

visitor
noun
a person who visits
The zoo has many *visitors* every day. People like to go there.

voice
noun
the sound made by speaking or singing
She has a lovely *voice*; she sang a beautiful song last night.

volleyball

noun
a ball game played over a high net
Our team of six players won the *volleyball* game yesterday.

vote
noun
a voice or support for someone running for an office or a position
Two persons were running for mayor of our city. The person who received more *votes* won the election.
verb: voting, voted, voted
give a voice or support for someone running for an office or a position
I *voted* for my friend to become our team captain.

vow
noun
a promise
She made a *vow* not to smoke cigarettes any more. She won't smoke at all.
verb
make a promise
She *vowed* never to smoke again.

vowel
noun
a sound or letter which is not a consonant
In the English alphabet, there are five *vowels* and twenty-one consonants. The *vowel* sound in *seat* is longer than the *vowel* sound in *sit*.

voyage
noun
a trip by sea or air
They were on board the ship for two weeks. Their *voyage* around the islands was wonderful.

Ww

wage
noun

a pay
All the workers received their *wages* at the end of the week; they were paid by check.

wagon

noun
a big carriage with one horse or more pulling it
In the past, travelers crossed the country in *wagons*.

waist

noun
the middle part of the body where a belt fits
His trousers were too big around his *waist*. He needed a belt to hold them up.

wait
verb
spend time expecting someone or something
We got to the station early; we *waited* half an hour for the train to arrive. I'm not ready; *wait* a minute.

waiter
noun
a male person who serves at tables
Our *waiter* in the restaurant was very good; he served us fast.

waitress
noun
a female person who serves at tables
That restaurant has a good *waitress*; she smiles and serves the customers politely.

wake
verb: waking, woke, woken
stop sleeping
I *wake* up at 6:00 a.m. every day, and I get out of bed. The mother *woke* her children up for school.

walk
noun
a stroll
We went for a *walk* to the park; we took our dog with us.
verb
take a stroll
We *walked* for a long time. When we got tired we took a taxi back home.

wall

noun
a flat structure that separates rooms or other areas
I have pictures of my family on the *walls* in my room. The soldiers built a *wall* around the city to protect it.

wallet

noun
a billfold
He keeps his money and cards in a black *wallet* in his pocket.

wander
verb
walk about without much purpose
He had nothing important to do; so he *wandered* around in the city before coming back home.

want
verb
desire, need
She *wants* a little more to eat; she is still hungry. She *wants* to play after she eats.

war
noun
fighting between countries
We learned about *wars*

in our history class.
All *wars* are bad; people get killed in them.

warm
verb
heat something a little
The mother *warmed* the milk for her baby.
adjective
not cold and not hot
I wear a *warm* coat in winter. It keeps me *warm.*

warn
verb
say or write something that tells of something bad or undesirable coming
Before they drove their car, I *warned* them about the weather. I told them that the weather might make it difficult for them to drive.

warning
noun
a statement about something bad that might be coming
The police gave the thief a *warning.* They said, "If you do it again, you will go to prison."

was
See **be** also.
verb
She *was* a nurse before becoming a teacher.
auxiliary verb
She *was* playing when I called her.

wash
noun
clothes and other things that have been cleaned or that need to be cleaned
The wife said to her husband, "You clean the house; I will do the *wash."*
verb
clean with soap and water
Wash your hands before you eat.

wasn't
See **be** and **was**.
verb
negative of was, was not
She *wasn't* at home when I phoned.
auxiliary verb
was not
She *wasn't* eating when I spoke to her.

waste
noun
a thing or things not used fully
To do nothing is a *waste* of time.
verb
not to use something fully
Don't *waste* your time or money. Get busy and save your money.

watch
noun
1. *an instrument that tells the time and can be worn by a person*

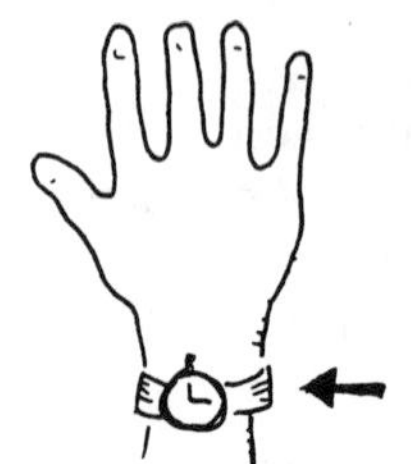

His wrist *watch* says it is 3:00; his pocket *watch* says it is 3:05.
2. *attention, observation*
The nurse kept *watch* over her patients in the hospital.
verb

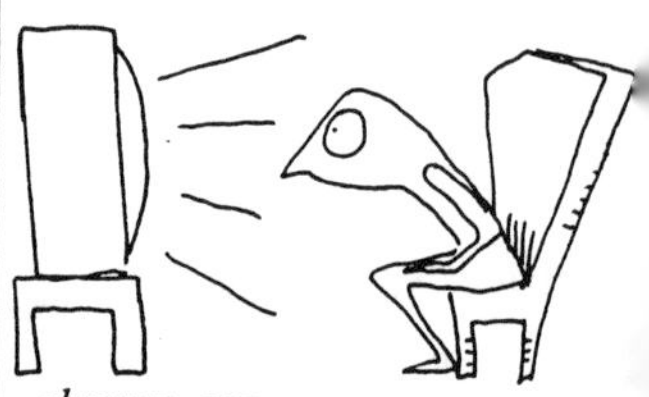

observe, see
We *watched* the game on television.

water
noun
the natural liquid (that we drink)
I had a glass of *water* with my lunch.
verb
pour water on, give water to
The lady *waters* her plants daily.

watermelon

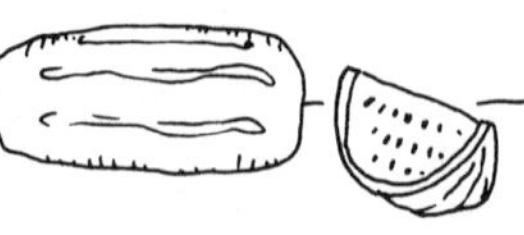

noun

a fruit that has a green or white peel, red or yellow flesh, and seeds
I like to eat *watermelon* in summer; it makes me feel cool.

wave
noun

1. *a movement of the hand or arm*
The policeman gave me a *wave* of the hand and let me drive on.

2. *a movement of the water in a lake or sea or pool*
The *waves* hit the rocks on the shore.
verb: waving, waved, waved
make a movement of the hand or arm
The policeman *waved* me on as I was driving. They *waved* good-bye to us as they walked to the plane.

way
noun
1. *route*
We know the *way* to the library. We've been there before.
2. *method, how*
He showed me the *way* to fix my bicycle.

we
pronoun (first person plural): us, our, ours
one person or a number of persons and I
I have one brother and two sisters. *We* live with our parents.

weak
adjective
opposite of strong
She cannot carry that bag; she is *weak*; she is not strong.

weakness
noun
opposite of strength
He was weak and ill; he stayed in bed and couldn't walk because of his *weakness.*

wealth
noun
richness
He shared his *wealth* with others; he gave a lot of money and goods to his friends and neighbors.

weapon

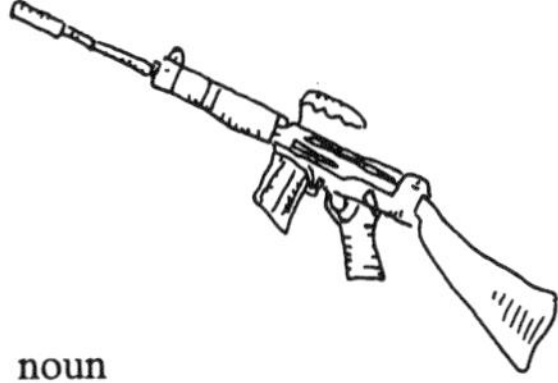

noun
an instrument to fight with like a knife or a gun
Students are not allowed to take any *weapons* with them to school.

wear

verb: wearing, wore, worn
put on
She *wore* a hat on her head and gloves on her hands in cold weather. What are you *wearing* today?

weary
adjective: wearier, weariest
tired
He felt *weary*; he worked all day and had no time to rest.

weather
noun
the condition of the atmosphere in a place
The *weather* today is very fine; it is not hot or cold, and it is not raining.

we'd
pronoun and auxiliary verb
1. *we had*
We'd been waiting one hour when they arrived.
2. *we would*
We'd like to see the

film you told us about.

wedding
noun
the occasion of a marriage
We attended their *wedding*. The bride and the groom looked very happy.

Wednesday
noun
a day of the week
She couldn't come on Tuesday. She came one day late. She arrived on *Wednesday*.

week
noun
a period of seven days
I see my friend once a *week*; I see him every Saturday.

weekend
noun
the end of the week; Saturday and Sunday (in the U.S.)
We went on a trip last *weekend*. We left on Saturday morning and returned on Sunday evening.

weep

verb: weeping, wept, wept
cry, let tears come down from the eyes
She *wept* when she heard the bad news.

weigh
verb

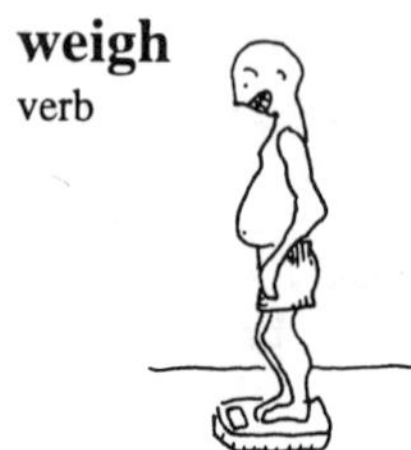

see how heavy something is, measure the weight of something
I *weighed* myself yesterday and knew that I had to lose two pounds. I was too heavy.

weight
noun
the measure of how heavy something is
The *weight* of the suitcase was 35 pounds.

welcome
noun
an expression of hospitality or happiness to receive people or things
We received a warm *welcome* from them when we got to their house.
verb
express hospitality or happiness to receive people or things
They *welcomed* us warmly when we got to their house. I *welcome* the idea of a free afternoon for games.

well
adverb
1. *feeling good and healthy*
He was sick, but he is very *well* now.
2. *in a good way*
He did all his work very *well.*

we'll
pronoun and auxiliary verb
we will
We couldn't see you yesterday, but *we'll* see you tomorrow.

went
See **go**.

were
See **be** also.
verb
I was in the garden, but my brother and sister *were* at home.
auxiliary verb
They *were* studying their lessons.

we're
pronoun and verb
we are
We're here now.
pronoun and auxiliary verb
we are
We're watching television in the evening.

weren't
negative of were
were not
They *weren't* in the house; they were in the garden.

west

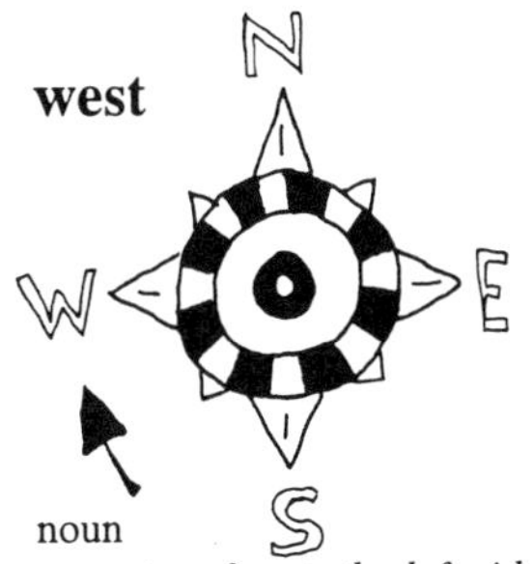

noun
opposite of east, the left side of a map
New York is in the east of the U.S. California is in the *west.*

western
adjective
related to the west
California is a *western* state.

wet
adjective
not dry
All his clothes are *wet.* He was playing in the water.

we've
pronoun and auxiliary verb
we have
We've done our work; now we can play.

whale

noun
a big sea animal
Some *whales* look like submarines.

what
question (interrogative) word
What are you doing now? I'm reading.
relative pronoun
I did *what* you told me to do.

whatever
pronoun
anything
The dogs I have eat *whatever* I give them.

what's
See **what** also.
1. *what is*
What's your name?
2. *what has*
What's happened to you?

wheat

noun
a grain from which we make bread
We turn the *wheat* into flour before we make bread.

wheel
noun

1. *a round thing on which things move or roll*
My car has four *wheels.*
2. *(important) person*
He is a big *wheel* in his company.
verb
move on wheels
We *wheeled* the food to the balcony on a trolley.

wheelchair

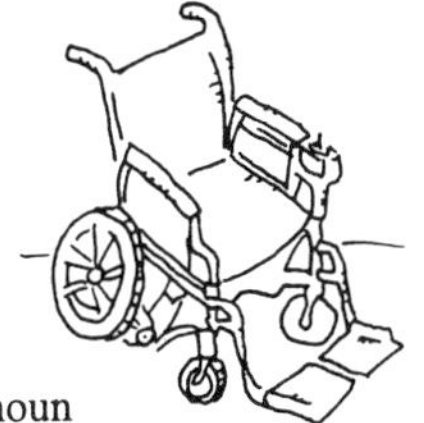

noun
a chair on wheels for people who cannot walk
The patient was taken to his hospital room in a *wheelchair.*

when
question (interrogative) word
about time
When are they coming? Tomorrow.
conjunction
at the time
They will come *when* I call them.

whenever
adverb
at any time
They use umbrellas *whenever* it rains.

where
question (interrogative) word
about place
Where is your friend?

He's in the library.

wherever
adverb
in any place
Try to find your teacher *wherever* she is.

whether
conjunction
if
We are going on our trip *whether* it rains or not.

which
question (interrogative) word
Which way did you go?
relative pronoun
This is the book *which* I wanted.

while
noun
time
You are in no hurry. Stay for a *while*.
adverb
during the time that
Wait for me here *while* I get my books ready.

whip

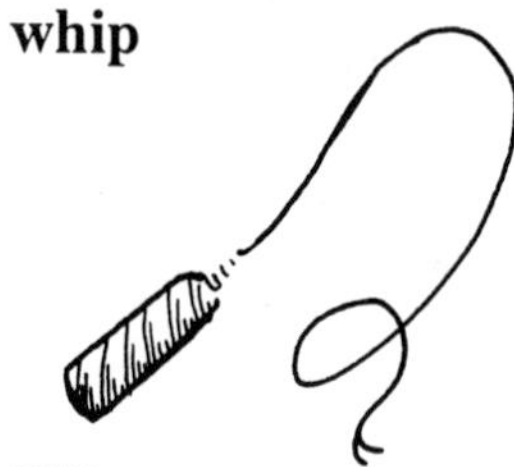

noun
a cord at the end of a stick used to hit animals
The driver of the horse carriage did not use his *whip* on the horse.
verb: whipping, whipped, whipped
hit with a whip
I don't like to see anybody *whipping* an animal.

whirl
verb
turn
The children *whirled* around as they played.

whisper
noun
soft spoken words in the ear
She didn't want anyone to hear her; so she told me in a *whisper* that she didn't want to eat her food.
verb
to speak softly in the ear
She *whispered* to me that she didn't want to eat her food. Nobody else heard what she said.

whistle

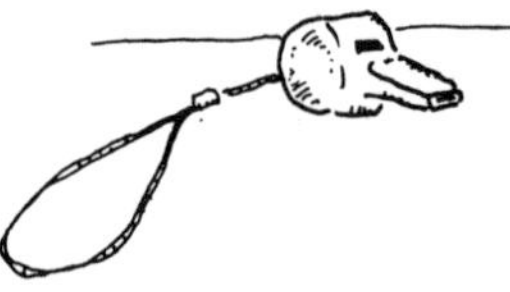

noun
an instrument that sends out a loud sound
The captain blew his *whistle* for the players to come to him.
verb: whistling, whistled, whistled
1. *blow such an instrument*
The referee *whistled* when the ball went out.

white
noun
a color, the opposite of black
White is the color of peace.
adjective
a color, the opposite of black
He likes *white* shirts and blue ties.

who
interrogative pronoun, question word about people
Who is at the door?
relative pronoun
This is the man *who* spoke to us yesterday.

whole
adjective
full, complete
He ate the *whole* apple; he left nothing of it.

whom
relative pronoun
My brother, *whom* you know very well, is in his office now.

who's
See **who** also.
who is
Who's he talking to?
who has
Who's done his work?

whose
interrogative pronoun, question word (showing

possession)
Whose book is this?
His.
relative pronoun
This is the boy *whose* book was stolen.

why
question (interrogative) word
what for
Why is he studying? Because he has a test.

wicked
adjective
bad, meaning to do harm
I don't like *wicked* people; they always want to hurt others.

wide
adjective
broad
This box is three inches long, two inches *wide*, and one inch high.

widen
verb
make wider
The road was very narrow; so the city *widened* it; now it is fine.

widow
noun
a woman whose husband is dead
Mrs. White is a *widow*, and she is living with her children.

widower
noun
a man whose wife is dead
The *widower* went to live with his daughter after his wife died.

wife
noun: wives
the woman of a married couple, the feminine of husband
Jack Brown and his *wife* Mary have two children.

wild
adjective
growing up without any care
We saw some beautiful *wild* flowers on our trip in the country. *Wild* animals are hard to catch.

wilderness
noun
open land without people, animals, or plants
They lived in tents for a week in the *wilderness* on their way south.

will
noun
intent
His *will* is to see his children get a good education.
verb
want, desire
You can *will* what you please, but you must work hard to earn it.
auxiliary verb (showing future action)
I can't see you now, but I *will* see you tomorrow.

willing
adjective
showing no resistence or objection
He doesn't want any money, but he is *willing* to help us if we ask him.

win
noun
victory, opposite of loss
Our basketball team had 24 *wins* and six losses last year.
verb: winning, won, won
be victorious
We *won* the basketball game last night: 92 87.

wind
noun
air blowing
I went inside; it was too cold in the *wind* outside.

wind
verb: winding, wound, wound
turn
He *winds* his watch every morning. It stops if he doesn't.

windshield
noun
the glass in the front of a car or bus

The driver couldn't see very well because his *windshield* was dirty.

window

noun

a space with glass in a wall to see out

My bedroom has one door and two *windows.*

windy

adjective: windier, windiest

with a lot of wind (air blowing)

Today is not a rainy day, but it is *windy.* The wind is blowing very hard.

wine

noun

a red, pink, or white drink made out of grapes

They served white *wine* with the fish and red *wine* with the meat.

wing

noun

1. *one of the two arms of a bird used for flying*

Some birds go for long distances without moving their *wings.*

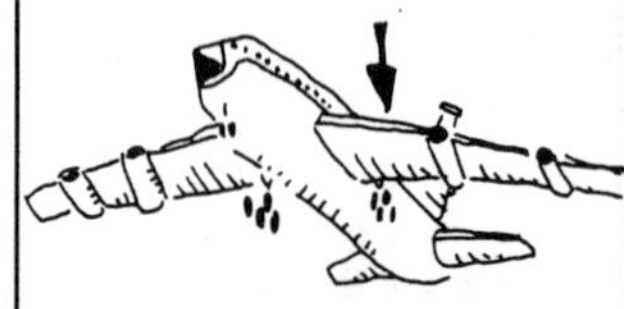

2. *one of the arms of a plane*

I couldn't see the city below; my seat on the plane was over the right *wing.*

winner

noun

a person who wins or is victorious

The *winner* in the race got first prize.

winter

noun

one of the four seasons of the year

They waited for the spring season after a cold *winter.*

verb

spend the winter season

Like some birds, they summer in the north and *winter* in the south.

wipe

verb: wiping, wiped, wiped

remove (something) with the hand or a piece of cloth

She *wiped* her tears with a handkerchief.

wiper

noun

an instrument that wipes

He has new windshield *wipers* on his car.

wire

noun

a metal string or cable

The lights went out because the electric *wires* broke.

wisdom

noun

great knowledge and understanding

We depend on his *wisdom*; he always gives us the best advice.

wise

adjective

having wisdom

A *wise* person studies a situation well before coming to a decision.

wish

noun

desire, hope, want

He has one main *wish*: he wants to see his children get a good

education.
verb
want, hope
He *wished* to succeed in his work.

wit
noun
quickness of mind, cleverness
I like her *wit*; she has a ready answer at any time.

with
preposition
The teacher is angry *with* them because they didn't do their work. She walked *with* me all the way. We talked *with* each other on the phone. She is pleased *with* my work; it is neat and correct.

within
preposition
inside
They live *within* the city limits.

without
preposition
in the absence of, leaving out
If he doesn't come soon, we will go *without* him.

witness
noun
a person who sees and knows something
The police asked the *witness* some questions, because he had seen the accident.
verb
see a situation
She *witnessed* the fight and was able to describe it.

wives
See **wife**.

woke up
See **wake**.

woken up
See **wake.**

wolf

noun: wolves
an animal that looks like a dog
We saw some *wolves* in the zoo.

woman

noun: women
a grown up female person, feminine of man
There are six people at the table: three men and three *women*.

women
See **woman.**

won
See **win**.

wonder
noun
surprise, a state of not knowing
How they climbed that high mountain alone is still a *wonder* to me.
verb
think and not know exactly
I *wondered* how they climbed that high mountain alone.

wonderful
adjective
very fine, amazing
We saw a *wonderful* film last night; the story was good and the acting was excellent.

won't
auxiliary verb
negative of will, will not
This is their last visit here. We *won't* see them again.

wood

noun
material that comes from tree trunks
Our dining room table

is made of very good *wood.*

wooden
adjective
made of wood
They sat on a *wooden* bench in the garden.

wool

noun
material made of animal hair
She has a beautiful sweater made of lambs' *wool.*

word

noun
a group of letters or sounds that can stand alone in a language
This sentence has five *words.*

wore
See **wear**.

work
noun
1. *product or production*
The poem he wrote was his own *work.*
2. *job*
His *work* is painting cars.
3. *effort*
High grades require hard *work.*
verb
1. *do labor*
He *works* in an office.
2. *make something go*
He *worked* his engine too long.
3. *put an effort*
Work hard if you want to succeed.

worker
noun
a person who works
The farmer has five *workers* in the field to help him.

world

noun
1. *the earth*
Our planet is our *world.*
2. *all of creation*
God created the *world* and everything that is in it.

worm

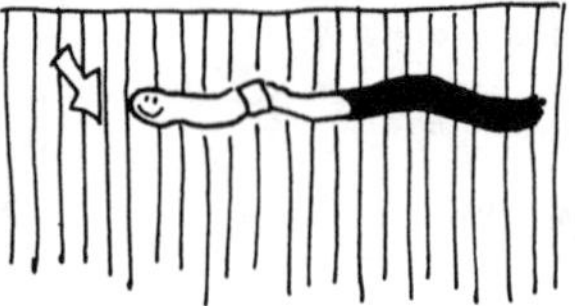

noun
an insect that crawls in the earth and in fruits and vegetables
He didn't eat his apple, because he saw a *worm* moving in it.

worn
See **wear** also.
adjective
old and used and not in good condition
She bought a new coat, because her old coat was *worn.*

worried
adjective
concerned and thinking about smething
The boy rode a bicycle for the first time, and his mother was *worried* about him; she was afraid he might fall and hurt himself.

worry
noun: worries
concern
She had one main *worry*: her children's health.
verb: worrying, worried, worried
be concerned
She *worried* about her children; they never left her mind.

worse
adjective
comparative of bad
The red bicycle is bad; it doesn't run very well.

The blue bicycle is *worse*; it doesn't run at all.

worship
verb
adore
A person can *worship* God by praying or by singing.

worst
adjective
superlative of bad
If you want to succeed, the *worst* thing you can do is to do nothing.

worth
noun
value
Does this old watch have any *worth*?
adjective
of value
This old watch is *worth* a lot; it is very expensive.

worthy
adjective: worthier, worthiest
deserving
This singer is *worthy* of praise; she sang very well.

would
auxiliary verb
I *would* like to read a new book. If you came early, I *would* go with you. *Would* you like some tea?

wouldn't
auxiliary verb
negative of would, would not
I *wouldn't* like to be out in the rain; I don't want to get wet.

wrap

noun
a cover
She felt cold; so she put a *wrap* around her shoulders.
verb: wrapping, wrapped, wrapped
cover
She *wrapped* the birthday present with colored paper.

wreck
verb
destroy
He *wrecked* his bicycle in the accident.

wrist

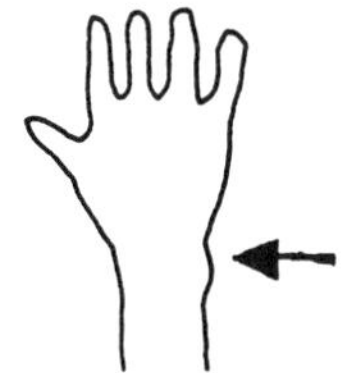

noun
a joint just above the hand
She wears bracelets on her *wrists*.

write
verb: writing, wrote, written
put on paper or another surface with a pen or a pencil
I *wrote* my name on the blackboard.

writer
noun
a person who writes
I like that story; the author is a good *writer*.

writing
noun
something written
I like that author; his *writing* is very good.
adjective
used to write on
I have a new *writing* pad. I use it to keep some notes.

written
See **write** also.
adjective
done in writing
We had two tests last week: an oral test and a *written* test.

wrong
adjective
opposite of right, incorrect
Of my five answers, four were right and one was *wrong*.

wrote
See **write**.

Xx

xerox

noun
a photograph copy (using electricity)
The manager made a *xerox* copy of the report I gave him.
verb
copy photographically (using electricity)
The manager *xeroxed* my report; he wanted a copy of it.

x-ray
noun
a picture by x-rays
The doctor said that the patient needed an *x-ray* of his arm to see if it was broken.
verb
take a picture by x-rays
The doctor *x-rayed* the patient's arm to see if it was broken.

Yy

yard
noun
1. *a measure of three feet*
A football field is 100 *yards* long.
2. *a garden or place to play*
The children are running in the school *yard*.

year
noun
12 months, 52 weeks, 365 days
The child is two *years* old.

yearly
adjective
every year, once a year
Birthdays are *yearly* events.
adverb
once a year, every year
They travel to Europe *yearly*; they usually go in August.

yellow
noun
a color
She doesn't like *yellow*; she prefers red and blue.
adjective
a color
She put a red rose on her *yellow* dress.

yes
opposite of no
Are you reading this sentence? *Yes*, I am.

yesterday
noun
the day before today
If today is Thursday, *yesterday* was Wednesday.

yet
adverb
up until now
Has he done his work *yet*?
conjunction
even so
It was raining; *yet* he walked to work.

yield
noun
product
The farmers say that their *yield* this year was good. They had plenty of corn and wheat.
verb
give in, give up
The weaker army *yielded* to the stronger army.

yonder
adverb
there
The field *yonder* is too far to walk to.

you
pronoun: you, your, yours
second person singular and plural
You can come to my house. I would like to see *you*.

you'd
pronoun and auxiliary verb
1. *you had*
I know you couldn't come; if *you'd* done your homework, you would have been able to come.
2. *you would*
I think *you'd* like to see what I have in my hand.

you'll
pronoun and auxiliary verb
you will
You'll see me in school tomorrow. I'll be there.

young
adjective
not old in age
They have two *young* children: one is three and one is five years old.

your
possessive pronoun
for you
My book is blue. What color is *your* book?

you're
pronoun and auxiliary verb
you are
I'm a teacher. *You're* a student. We're teachers. *You're* students.

yours
possessive pronoun
for you
This book is mine. Where is *yours*?

yourself
emphatic pronoun (plural: yourselves)
you alone
I didn't help you with your work. You did it *yourself*.
reflexive pronoun (plural: yourselves)
your own self
You hurt *yourself* when you fell.

yourselves
See **yourself**.

youth
noun
young age
In his *youth*, he was foolish. Now he is wise.

you've
pronoun and auxiliary verb
you have
You've been a very good student.

Zz

zeal
noun
eagerness
He likes his work very much. He shows great *zeal* in it.

zebra

noun
an animal with black and white stripes on the skin
We saw some *zebras* in the zoo.

zero
noun: zeros or zeroes
1. *the digit 0*
The number 70 is made up of seven and *zero*.
2. *nothing*
He has *zero* in his bank account.

zip code
noun
the number of a postal area
If their *zip code* is 22307, they must be living in northern Virginia.

zone
noun
a special area of a land or country
They lived in a war *zone* for many years.

zoo
noun
an animal garden
I like the monkeys in the *zoo*.

APPENDICES

A. MEASUREMENT OF TEMPERATURES: Centigrade & Fahrenheit

	Freezing Point	Boiling Point
Centigrade	O° C	100° C
Fahrenheit	32° F	212° F

Steps for Changing from Centigrade to Fahrenheit

1. Take any temperature. Example: 35° C
2. Divide by 5: 35/5 = 7
3. Multiply by 9: 7 x 9 = 63
4. Add 32: 63 + 32 = 95° F

Steps for Changing from Fahrenheit to Centigrade

1. Take any temperature. Example: 95° F
2. Subtract 32: 45-32=63
3. Divide by 9: 63/9 = 7
4. Multiply by 5: 7 x 5 = 35° C

B. MEASUREMENT OF WEIGHTS: Pounds & Kilograms

1 pound = 16 oz. (ounces) 1 kilogram = 1,000 grams

Steps for Changing from Kilograms to Pounds

1. Take any weight. Example: 30 kilograms
2. Multiply by 2.2: 30 x 2.2= 66 pounds

Steps for Changing from Pounds to Kilograms

1. Take any weight. Example: 66 pounds
2. Divide by 2.2: 66 / 2.2 = 30 kilograms

C. MEASUREMENT OF LENGTHS AND DISTANCES

1 mile = 1760 yards
1 yard = 3 feet
1 foot = 12 inches

1 kilometer = 1,000 meters
1 meter = 100 centimeters
1 centimeter = 10 millimeters

1 mile = 1.609 kilometers
1 inch = 2.54 centimeters

D. MEASUREMENT OF LIQUIDS

1 gallon = 8 pints
1 pint = 16 fluid ounces

1 liter = 10 deciliters
1 deciliter = 10 milliliters

1 liter = 1.76 pints

E. ROMAN NUMERALS

1.	I	11.	XI	30.	XXX
2.	II	12.	XII	40.	XL
3.	III	13.	XIII	50.	L
4.	IV	14.	XIV	60.	LX
5.	V	15.	XV	70.	LXX
6.	VI	16.	XVI	80.	LXXX
7.	VII	17.	XVII	90.	XC
8.	VIII	18.	XVIII	100.	C
9.	IX	19.	XIX	500.	D
10.	X	20.	XX	1,000.	M

Other Examples

320	CCCXX
518	DXVIII
631	DCXXXI
1995	MCMXCV

About the Author

Dr. Raja T. Nasr has held several academic and administrative positions in different parts of the world. He was at one time Director of the Center for English Language Research and Teaching at the American University of Beirut, Professor of Education and Applied Linguistics at Beirut University College, educational and language consultant to a number of Ministries of Education in the Arab world, and teacher trainer in over twenty countries of the Middle East, North and East Africa, Europe, England, and the U.S.A.

Professor Nasr is currently teaching graduate education courses at Marymount Universtiy in Arlington, Virginia. He is also an educational and language consultant and public speaker.